THEORY OF EDUCATIONAL EVALUATION

Payment and Settlement System Act, 2007, 51
Payment and Settlement Systems (PSS) Act, 2007, 54
Payment and Settlement Systems in India: Vision 2018, 60
Payment and Settlement Systems in India: Vision 2019-21, 61
Payment Orders, 83
Peer-to-peer (P2P) Lending, 16
Phishing, 156
Point-of-Sale (PoS) Terminals, 99
Pre-Independence Payment Systems, 49
Pre-paid Cards, 94
Proxy Servers, 167
Public Debt Office (PDO), 67
Public Key Infrastructure (PKI), 107, 168

R

R. Gandhi, 103
Ratan P. Watal, 73
Real Time Gross Settlement (RTGS), 104
Registration Authority (RA), 169
Reserve Bank of India (RBI), 7, 18
Robo Advisors, 6
Robotics, 19
Role of RBI in Promoting Digital Payments, 37
RuPay, 100

S

S.C. Garg, 38
Scamming, 156
Secure Socket Layer (SSL), 171
Securities and Exchange Board of India (SEBI), 17
Self-help Groups (SHGs), 102
Shyamala Gopinath, 111
Significance of Digitization, 33
Simple Transactional Systems, 131
Smart Cards, 165
Smart Contracts, 17
Sniffer Attack, 141
Sniffing, 145, 156
Spoofing, 145, 156
Stateful Inspection Firewall, 167
Sudarshan Sen, 7, 38
Symmetric Key Encryption, 168
Systemically Important Payment Infrastructure (SIPI), 71

T

Technical Committee on Mobile Banking, 153

Telecom Regulatory Authority of India (TRAI), 162
Token Technology, 165
Travellers Cheques, 83

U

Unified Payments Interface (UPI), 115
Uniform Regulations and Rules (URR), 79
Unique Identification Authority of India (UIDAI), 121
Unstructured Supplementary Service Data (USSD), 117

V

Village Level Entrepreneur (VLE), 102
Virtual Banks, 173
Virtual Payment Address (VPA), 116
Vision Document for Payment Systems, 2005-08, 57
Vision Document for Payment Systems, 2012-15, 59

W

White Label ATMs (WLAs), 98
Wireless Application Protocol (WAP), 138
Working Group on FinTech and Digital Banking, 7
Working Group on Regulatory Mechanism for Cards, 103
World Bank, 10
World Digital Competitiveness Ranking, 2019, 39

THEORY
OF
EDUCATIONAL EVALUATION

Edited by

S.R. VASHIST

ANMOL PUBLICATIONS PVT. LTD.
NEW DELHI - 110 002 (INDIA)

ANMOL PUBLICATIONS PVT. LTD.
4374/4B, Ansari Road, Daryaganj
New Delhi - 110 002
Ph.: 23261597, 23278000
Visit us at: www.anmolpublications.com

Theory of Educational Evaluation

ISBN 81-7041-750-3

PRINTED IN INDIA

Published by J.L. Kumar for Anmol Publications Pvt. Ltd., New Delhi - 110 002 and Printed at Tarun Offset Press, Delhi.

Preface

Measurement and evaluation have found a solid place in educational psychology. Inspite of the fact that the new tests profess validity and reliability, there has not been the absence of criticisms. Criticism of the limitations of objective tests, in particular, have focused attention on the relationship between teaching objectives and test instruments.

Besides the conventional techniques of evaluation, the new techniques of questionnaire, inventories, and interviews, personal reports and projective techniques have been discussed in this volume. A relatively new theory of evaluation has emerged and has been included in this book.

The editor is grateful to all those sources which have been used in this volume, which are mostly American.

Editor

Contents

Preface v

1. Introduction : Origins and Trends in Evaluation 1
2. Needs of the Future 17
3. Methodology of Evaluation 37
4. Major Evaluation Techniques 55
5. Administrative Aspects of Evaluation 95
6. Short Answer Tests 115
7. Essay and Oral Examinations 145
8. Observation and Anecdotal Records 163
9. Questionnaires, Inventories and Interviews 189
10. Checklists and Rating Scales 215
11. Personal Reports and Projective Techniques 239
12. Sociometric Methods 273
13. Case Studies 291
14. Cumulative Records 305
15. Evaluating Achievement in Language, Arts and Mathematics 317
16. Evaluating Achievement in Selected Courses 353
17. Evaluating Interests 383
18. Evaluating Aptitudes 403

1

Introduction : Origins and Trends in Evaluation

The modern concept of evaluation which has evolved largely, though gradually, in recent decades, stemmed from a newer philosophy of education which called for the development of more adequate techniques of assessing pupil growth and development. This recent philosophy of education has emphasized the responsibility of the educator not only for the development of concepts, information skills. and habits, but also for the stimulation of pupil growth in attitudes, appreciations, interests powers of thinking, and personal-social adaptability. As these objectives have become clarified and defined in instructional practices, appropriate methods of assessment—both formal and informal—have been devised to guage the adequacy of the schools' programs. For example, evaluative tests have been devised to test such works-study skills as map reading; finding topics in reference book; using indexes or tables of contents; and reading charts, graphs, or tables.

Modern evaluation differs from older forms of appraisal in several ways. First, it attempts to measure a comprehensive range of objectives of the modern school curriculum rather than subject-matter achievement only. Second, it used a variety of techniques of appraisal, such as achievement, attitude, personality, and character tests. Included also are rating scales, questionaries, judgment scales of products, interviews, controlled-observation techniques, sociometric techniques, and aneedotal records. Third, modern evaluation includes integrating and interpreting these various indices of behaviour into an inclusive portrait of an individual or an educational situation.

Differences Between Measurement and Evaluation

Monroe (8) has distinguished between measurement and evaluation by indicating that in measurement the emphasis is upon single aspects of subject-matter achievement or specific skills and abilities, whereas in evaluation the emphasis is upon broad personality changes and major objectives of the educational program. In function, *evaluation* involves.

1. the identification and formulation of a comprehensive range of major objectives for a curriculum,
2. their definition in terms of pupil behaviour to be realized, and,
3. the selection or construction of valid, reliable, and practical instruments for appraising major objectives of the educative process or characteristics of personal growth and development. On the other hand, *measurement*, through the use of achievement tests, yields measures of pupil attainment in subject-matter areas, especially in acquisition of skills and information. Although earlier test technicians recognized both the ability to apply information and skills in problem-solving and related factors, such as interests, attitudes, and personal-social adjustment, as learning outcomes, these technicians showed little concern about the measurement of the less tangiable aspects of educative growth. For this reason the term "measurement" as used by them in connection with achievement tests meant the measurement of skills, factual information, and the like.

THE DEVELOPMENT OF MODERN EVALUATION

The origins of modern evaluation go back many decades. In the United States the concept of evaluation as related to measurement extends from rudimentary approaches beginning before 1900 to the comprehensive programs of the present day.

Seates (12) has traced the trends in measurement and evaluation through five deeades. The incubation period extending from 1897 to 1906 began with the proposals of Rice and culminated in the publication of the first Binet Intelligence Scale. The second period, from 1907 to 1916, was characterized by the work of Thorndike and his students, the publication of the first standardized scales and achievement tests, and the fight for objectivity in testing educational achievement.

The third period, from 1917 to 1926, was one of rapid expansion for educational measurements; during this time the exigencies of World War I contributed directly to the introduction of group intelligence tests and stimulated their postwar development. The fourth period, from 1927 to 1936, was characterized by direct attention to the objectives of instruction, to the evaluation of instructional outcomes of all aspects of growth, and by the construction of many new and improved tests and techniques for personality assessment as well as for intelligence and achievement measurement. The period from 1937 to 1946 was marked primarily by the emphasis on projective personality techniques, differential aptitude tests, and application of techniques of factor analysis to a wide variety of test batteries. These trends are described more fully in subsequent paragraphs.

The First Decade – Rise of Testing (1900 –1910)

In 1897, Joseph M. Rice (11) had published his studies entitled, "The Futility of the Spelling Grind." In his investigation, Rice set up the design of an experiment for comparing the achievement of pupils who spent a considerable amount of time on spelling drill with that of others who spent less time. To obtain a measure of achievement, he devised a spelling test which may be considered the first modern, formal type of test. Rice was interested not only in the measurement of spelling as such but also in evaluating the strengths and weaknesses of the educational practices of his time. This interest represented a break with the idea, generally prevalent prior to 1900, that learning products were intangible and could be appraised only by the teacher of a particular class.

During the first decade of this century, some experimentation was initiated with the Binet scale for evaluating intelligence, and some beginnings of achievement tests in the basic skills of arithmetic and the language arts can be discerned. Stone in 1908 and Courtis in 1909 published tests to measure achievement in elementary arithmetic. One can trace, in the decades which follow the initial formal test construction, the rise of modern measurement and evaluation. Ayres (1) and Freeman (5) have described in detail these early stages in educational measurement.

The Second Decade—Development of Testing (1910—1920)

The second decade of the century was marked by the development of some of the early standardized tests of intelligence and achievement and the struggle to get them accepted by both educators and the public. An important milestone in the use of achievement tests was reached when standardized tests were employed on a large scale for the first time in a survey conducted by the City of New York in 1911-13. After this, standardized tests were used in other large cities.

During this period many scales and tests were devised. Thorndike's (15) handwriting scale appeared in 1910. This scale included a series of samples of handwriting presented on a chart in order of merit. Based on the judgment of a jury of experts, each sample was assigned a statiscally determined numerical value or score. Thus a teacher could compare a sample of a pupil's writing with the scale samples and assign to it the numerical score of the scale sample that it most closely resembled. This may appropriately be called the first scientifically constructed test or measure of educational achievement.

In 1911, Ayres published a scale in which the samples of handwriting were arranged in order of increasing legibility, but the scores for samples were established by less rigorous statistical methods than those of the Thorndike scale. The Hillegas Composition Scale, published in 1912, followed the Thorndike quality-scale pattern. In 1913, Buckingham published a spelling scale in which the words were arranged in order of increasing difficulty. The criterion of difficulty was used by Woody in building an arithmetic scale and by Trabue in constructing a language scale, both published in 1916.

Tests published before 1916 also included a series by Starch which embraced his Reading Tests, Grammatical Scales, Punctuation Scale, Grammar Tests, and Latin Vocabulary and Reading Tests. About the same time, Thorndike constructed a Scale for the Merit of Drawing by Pupils Eight to Fifteen Years Old. Although Goddard had translated Binet's intelligence Scale as early as 1908, Terman did not make his famous Stanford Revision until 1916.

The Third Decade—Extension of Standardized Testing (1920 – 1930)

In the third decade, tests both of intelligence and of achievement advanced rapidly. The use of intelligence tests during World War I for classifying personnel in the armed forces provided an opportunity for the employment of new tests and gave impetus to the testing movement. In 1919, achievement-test batteries and intelligence tests were issued for the first time by commercial publishers for purchase by school systems. Notable among these were such pioneer tests as the Otis Intelligence Test and the Stanford Achievement Test batteries. Before 1930, more than one thousand standardized tests had appeared. During this period the development of statistical techniques of test analysis also received considerable attention.

The Fourth Decade—Rise of Evaluation (1930—1940)

During the 1930's, measurement and the evaluation movement continued to expand. It was during this decade that the Cooperative Test Service began to publish a large number of parallel forms of tests for secondary schools. Many new batteries of tests appeared. During this period, also, appeared such personality tests as the Rorschach and other projective techniques. Interest inventories were devised. Attitude scales and sociometric techniques were developed. Anecdotal records were introduced as evaluation techniques. All of these were evidence of a serious attempt to find ways to test not only tangible skills and knowledges, but also the less tangible objectives of the modern educational program.

It was during this period also that Tyler, Wrightstone, and others carried on studies evaluating newer practices in elementary and secondary schools, while Eurich conducted several studies at the college level to appraise the effectiveness of college curricula and to guide the revision of such curricula to meet more adequately the needs of college students. At the same time, evaluative criteria which recognized the comprehensive and flexible nature of the schools' curricula were set up for accrediting high schools and colleges.

The Fifth Decade—Extension of Measurement and Evaluation (1940—1950)

The decade of the 1940's was marked by a maturing and a refinement of the techniques developed during the 1930's. Various evaluation studies will indicate the scope and nature of these evaluation programs. In New York City the appraisal of the activity program in the elementary schools (9) involved a comprehensive design of evaluation. In the secondary schools the "Eight-Year Study" of thirty high schools (14) illustrates the broad scope of a modern evaluation program, The Cooperative Study of Evaluation in General Education of the American Council on Education for colleges used similar techniques. The Commission on Teacher Educational also formulated a broad program of evaluation.

SCOPE OF MODERN EVALUATION—ILLUSTRATIVE STUDIES

Designs for Secondary and Elementary Schools

Most comprehensive in design of the plans for evaluating secondary and elementary schools in the Eight-Year Study directed by Tyler. The report on the appraisal (14) provides a detailed description of the development and application of present-day evaluation instruments. These instruments were designed to measure the major objectives of high-school instruction, as follows :

1. For aspects of thinking : tests of interpretation of data, application of principles, logical reasoning, and nature of proof.
2. For social sensitivity : tests of application to social problems of social values, social facts, and generalizations.
3. For civic and social beliefs : scales of social, political and economic beliefs.
4. For aspects of appreciation in literature and art : a variety of techniques.
5. For interests : an inventory of personal, social, and school interests.
6. For personal and social development : various self-reporting scales and anecdotal records.

In addition, various pupil-record forms for noting reading and listening were used. These tests, scales, inventories, questionnaires, check-lists, pupil logs, and other records were applied as requiied in gathering evidence about the achievement of objectives in the curriculum in each of the thirty schools participating in the study.

In connection with this study, Raths (10) has described and illustrated how the newer concepts of evaluation are applied in evaluating the program of a progressive high school. He shows how various tests and instruments of appraisal for such objectives as interpreting data, applying scientific principles, and evaluating data may be used to analyze both individual pupil behavior and class performance. He illustrates, by case studies, the integration of various indices of behavior into an inclusive appraisal portrait of the individual student.

On the elementary level, the appraisal of the activity program in the New York City schools (9, 17) illustrates the measurement of a variety of objectives, regarding basic skills in reading, language arts, and arithmetic, and selected work-study skills, such as map reading, finding references, using indexes, and interpreting charts, graphs, and tables. Interests were evaluated by a specially devised interest inventory. Powers of thinking were measured by a special test based upon interpretation of data and application of generalizations to new situations. For personal and social adjustment, various observational techniques, anecdotal records, and sociometric were employed. For evaluating creative expression in language, a scale for assessing the originality of written compositions was devised. Smith (13) describes procedures in the evaluation of language arts programs.

At the elementary-school level, the most comprehensive effort in recent years to get suggestions for objectives from subject-matter specialists, psychologists, teachers, and school supervisors is summarized in the report of the Mid-Century Committee on Outcomes in Elementary Education (7). This committee asked recognized authorities to submit statements concerning desirable outcomes in subject-matter learning and intellectual competence. In addition, the committee obtained statements of objectives from recognized authorities or personal development and social maturation. The committee used the contributions of all the specialists, as well as of general educators, in preparing a comprehensive statement of objectives for the modern elementary school. In summary form here are the nine goals for the elementary-school years which were formulated :

(*a*) Health, safety, and physical development.

(*b*) Social and emotional development.

(*c*) Ethical behavior, personal standards, and moral values.

(*d*) Ability to assume leadership, to choose leaders wisely, to work in teams in neighborhoods, communities, and states.

(*e*) Becoming a citizen valuable in his home, school, and community today, and a good neighbor, good community member, and good American citizen in the world of tomorrow.

(*f*) Knowledge of the physical world of plants and animals, nature, science, conservation, machines.

(*g*) Esthetic development as both consumer and producer, as enjoyer and creator—in art, music, literature, drama, radio and television, crafts, home and community beautification.

(*h*) Competence in communicating with other people through speaking, listening, reading, and writing.

(*i*) Ability to count, measure, compute, estimate, and reason quantitatively.

Each objective is defined in detail in the committee report. This report points out the need to review and classify the kinds of measurement and evaluation now available to appraise these objectives. For some of the objectives, it is recommended that new instruments of appraisal be constructed.

Follow-Up Studies as Evaluation Methods

The follow-up study is used as another phase of a larger

pattern of evaluation. Two illustrative studies of this type may be mentioned. Bell's study (2) for the American Youth Commission was a pioneer attempt to determine and analyze the status of a representative sample of Maryland youth, aged sixteen to twenty-four. Interviews were held with more than thirteen thousand young people, sampled on the basis of sex, race, school status, job status, social and economic status, marital status, type of community, and other factors. The study was concerned with youth at school, home, work, play, and church.

The follow-up phase of the Eight-Year Study has been reported by Chamberlin and others (3). Graduates from thirty experimental high schools were matched with graduates of traditional high schools on the basis of such matters as scholastic aptitude, sex, race, age, religious affiliation, size and type of high school, size and type and location of community, socio-economic status of family, and extracurricular activities in high school.

A comparison was made between the subsequent success of both groups in college. College records and reports, special questionnaires and tests, and personal interviews were used to gather evidence about nine aspects of college success : intellectual competence, cultural development, practical competence, philosophy of life, character traits, emotional balance, social fitness, sensitivity to social problems, and physical fitness. In many of these areas, the mass of data for each student was correlated to behavior levels or types which were described briefly.

RECENT TRENDS IN EVALUATION

The modern teacher and the supervisor are concerned with important functional learning outcomes, many of which are less tangible and less easily measured than the concepts, skills, and abilities represented in subject-matter tests of the past several decades. The concern for the total development of the child—physical, emotional, social, and intellectual—has resulted in an emphasis upon a sound understanding of child growth and development and of individual and group differences, as well as upon the personal and social adjustment of the pupils. This represents an emphasis upon Gestalt, or organismic, psychology, which recognizes the interrelationships of the multiple aspects of growth in an individual.

An increasing emphasis on the measurement of understanding and interpretation, rather than upon isolated information, skills, and abilities is particularly observable in present-day tests of general educational development. These are represented by such test batteries as the United States Armed Forces Institute Tests of General Educational Development Tests of Educational Development. A similar trend is evident in the tests recently constructed by the College Entrance Examination Board and other tests devised by the Educational Testing Service. At the college level, measurement of understanding is stressed in the examinations constructed for the Graduate Records Examination.

Tests of general educational development usually present information in verbal, graphic, or other form, with the test exercises devised to measure the ability of the individual to comprehend and interpret the material presented. This contrasts with the isolated test item which emphasizes the recall or recognition of items of information. General educational development tests usually cover such areas as language arts, including literature, social studies, science, and mathematics.

The increased use of informal, or teacher-made, test exercises to supplement formal or standardized tests is also characteristic of recent evaluative programs. Some surveys show that the average classroom teacher uses five or six teacher-made tests for every standardized test employed. Informal tests are valuable in the day-by-day appraisal and guidance of pupils in specific units of classroom study.

The development of factor analysis of mental abilities, in which Dr. L.L. Thurstone has been a leader, is another important new approach. By statistical analysis of many mental ability tests, Thurstone isolated seven primary mental abilities.

These include : a verbal factor, which involves vocabulary and reading comprehension ; a number factor, which involves speed and accuracy in computation ; a space factor, which involves visualization of space relationships : a rote memory factor ; a perceptual factor, which involves discrimination of likenesses and differences ; a word factor, which involves naming isolated words at a rapid rate ; and a reasoning factor, which involves finding a rule or principle governing a series of numbers, letters, or words.

The mental ability tests incorporating the results of this analysis, called Tests of Primary Abilities, are published in batteries for various age levels by the Science Research Associates of Chieago. Constructed along somewhat similar lines are the Differential Aptitude Tests, published by the Psychological Corporation. The Differential Aptitude Tests measure similar abilities and are especially useful for guidance work and counseling of high-school students, for both educational and vocational guidance purposes.

One study concerning the measurement of reading achievement analyzed the factors involved in reading comprehension, and served as the basis for the development of the Cooperative Reading Comprehension Tests. In this analysis, Davis (4) identified two general factors and six specific factors in reading comprehension. The general factors are word meaning and reasoning in reading, which requires the ability to weave together several ideas and to show their relationships, as well as the ability to draw correct inferences from written statements. The specific factors isolated are :

(*a*) ability to determine the writer's purpose, intent, or point of view.

(*b*) ability to understand the writer's explicit statements or to get the literal meaning,

(*c*) ability to follow the organization of a passage,

(*d*) ability to select the main thought or idea of a paragraph or passage,

(*e*) ability to determine from context the meaning of an unfamiliar word, and

(*f*) ability to determine the tone and mood implicit or explicit in a passage.

Another development in recent evaluation studies is measurement of the role of the individual, as well as of small groups, in studies of group dynamics. This trend has shown itself in several ways. One is the measurement of the social status of groups and individuals. Warner (16) and Hollingshead (6) are particularly noted for this type of work. A second manifestation is the work on group dynamics that has been carried on by various organizations, especially the Research Center for Group Dynamics at the University of Michigan. Another manifestation is the various sociometric analyses that have been made in the studies of intergroup education.

The increasing attention that has been given to the unstructed, projective tests of personality is also typical of recent approaches to evaluation. Techniques developed for evaluating personal-social behavior range from the analysis of paintings and drawings, play techniques, and sentence completion to more formal methods such as the Rorschach and Thematic Apperception Tests.

SUMMARY

This brief survey of the origins and development of measurement and evaluation provides an appreciation of five decades of effort and research. Testing with emphasis upon the measurement of single aspects of subject-matter achievement or of specific skills and abilities was markedly different from the newer concept of evaluation, with its emphasis upon the appraisal of broad personality changes, including interests, attitudes, powers of thinking, and personal-social adaptability.

For convenience in discussion, the development and refinement of methods of measurement and evaluation are classified into five periods or decades. During the first decade, the modern concepts and methods of testing had their origin in the contributions of Joseph M. Rice and his test of spelling, in experimentation on the Binet scale for evaluating intelligence, and in the beginnings of achievement tests for the basic skills of arithmetic and language arts. During the second decade, beginning about 1910, testing was characterized by the contributions of E.L. Thorndike and his associates, who introduced concepts of objective scoring, scaling of items according to difficulty, and statistically determined norms for achievement tests. During this period, Terman made his famous revision of the Binet scale for measuring intelligence.

The third decade was characterized by the rapid growth of educational measurements. There appeared group intelligence tests for children, patterned after the group intelligence tests used for adults in World War I. Achievement test batteries of basic academic skills were published for purchase by school systems. Statistical techniques of test analysis received considerable attention. During the fourth decade, attention was directed to the formulation of methods and techniques for assessing growth in such objectives as attitudes, interests, powers of thinking, and personal-social adaptability, as well as to the measures of intelligence and achievement. Personality tests, projective techniques, interest inventories, attitude scales, and anecdotal records were introduced as instruments of evaluation in schools. During the fifth decade, a refinement of the techniques developed during the previous decade was apparent. The application, as well as the construction, of these newer techniques is illustrated in such studies as the Eight-Year Study of secondary schools and the appraisal of the activity program in the New York City schools.

In more recent years, the following trends in evaluation have become evident :

(*a*) The modern teacher and the supervisor are concerned with important functional learning outcomes, many of them less tangible and less easily measured than the subject-matter concepts, skills, and abilities of previous decades.

(*b*) An increasing emphasis on the measurement of understanding and interpretation rather than upon isolated information, skills, and abilities is particularly observable in present-day tests of general educational development.

(*c*) The increased use of informal, or teacher-made, test exercises for instructional purposes to supplement formal or standardized tests is also characteristic of recent evaluation programs.

(*d*) The development of factor analysis of mental abilities may also be cited as an important new approach in measurement and evaluation.

(*e*) The development of techniques for measuring the role of the individual, as well as of small groups in studies of group relationships.

(*f*) Increasing attention has been given to the development and refinement of unstructured, or projective, tests of personality.

PROBLEMS FOR CLASS DISCUSSION

1. In parallel columns, under the captions "Measurement" and "Evaluation," list the major differences between these two concepts.
2. On a graphic time line or chart from 1900 to 1950, indicate for each decade the major trends in the measurement and evaluation movement in the United States.
3. Select two of the recent trends in evaluation. For each of these trends, explain the educational or psychological factors contributing most directly to the trend.

2

Needs of the Future

Measurement and evaluation have earned a solid place in educational psychology. However, there is so much information in this area that is basic to a good teaching-learning situation that the author has been able to include only a few papers discussing issues of genuine importance for the teacher.

Although an old problem, there has been a revival of interest in ascertaining the validity of test items. Criticism of the limitations of objective tests, in particular, have focused attention on the relationship between teaching objectives and test instruments. Nelson's article in Chapter 15 illustrates how items can be constructed to measure complex behaviour. Fishman makes it clear that no matter how well a test instrument is constructed for middle-class children, it may not produce valid results for children who have been at a cultural or social disadvantage. He discusses three critical issues that must be considered in testing these disadvantaged groups.

After we measure behavioural change, we must then interpret these changes in the light of the goals we have specified. Did achievement occur ? Was it adequate ? The feedback that we get through measurement helps us to evaluate progress and aids us in determining the effective aspects of teaching and what remains to be done. Glock and Millman call attention to errors in procedure and suggest methodology for doing one kind of evaluation – the giving of grades.

Chapter 16 should help the reader to become aware of the public's concern with testing Test results exert a powerful influence over our lives today. To a large extent they determine school progress, admission to quality institutions, and the jobs we are able to obtain and progress in after graduation. This places a heavy obligation on those who use tests. Strengths and weaknesses of these instruments must be carefully considered. Anastasi's and Ebel's papers clarify the issues.

The last chapter of the volume emphasizes the need to use criterion-referenced tests with the new technology and for determining the status of educational achievement in the nation. This type of measurement is unlike that dercribed by Glock and Millman for the typical grading situation. They suggest the use of norm-referenced tests, which enable one to relate an individual's performance to that of others on the same test. On the other hand, criterion-referenced tests are used for comparing an individual's performance with respect to some criterion, such as an established performance standard. They enable us to determine what the pupil can do, rather than how he compares with others. Test specialists are not argreed on the advantages of using the criterion-referenced tests suggested by Glaser and Tyler. They have presented arguments both pro and con.

Those who teach science courses at the college and university level have perhaps been even less objectives-conscious than their secondary and elementary school counterparts. This seeming apathy has no doubt been due in part, at least to the chaotic and confused status of higher education objectives. A committee of university and college examiners has in recent years undertaken to bring some order out of the prevailing chaos by organizing and classifying various objectives under carefully conceived headings in the hierarchy listed in the following taxonomy :

Taxonomy of Educational Objectives

By A Committee of university and College Examiners

Benjamin S. Bloom, Editor

Max D. Engelhart Walker H. Hill

Edward J. Furst David R. Krathwohl

Pub. by Longmans, Green & Co. New York

Cognitive Domain

1.10 Knowldge of specifics.

1.11 Knowledge of terminology.

1,12 Knowledge of specific facts.

1.20 Knowledge of ways and means of dealing with specifics.

1.22 Knowledge of trends and sequences.

1.22 Knowledge of trends an sequences.

1.23 Knowledge of classifications and categories.

1.24 Knowledge of criteria.

1.25 Knowledge of methodology.

1.30 Knowledge of the universals and abstractions in a field.

1.31 Knowledge of principles and generalizations.

1.32 Knowledge of theories and structures.

Intellectual Abilities and Skills

2.00 Comprehension – ability to make use of materials or ideas.

2.10 Translation.

2.10 Interpretation.

Table 1

Two-Axis Chart of Specifications for Nat. Sci. 181 Examination, Fall Term, 1955

Course Content / *Course Objectives*	*1.00 Knowledge of Terminology, Facts, Conventions, Trends, Sequences, Categories, etc.*	*2.00 Comprehension (Translation, Interpretation, Extrapolation)*	*3.00 Application*	*4.00 Analysis*	*5.00 Synthesis Production of a Unique Communication*	*6.00 Evaluation—Satisfacing Criteria, Ability to Indicate Logical Fallacies in Arguments*
I. Preception, symbolination, and methods of science	3, 7, 8	1, 2, 6, 11	4, 9, 10		(No items for these two categories of objectives were included in this particular objective test. Attainment of ability in synthesis and evaluation	
II. The cell—structure and functions; cell principle	12, 13, 15, 16, 17, 19	14		20-27		

III. Spontaneous generation—Biogenesis				46		can better be demonstrated in non-structured, free-response testing situations in which the students create their own answers.)
IV. Sexual reproduction in animals and plants; human production and sex hormons	28-31	32-35		5		
V. Cellular reproduction—mitosis	41-43					
VI. Meiosis—chromosomes and genes	36-40,	47, 89, 90	48-52	44, 45		
VII. Single-factor cross			55-57	53		
VIII. Two-Factor cross				58-62, 69-72, 63-68		
IX. Blood group inheritance; heredity in man			73-82	54		
X. Linkage and crossing-over	87		83, 85, 88	84, 86		
XI. Sex determination Sex linkage				91-94	95-100	

2.30 Extrapolation.

3.00 Application—The use of abstractions in particular and concrete situations.

4.00 Analysis—Making clear the relative hierarchy of ideas in a communication.

4.10 Analysis of elements.

4.20 Analysis of relationships.

4.20 Analysis of relationships.

4.30 Analysis of organizational principles.

5.00 Synthesis—The putting together of elements and parts so as to form a whole.

5.10 Production of a unique communication.

5.20 Production of a plan, or proposed set of operations.

5.30 Derivation of a set of abstract relations.

6.00 Evaluation.

6.10 Judgments in terms of internal evidence.

6.20 Judgments in terms of external criteria.

The above outline is the summary of a 192-page volume which contains extensive discussions as the meaning of each objective and its sub-headings. In addition to the explanatory material, test items are included which illnstrate how the attainment of each objective could be measured.

Table 1, a two-axis of specifications for a Natural Science Examination, lists the major objectives on the horizontal axis (across the top) and the subject-matter content topics on the vertical axis at the left. Each number in the columns under the objectives is the number of an item in this examination which embodies the objective listed above it as well as the subject-matter topic listed to its left. Thus each item in the examination is keyed to a specific objective as well as to a specific of course content.

While limitation of space forbids reprinting the entire examination, one set of items to illustrate each objective is presented herewith as follows :

1.00 Knowledge of terminology, facts, convention, trends, sequences, categories, etc.

Items 36–40 involve a comparision of mitosis and meiosis, For each item select from the Key the most appropriate response.

Key : 1. Meiosis.

2. Mitosis.

3. Both mitosis and meiosis.

4. Neither mitosis nor meiosis.

36. A sperm and an egg unite by......
37. The nuclear membrane disappears in .....
38. Haploid cells are formed by......
39. Diploid cells are formed by... ..
40. The zygote undergoes .....

2.00 Comprehension – Translation, Interpretation, Extrapolation.

Items 48-52 are concerned with the life cycle of a typical plant (corn). Study the diagram carfully before you begin to answer these items.

48. Meiosis takes place between Stages.

    1. A and B. 2. B and C. 3. C and D. 4. C and E. 5. D and E.

49. If the polar or endosperm nuclei of Stage C fuse, how many chromosomes will there be altogether within the embryo sac ?

    1. 163 2. 90 3. 80 4. 50 5. 20.

50. The total number of chromosomes in all the microspores and all the megaspores shown in Stage *B* – all

added together – would be.
1.10 2. 20 3. 30 4. 40 5. 80.

51. How many chromosomes are there altogether in all the nuelei shown in the pollen grain plus all the nuclei shown in the embryo sac in Stage C ?
1. 220 2. 110 3. 40 4. 30 5. 20.

52. The number of chromosomes in the nucleus of the microspore mother cell plus the number of chromosomes in the nucleus of the megaspore mother cell will total.
1. 10 2. 20 3. 30 4. 40 5. 80.

3.00 Application

Items 91-94 are based on the following situations which involves the inheritance of baldness, a sex-influenced trait.

A young female circus acrobat who hangs by her hair as part of her act is wondering whether she should change her profession, if necessary, before it becomes too late. Her problem is this : Her mother is bald, but her father has a normal head of hair. Her older brother is rapidly losing his hair and will soon be bald.

Let B represent the gene for baldness and b the gene for non-baldness. In the heterozygous condition B is dominant in males, but b is dominant in femals. A heterozygous man will be bald, but a heterozygous woman will not be bald.

91. Which of the following matings represents the parents of the young female circus acrobat ?

1. BbXX x BbXY.
2. bbXX x BBXY.
3. BbXX x bbXY.
4. BBXX x bbXY.
5. BBXX x BbXY.

92. The genotype of the young female circus acrobat is represented by.

 1. BbXY.
 2. BBXY.
 3. bbXX.
 4. BBXX.
 5. BbXX.

93. The genotype of the older brother of the young female circus acrobat is represented by.

 1. BbXY.
 2. bbXY.
 3. BbXX.
 4. BBXY.
 5. BBXY.

94. On the basis of the data, which of the following suggestions to the young female circus acrobat would be most justifiable ?

 1. You need not change your profession—according to the genetic evidence there is no likelihood at that you will become bald.
 2. The chances are 1 in 4 that you will become bald.
 3. The chances are 3 in 4 that you will become bald.
 4. There is a 50 per cent chance that you will become bald.

4.00 Analysis.

Items 20-27 are based upon the following passage which describes some of Pasteur's later experimental work on spontaneous generation.

After some preliminary experimentation Pasteur developed a refinement in his method which was designed to meet various objectives raised by his critics. This time he boiled the sugared yeast water in a swan-neck flash like flask A below.

Pasteur's swan-neck (A) and open-top flask (B). The sugared yeast water in both flasks was boiled, then allowed to cool and stand for several weeks. Air could enter flask A via the long bent tube. The contents of flask B were exposed to the air through its open top. A dense clouding soon appeared in flask B, but none developed in flask Y.

Pasteur allowed the contents of flask A to cool very slowly. This time the end of the stem was not sealed. Any air entering the swan-neck was believed to have lost its load of dust, microorganisms, and other suspended debris when it began ascending the long uphill part of the swan-neck. In all likelihool only air frce of microorganisms came into contat with the sugared yeas water inside the swan-neck. No clouding appeared in flask A, even after months of standing.

Pasteur believed that any microorganisms borne by the air entering the swan-neck tube may have lodged in the lowermost curve near the entrance of the tube. To find ont if this were indeed true, he tilted the flask in such a way as to allow some of the fluid within the flask to run down into the portion of the curve designated by "X" in the sketch. When this fluid was subsequently drained back into the flask and the flask had been incubated for a week longer, clouding of the formerly clear liquid in the flask gradually occurred. For items 20-24 select from the Key the most appropriate category.

Key : 1. Generalization.

2. Experimental observation.

3. Deduction.
4. Analogy.
5. None of the above·

20. The liquid is flask A remained clear even after months of standing.

21. Whenever sugared yeast water is kept sterile it remains clear but whenever microorganism-laden air comes into contact with sugared yeast water, the liquid becomes clouded.

22. Since clouding occurred in flask A after fluid had been drained back into the flask from point "X" of the swan neck tube, micro-organisms must have been present in the tube in the vicinity of point "X".

23. Since the liquid in flask A showed no growth of microorgainsms, the air which entered the body of the flask must have been sterite.

24. Since the liquid in flask A remained clear, it contained no growth of microorganisms.

25. Pasteur allowed the contents of flask A to cool very slowly in order to.
    1. give himself time to make observations while the contents of the flask were cooling.
    2. prevent the flask from cracking and spillings its contents.
    3. avoid the danger of an explosion inside the flask.
    4. prevent an inrush of air and microorganisms.
    5. avoid shock to the microorganisms by sudden temperature change.

26. No critic could rightfully say of Pasteur's swan neck flask experiment that.
    1. Pasteur deserved the prize offered by the French Academy.

2. air entering the flask had been deprived of its vegetative force or vital spirlt by heating or treatment with harsh acids.

3. microorganisms would have appeared had he used mutton broth instead of sugared yeast water as culture medium.

4. Pasteur's success was due in part to a fortunate choice of culture medium

5. the question of spontaneous generation of microorganisms was any nearer settlement now than it had been prior to Pasteur's experimentation.

27. By this experiment Pasteur.

1. obtained conclusive evidence that sterile sugared yeast water in contact with germ-free air does not engender microorganisms.

2. proved that spontaneous generation has never occurred on the earth.

3. proved that microorganisms arise by spontaneos generation in a culture medium if the experimenter is careless but they do not arise if he is careful.

4. demonstrated that no culture medium. if it has been boiled, will become contaminated with microorganisms even if germ-free air comes into contact with the fluid inside the flask.

5. went down to defeat from which he never recovered.

Those who are acquainted with objective testing only in its worst manifestations vociferously maintain that (1) objective tests can measure only the attainment of minute, disjointed factual information, and (2) the only means by which one can measure the student's understanding of a somewhat extended and involved concept, theory, or principle is to give the student an essay test ; it is impossible to measure understanding of an organized sequence of ideas by using objeetive test items. The following set of 21 objective test items pursue one major idea, disposing first of prevailing miscoceptions, then presenting hypotheses which evidence tends to support, until a chain of proof has been established. The student must work through the items and accept or reject each of the four hypotheses in turn, then select the best single conclusion that can be drawn from the data. (Answers are indicated in parentheses foilowing each item.)

Problem. What role do the sex chromosomes play is determining sex in Drosophila ?

Hypothesis I. Maleness in Drosophila can be attributed to the presence of chromosome in the genotype.

Data. Occasionally, during gamete formation in the female, the two X chromosomes do 'not' separate. Instead, both go to a single gamete, and the corresponding gemete receives no X chromosome. In such cases the mating with a normal male would be as follows :

The results of such a mating show 50 per cent males and 50 per cent females, but the number of offspring is only

♀ / ♂	XX	——
X	XXX	X—
Y	XXY	Y—

one-half the usual number obtained. A cytological examination of the chromosomes showed that there were only XXY and X—individuals among the offspring. For reasons as yet unknown, XXX individuals and Y— individuals died before birth ; these combinations are apparently lethal. Among the offspring that survived,

however, 'females' were XXY and males were X—.
For items 80 – 85 mark space

1. if the item is true according to the data and tends to support Hypothesis I ;
2. if the item is true according to the data but tends to refute Hypothesis I ;
3. if the item is false according to the data, but if true, would tend to support Hypothesis I ;
4. if item is false according to the data, but if true, would tend to refute Hypothesis I ;
5. if the item is irrelevant to Hypothesis I, regardless of its truth or falsity according to the data.

Suggestion. It will be easier if you decide first whether each statement is true or false according to the data.

80. The presence of a Y chromosome in the genotype inevitably produces a male individual. (3)
81. An individual that inherits a Y chromosome cannot be a female. (3)
82. The presence of a lone Y chromosome in the genotype is lethal. (2)
83. An individual that lacks a Y chromosome cannot be a male. (3)
84. The presence of three X chromosomes in the genotype is lethal. (5)
85. What is the status of Hypothesis I at ths point ?
    1. It is established as true beyond doubt.
    2. It is probably true – the evidence tends to support it.
    3. It is probably false – the evinence tends to refute it.

4. It is definitely false without any doubt.

5. It remains as much unsettled as at the outset. (3)

Hypothesis II. Maleness in Drosophila can be attributed to the presence of one X chromosome and the lack of a second X chromosome in the genotype.

For items 86-88 mark space.

1. it the item is true according to the data and tends to support Hypothesis II ;
2. if the item is true according to the data but tends to refute Hypothesis II ;
3. if the item is false according to the data, but if true, would tend to support Hypothesis II ;
4. if the item is false according to the data, but if true, would tend to refute Hypothesis II ;
5. if the item is irrelevant to Hypothesis II, regard- less of its truth or falsity according to the data.

86. An individual with a lone X chromosome in its genotype is a male. (1)

87. The presence of three X chromosomes in the genotype is lethal. (5)

88. An individual with two X chromosomes and one Y chromosome in its genotype is not a male. (1)

89. What is the status of Hypothesis II at this point ?

1. It is established as true beyond doubt.
2. It is probably true – the evidence tends to support it.
3. It is probably false – the evidence tends to refute it.
4. It is definitely false without any doubt.
5. It remains as much unsettled as at the outset. (2)

Hypothesis III. Femality in Drosophila can be attributed to the absence of a Y chromosome in the genotype.

For items 90-93 mark space.

1. if the item is true according to the data and tends to support Hypothesis III ;
2. if the item is true according to the data but tends to refute Hypothesis III ;
3. if the item is false according to the data, but if true, would tend to support Hypothesis III ;
4. if the item is false according to the data, but if true, would tend to refute Hypothesis III .
5. if the item is irrelevant to Hypothesis III regardless of its truth or falsity according to the data.

90. An individual with two X chromosomes and one Y chromosome in its genotype is a female. (2)
91. An individual with a lone X chromosome in its genotype is not a female. (2)
92. The presence of three X chromosomes in the genotype is lethal. (5)
93. The presence of a lone Y chromosome in the genotype is lethal. (5)

1. It is established as true, beyond doubt.
2. It is probably true—the evidence tends to support it.
3. It is probably false—the evidence tends to refute it.
4. It is definitely false without any doubt.
5. It remains as much unsettled as at the outset. (3)

Hypothesis IV. Femality in Drosophila can be attributed to the presence of two X chromosomes in the gentype.

For items 95-98 mark space.

1. if the item is true according to the data and tends to support Hypothesis IV ;

2. if the item is true according to the data but tends to refute Hypothesis IV ;

3. if the item is false according to the data, but if true, would tend to support Hypothesis IV ;

4. if the item is false according to the data, but if true, would tend to refute Hypothesis IV ;

5. if the item is irrelevant to Hypothesis IV, regardless of its truth or falsity according to the data.

95. An individual with two X chromosomes and one Y chromosome in its genotype is a female. (1)

96. The presence of three X chromosomes is the genotype is lethal. (5)

97. An individual with a lone X chromosome in its genotype is not a female. (1)

98. The presence of a lone Y chromosome in the genotype is lethal. (5)

99. What is the status of Hypothesis IV at this point ?

1. It is established as true beyond doubt.

2. It is probably true – the evidence tends to support it.

3. It is probably false – the evidence tends is refute it.

4. It is definitely false without any doubt.

5. It remains as much unsettled as at the outset. (2)

100. On the basis of the foregiong data and its analysis in the preceding 20 items, which one of the following is the best single conclusion that can be drawn ?

1. Maleness is due to the presence of a Y chromosome in the genotype and femaleness is due to absence.

2. No individual that bears a Y chromosome in its genotype can be female and no individual lacking a Y chromosome can be a male.

3. An individual with more than two X chromosome is a super female and an individual with two X chromosomes and one Y chromosome is a super male.

4. Femaleness in Drosophila is due to the presence of a second X chromosome in the genotype, and maleness is due to its absence.

5. None of the above conclusions fit the data. (4)

In evaluating the outcomes of science teaching we have not begun to exhaust the potentialities of the measuring devices that we have known for years. Testing in many quarters persists at the most primitive and slip-shod levels. To raise the level of testing and evaluation would require a re-study of objectives and teaching methods in an attempt to implement the objectives in the teaching. This is largely a matter of establishing an atmosphere in the classroom that is appropriate to science teaching—an atmosphere in which inquiry, exploration and discovery are encouraged: With adequate planning well in advance of examination time, the teacher who can create the appropriate teaching situation should also be imaginative enough to be able to develop adequate measuring devices.

If the semester examination were planned and begun the first week of school and an average of two questions per day were to be written while the material is fresh in mind, by the end of the semester it should be possible to have a creditable final examination ready for use. An excellent reference for aid in test construction is the book entitled *Educational Measure-*

ment, edited by E. F. Lindquist and published by American Council on Education, Washington, D.C. Attention is especially called to Chapter 7 which is entitled, "Writing the Test Item," Recent extensive biographies on educational and psychological testing may be found in *Review of Educational Research*, Vol. 26 (1), Feb 1956. With these aids any resourceful teacher should be able to develop aehievement tests that will adequately evaluate the degree of attainment of the objectives of sciencee teaching.

3

Methodology of Evaluation

Evaluation has been practiced by teachers for many years, but the purposes, functions, and techniques of evaluation have gradually been modified and improved. Through research there have been developed and refined new techniques and methods for the measurement of attitudes, interests, critical thinking, and personal-social adaptability.

Broadly defined, educational evaluation is the estimation of the growth and progress of pupils toward objectives or values in the curriculum. The purposes of evaluation are to provide for the collection of evidence which will show the degree to which pupils are progressing toward curricular goals, and to permit teachers and supervisors to evaluate the effectiveness of curricular experiences, activities, and instructional methods. The functions of evaluation are to make provisions for guiding the growth of individual pupils, to diagnose their weaknesses and strengths, to point out areas where remedial measures may be desirable, and to provide a basis for the modification of the curriculum or for the introduction of experiences to meet the needs of individuals and groups of pupils.

Techniques of evaluation range from such information measures as teacher ratings on oral recitations and teacher-made tests to more refined and standardized measuses of aptitudes, abilities, skills, interests, and attitudes. Formerly, the major emphasis in measurement was on appraisal of pupil mastery of information and the skills. The changing concepts of the curriculum have required the evaluation of pupil growth in other areas as well, such as physical and mental health, social relationships, critical thinking, appreciations and creative expression, interests, and attitudes. In other words, new curricular emphases have required the development of new techniques of measurement and evaluation.

STEPS IN THE PROCESS OF EVALUATION

It is possible to indicate here only the broad steps that should be taken in working out an evaluation program fitted to the conditions and needs of a particular school. These steps are arranged roughly in the sequence which would be followed in planning and in implementing an evaluation program. They overlap at various places, and in some situations, of course, the sequence might need to be modified.

1. Formulation of the Major Objectives of the Curriculum

Teachers and supervisors must first define the values—the objectives—toward which they wish to guide pupil growth and development. The philosophy of education in any school will be important in determining the values or objectives to be set up as goals for curriculum-making and, consequently, for evaluation in that school. Though the pattern of objectives will vary from school, a comprehensive range of major objectives would be concerned with physical and mental health, social relationships, skills and knowledges, appreciations and creative expressions, critical thinking, interests, and attitudes.

A school which preferred a less comprehensive range of objectives might choose to stress skills and knowledges, interests and attitudes. In any event the major objectives operate directly or indirectly in all of the subjects or areas of the curriculum. It, is essential, therefore, that the staff of a school agree as clearly as possible upon those objectives which it feels are appropriate to its local needs. These objectives then become the guideposts in both curriculum development and evaluation. Techniques of evaluation will be selected or methods constructed to measure pupil growth in each major objective.

Three methods have been used in identifying and defining curricular objectives for purposes of evaluation. These are:

(*a*) curriculum analysis,
(*b*) conference, and
(*c*) questionnaire and interview.

The curriculum analysis method may be illustrated by the studies of Wrightstone (8, 9), Tyler (6, 7), and Smith (5). In these studies, the general purpose of a curriculum is analyzed into relatively independent objectives. The analysis continues to a point where the objectives become clear and useful in teaching and in appraisal, and is suspended after each objective has been defined explicitly in terms of the student behavior leading to its attainment. Smith (5), in reviewing recent evaluation studies, found nine recurring major objectives: mastery of basic skills, effective ways of thinking, development of understandings and insights as revealcd in social behavior, gains in knowledge as exhibited through conduct in personal and social situations, development of interests as related to activities, fostering of personal initiative, creative power, sincerity and potency of attitudes, and post-school vocational competence. In the social studies, Wrightstone (10) has defined such major objectives as acquiring functional information, interpreting facts, applying generalizations, developing work-study skills, organizing facts, and developing social attitudes.

The conference method was used in the Eight-Year Study of the Progressive Education Association. Inter school committees were set up to indicate those objectives for which instruments of evaluation were available. Many of the objectives proposed were so vague that their meanings had to be clarified through definition in terms of student behavior.

Raths (4) reported for the Eight-Year Study these major objectives :

(*a*) Thinking, which was defined broadly to include ability to interpret data, ability to apply principles of science, social facts, and generalizations to specific situations, ability to analyze the nature of proof in reasoning, and sensitivity to social problems and situations.

(*b*) Interests, Aims, and appreciations : which were broadly defined to include a liking or preference for various activities, insight into an activity, realizing its true values, and distinguishing the better activities from the worse.

(*c*) Attitudes : which were defined broadly as beliefs or opinions about social, economic, and political issues, and about school life.

(*d*) Study skills and work habits : such as effective use of study time, effective use of various sources of data, and effective recording, organization, and presentation of data.

(*e*) Social adjustment : which involved such aspects of behavior as acceptance of one's own impulses, agressions, human relationships, identifications with others, fantasies, and reactions to authority.

(*f*) Creativeness, as characterized by original and personal expression in language arts, graphic arts, and industrial arts.

(*g*) Funclional, Information : as represented in the acquisition of concepts, understandings, and skills related to the various secondary-school subjects or curriculum areas.

(*h*) Functional Social Philosophy : which involves the integration of all aspects of growth and development into an intelligent and co-ordinated way of living in one modern society.

The questionnaire and interview method is best illustrated by the University of Minnesota study (1), wherein a questionnaire was sent to graduates of the college and an interview follow-up was made to determine the validity of the method. From an analysis of the responses to the questionnaire, the objectives of the college were determined. In a simllar study at Bennington College (2), the college records and opinions of trustees, students, and faculty were used in analyzing the objectives. These objectives, once they had been defined through extensive deliberations and conferences, provided the basis for a program of evaluation which used questionnaires, tests, rating scales, records, and interviews.

2. Definition and Clarification of These Major Objectives

It is not sufficient to make a list of major objectives; it is necessary to define these objectives so that their meaning will be clear. For example, it is essential to outline more or less specifically the skills and knowledges in reading, in mathematics, or in science. It is equally important to define as clearly as possible the proper types of critical thinking and attitudes that should be developed in subjects such as social studies and science. This definition and clarification makes possible specific application of the broad objectives to particular types of curriculum content and experiences, and thus constitutes a guide to the methods of presentation of such experiences to the pupils. Following are examples of such definitions for several objectives in reading.

Vocabulary—Accurate word recognition and word meaning in both recreational and work-type reading of an appropriate level of difficulty.

Comprehension—Adequate ability to get literal meaning, to follow the organization of a selection, to define new words in context, to identify the main idea, to see relationships among ideas, and to judge the tone of a passage.

Study Skills—Locating Information—Among the many skills, some of those most commonly used in the average classroom include:

(*a*) using indexes,

(*b*) using tables of contents,

(*c*) using dictionaries,

(*d*) using card files, and

(*e*) using such reference sources as atlases, maps, encyclopedias, yearbooks (such as *The World Almanac*), textbooks, magazines, and newspapers.

Interests—Balanced reading diet of various types of reading materials—light and fantastic to serious and technical.

Attitudes—Assimilation and critical appraisal of attitudes implicit or explicit in reading content.

3. Selection of Available Tests or Measures for Each Major Objective

After the major values or objectives have been identified and clarified for each area of the curriculum, the next logical step is to select available tests or measures that will provide evidence about the growth and development of pupils toward each major objective. Thus, one must determine the applicability of various standardized or published tests and scales for measurement of achievement in the major objectives in each subject-matter area. In such subjects as reading, mathematics, social studies, science, and language arts, some, but not all, of the many standardized tests published will be found to fit the definition of the objectives as they have been developed by the staff of the school.

For example, in the field of social studies there are available tests of social studies concepts by Kelty and Moore for elementary-school and by Wesley for secondary-school children. Study skills may be measured by the Iowa Every-Pupil Test of Work-Study Skills.

Critical thinking may be measured at the secondary-school level by the Watson-Glaser Test of Critical Thinking, the Co-operative Test of Social Studies Abilities, or the battery of tests devised in the Eight-Year Study under the titles of Interpretation of Data. Applying Principles and Generalizations, and Nature of Proof. Attitudes or beliefs may be measured by the series of attitude scale devised by H.H. Remmers and his associates. Beliefs on Social Issues devised by the staff of the Eight-Year Study, or the Scale of Civic Beliefs by Wrightstone.

4. Construction of Needed Test Scales or Techniques

For some of the objectives, standardized or published tests, scales, or other techniques will not be available. It is essential, therefore, to begin construction of necessary measurement techniques which will help to appraise growth and development in such objectives. For example, very few published tests are available to measure growth and development in appreciations or in creative expression. and the staff of a school might work cooperatively with test technicians in order to develop the needed scales or techniques to permit measurement of pupil progess in these areas.

In one large city, as an illustration, a committee of mathematics teachers cooperated with school psychologists and research personnel in the construction of tests covering arithmetic computation and arithmetic judgment. Another committee of teachers cooperated in the construction of a battery of tests to measure critical thinking in chemistry. Several teachers from one high school cooperated in the construction of scales of attitudes to measure the effectiveness of a curriculum stressing intellectual relationships.

Another committee of teachers from several vocational high schools cooperated in the construction of a battery of tests for courses in each of the following areas of vocational education : automotive trades, machine shop trades, electrical trades trade dressmaking, commercial education, and cosmetology. For each trade, the battery included tests for trade knowledge required in the particular industry, trade performance, related drawing, related mathematics, and related science.

5. Application of the Various Formal and Informal Tests and Techniques to the Appraisal of Individual Growth and Development

The final step in the process of evaluation is to apply the various formal and informal tests and techniques in order to make judgments about individual growth and development in each of the major objectives. This application and the subsequent interpretation of the results will permit teachers and supervisors to guide the growth and development of each pupil to the best of his individual capacities, abilities, and goals. It will also permit the teachers and supervisors to judge the effectiveness of the curriculum and the instructional techniques that are being used, and to make desirable modifications in them. Of these two major purposes the more important is to provide some data or evidence that will permit the teacher to guide the individual more wisely than would be possible without such information about his growth and development over a period of time.

CHARACTERISTICS OF AN ADEQUATE PROGRAM OF EVALUATION

A modern program of evaluation can be recognized by certain characteristics. Four questions may be applied to judge the adequacy of a program of evaluation in a modern school :

1. Is the Design of the Evaluation Program Comprehensive ?

The major objectives to be appraised should include not only concepts, skills, and knowledges, but also appreciations, attitudes, interests, critical thinking, and personal-social adaptability. Such a design of evaluation is comprehensive when it includes the major values or objectives that the modern school attempts to achieve for each individual pupil. The teacher must regard his task as guiding the pupil's growth and development not only in academic subjects, but also in the more intangible areas of interests, attitudes, appreciations, and emotional and social adjustment. His concern is with the whole child and not merely with the intellectual or academic growth of the child. This is hallmark of the modern design of evaluation.

One must remember, however, that valid and reliable techniques of measurement or appraisal are by their very nature restricted to an evaluation of major aspects of learning-concepts, skills, attitudes, things, and personal-social relationships. It is impractical to attempt to measure the whole result of an educative experience because it involves expending an unreasonable amount of time and energy.

The types of behavior measured in a comprehensive evaluation of pupil growth represent a sampling, not the total of all behavior that might be measured. This sampling should be sufficiently comprehensive to give an accurate appraisal of a pupil's over-all growth and development, provide the design of the evaluation includes the major objective of the course or curriculum. Likewise, the items of a test or scale represent a sampling, not the total of the concepts, information, attitudes, interests, or powers of thinking acquired by a pupil. This sampling, however should be sufficiently comprehensive to give an accurate index of a pupil's status and growth.

For certain of the objectives of the educative process, fairly satisfactory tests and measures have been devised. This is especially true for skills, concepts, and information. To some degree, it is true for various aspects of critical thinking, such as interpreting data, applying principles, and identifying faults in thinking or logic. In physical health, fairly satisfactory tests and measures have been devised for important areas of growth. In mental health, in appeciations and creative expression, and in interests and attitudes, our present measures are less well developed and need considerable refinement. Such measures, however, despite their technical faults and shortcomings, do provide some evidence that is valuable in judging the growth of the individual and in guiding his future growth and development. Some of these measures may be rather subjective, for example, rating scales, anecdotal records, essay examinations and the like. As more technical advances are made, these instruments will be improved. The fact that they are now only tentative, however, should not discount their present values for the teacher.

2. Are Changes in an Individual's Behaviour the Basis for Evaluating His Growth and Development ?

The total behavior of the individual—intellectual, physical, emotional, and social—should be the concern of the teacher and the supervisor in every learning situation. When the child is learning arithmetic, or science, or history, he is at the same time learning attitudes, developing interests, and making emotional and social adjustments. If he is frustrated by too-difficult tasks, or if he is bored by too easy tasks, then his attitudes and emotional and social edjustments will be adversely affected in the learning situations. The teacher, therefore, must remain aware of the various aspects of a pupil's behavior, even though the major purpose of a particular learning experience may be to master the formula for finding the area of a rectangle, or to recognize the chemical symbol for salt. Every learning situation includes multiple learning, involving not only intellectual concepts and skills but also physical, emotional and social adjustment. The total behavior of the child, therefore, is affected to some degree by every learning experience. If the curriculum is designed with the broad objectives in mind, it follows that pupil behavior will be evaluated in terms of these multiple objectives or values.

3. Are the Results of Evaluation Organized and Integrated into a Meaningful Interpretation ?

The quantitative and qualitative results stemming from an evaluation program should be summarized into a meaningful pattern of scores - statistical, graphic, and verbal—so that a portrait of the individual may be gained and compared with previous portraits. The directions and areas in which he is growing, as well as the rate of growth, should be evident. In this interpretation, an effort should be made to see the relationship between the scores on tests and such qualitative entries as ancedotal records, so that the total growth and development of the pupil may be guided wisely.

This implies that data about physical health, emotional and social adjustment, interests, attitudes, and the results from achievement tests in various subjects will not be treated as separate and unrelated entities, but will be correlated or integrated into a unified description of the individual. A hypothetical and simple illustration can be cited.

> Data from a cumulative record card show that James Morris has good physical health and vitality, except that his vision has been impaired so that this year he needs glasses for reading. His emotional and social adjustment was slightly less favorably rated than in previous years, perhaps because he was disturbed by his less successful achievement in subjects requiring reading—languages, history, and science. His interests are mainly academic. His attitudes are rather liberal and broadminded. His academic achievement, except in mathematics, is slightly below previous years, but it has improved since he obtained glasses.

4. Is the Evaluation Program Continuous and Interrelated with the Curriculum?

In the modern school, evaluation is considered an ongoing process. Day-by-day observations, ratings, and tests should constitute the appraisal procedures by which the teacher attempts to evaluate and guide the pupil's growth. This is a concept different from the older approach, which considered testing as an end product rather than as a means for guiding growth, and looked upon measurement as an end-of-term activity.

An evaluation program is interrelated with the curriculum because it is an integral part of guiding pupil experiences. The tests, questionnaires, and other instruments by means of which evidence is gathered, provide the basis for judging growth toward the curriculum objectives. The evidence which is gathered for individuals or for groups in turn affects the curriculum by indicating those areas in which pupil achievement is not as effective as may be desirable, and by indicating those activities and experiences which may not be as conducive to pupil development as others. Thus, the evaluation program becomes a means not only for guiding the pupil's growth, but also for judging changes that may be necessary in the design of the curriculum and in the conduct of instructional practices. Evaluation also throws a further light on the meaning and redefinition of objectives of the curriculum. It helps in any refinement or modification that may be desirable in the objectives that are set up for the curriculum.

THE USE OF EVALUATIVE TECHNIQUE IN SCHOOL SYSTEMS

One of the most systematic surveys of evaluation programs in action was conducted by Michaelis and Howard (3). The purpose of their survey was to review current practices in programs of evaluation in unified city school districts in California. Thirty-eight city school systems provided data for the study. It seems reasonable to assume that the conditions and practices discovered in California prevail in modern school systems in other parts of the nation.

Among the major findings of the study are the following: Thirty-two per cent of the school systems provide handbooks to guide the teachers and to keep them informed about the program of evaluation. These handbooks generally have sections on the relation of evaluation to the educative process, purposes of evaluation, basic needs and differences of children, guiding principles of evaluation, and practical suggestions for using such informal devices as observations of behavior, anecdotal records, sociograms, interviews, checklists, rating scales, and inventories.

Of particular interest is the summary table of data (3:252) indicating the number and percentage of school systems using various evaluative devices. One hundred per cent of the school systems, for example, use psychological and educational tests, but only about ten per cent use sociograms. More detailed information is provided in the table below which is quoted from the published study

Table 1

California School System Reporting the Use of Various Evaluative Devices

Evaluation Devices	*School System Using*	
	Number	*Per Cent*
Tests	38	100.0
Interviews	34	89.5
Case Studies	32	84.2
Case Conferences	31	81.6
Group Discussion	26	68.4
Anecdotal Records	24	63.2
Observation	23	60.5
Files of Sample Materials	22	57.9
Questionnaires	21	55.3
Rating Scales	17	44.7
Check Lists	14	36.8
Inventories	12	31.6
Logs	5	13.2
Diaries	5	13.2
Sociograms	4	10.5

Michaelis, John U., and Howard, Charles, "Current Practices in Evaluation in City School System in California," *Journal of Education Research.*

In addition to the devices listed in Table 1, the authors report that individual school systems indicated the use of follow-up studies, autobiographies, clinics, social case work, evaluative criteria, stenographic reports, recordings, interaction content records, photographs, movies, and pupils' graphs.

From the data reported in the study, it is evident that the school systems generally are using a wide range of techniques and methods to evaluate the growth and development of pupils. It is significant that more than fifty per cent of the school systems are using not only tests of intelligence and achievement, but also interviews, case studies, anecdotal records, observational methods, files of sample materials, and questionnaires to evaluate the development of various aspects or objectives of learning and instruction. It is equally interesting to note that even such new techniques as logs, diaries, and sociograms are being used in slightly more than one out of every ten school systems, a significant comparison with the practices of ten years ago. The trend represents a distinct movement toward more comprehensive evaluation programs.

SUMMARY

A comprehensive evaluation program for a school or school system requires careful planning and effective administration. The steps in careful planning of an evaluation program are ; *First*, formulation of the major objectives of the curriculum. These objectives become guideposts in both curriculum development and evaluation. The formulation of the particular pattern of objectives for a school may be accomplished by :

1. the curriculum analysis method, wherein the general purposes of a curriculum are analyzed into relatively independent objectives,

2. the conference method, in which committees are set up to indicate those objectives to be realized, or

3. the questionnaire and interview method, wherein a questionnaire may be used with students, groups, or patrons of a school, and an interview follow-up made to check the validity of the questionnaire in determining the purposes and aims for the curriculum.

The *second* step in planning a program is the definition and classification of the major objectives. These definitions should outline more or less specifically the skills, abilities, understandings, attitudes, and interests that are to be achieved. The *third* step is the selection of available tests or measures and the determination of the appropriateness of the selections for each of the major objectives as outlined. The *fourth* step is the construction of tests, scales, or techniques needed to evaluate those objectives for which no standardized or published measuring devices are available. The *fiifth* step in the evaluation process is the application of the various formal and informal tests and techniques in order to make judgments about individual and group growth and development in each of the major objectives.

The characteristics to be used for appraising the adequacy of a program of evaluation in the modern school may be embodied in the four questions which follow :

1. Is the design of the evaluation progrm comprehensive so that it includes not only abilities, skills, and understandings, but also the less tangible objectives of learning and instruction ?

2. Are changes in the behavior of the individual the basis for evaluating his growth and development, since the total behavior of the individual—mental,

physical, emotional, and soccial—should be the concern of the teacher and supervisor in every situation ?

3. Are the results of the evaluation organized into a meaningful interpretation so that a portrait of the individual's growth and development and the interrelationships of such growth become evident ?

4. Is the evaluation program continuous and interrelated with curriculum development ?

Surveys of evaluation programs in schools reveal that, compared with practices of ten years ago, the modern school or school system is using a wider variety of evaluation techniques or devices to assess pupil growth and development. Practically every school system uses tests of intelligence and achievement, but, in addition, over eighty per cent use interviews, case studies, and case conferences. Approximately two out of every three schools use group discussion and anecdotal records, as well as observational methods. About one out of every two schools uses files of sample materials, questionnaires, and rating scales. One out of every ten schools uses logs, diaries, and sociograms.

PROBLEMS FOR CLASS DISCUSSION

1. Formulate the major objectives of a course of study or a subject in which you are interested and define each major objective briefly in terms of pupil behaviors that would indicate growth in the objective.

2. For a course in secondary-school science or social studies, list at least one available test or measure for

each of the following; mastery of information, attitudes, critical thinking, and interests.

3. Using an adaptation of the list of evaluation devices in Table 1 in this chapter, make a survey of the teachers in one or more schools to determine which devices are used most frequently.

4

Major Evaluation Techniques

In a comprehensive program of appraisal in the modern school, objective tests constitute one of the major techniques of evaluation. Other major techniques by which data for assessing pupil growth and development may be obtained include, as previously noted : anecdotal records and observational methods; oral and essay examinations; questionnaires, inventories, and interviews; checklists and rating scales; personal reports and projective techniques; sociometric methods; and, case studies and cumulative records

For each of these evaluation techniques, a variety of uses may be discerned in current practice. These include interpretation of data and results for :

(*a*) administrative uses

(*b*) instructional uses,

(*c*) guidance uses, and

(*d*) research uses.

These uses overlap because the categories are not mutually exclusive and the same evaluation data may serve multiple purposes. The adequacy of each evaluation method should be judged on commonly accepted criteria – validity, reliability, objectivity, norms, and practicability—as these apply to the educational situation and the purposes of the educators.

CLASSIFICATION AND DEFINITION OF MAJOR EVALUATION TECHNIQUES

For convenience in discussion, the large number of specific evaluation techniques, methods, and devices have been classified into categories. While it may be argued that these categories are somewhat arbitrary, any other classification scheme would be equally dependent upon the purposes and logic of an author, the present classification follows closely.

Objective Tests

Psychological tests, variously termed mental or educational tests, are designed to present an organized series, or pattern, of items exercises, or stimuli to elicit responses which will reveal the relative degree of the Psychological characteristics proposed by the individual to whom such tests are administrered. Among the psychological characteristics frequently tested are general mental ability, achievement in particular subjects, reading abilities and skills, motor coordination, and aptitude for music or art. Other types of measures frequently included under the category of psychological tests are scales or inventories of attitudes, interests, and personality. The responses required in tests may be selecting the one word or statement among several which best answers a question, filling in by word or phrase an incomplete sentence or statement, the drawing of a simple figure, or marking each of a series of beliefs or opinions to indicate agreement, uncertainty, or disagreement with a statement.

Classification of Objective Tests By Psychological Charactersistics

A variety of scheme may be used to classify objective tests; the psychological characteristics measured, the purposes of the test, the content of the test, or the technical features of the test. For purposes of discussion the chart on page 57 presents a classification of objective tests according to the psychological characteristics that they purport to measure.

It will be noted in this illustrative chart that the general psychological characteristics by which objective tests have been classified include those terms commonly used in educational practice. Among these are tests of intelligence or mental ability; achievement as measured by mastery of abilities, skills, and concepts in the various school subjects of reading, mathematics, language arts, social studies, and science; performance tests and aptitude tests for art, music, language, and mechanical fields. Included under the category of tests are scales, inventories or questionnaires of attitudes, interests, and personality. The second column in the chart illustrates titles of some tests of more specific characteristics. Thus, intelligence has been broken down into tests of verbal intelligence and tests of non-verbal intelligence. Tests of achievement have been broken down into tests of reading comprehension, vocabulary, work-study skills, and tests of critical thinking. Mechanical aptitude tests have been broken down into tests of manual dexterity and tests of spatial relationships.

It is not intended that the list of test titles in the chart should be inclusive. Rather, the intention is to illustrate some of the types of tests available when these are classified by both general and specific psychological characteristics.

CHART ILLUSTRATING CLASSIFICATION OF OBJECTIVE TESTS

According to Psychologisal Characteristics

General Characteristics	*Specific Characteristics*
Intelligence or mental ability	Verbal intelligence Non-verbal intelligence
Achievement, or abilities, skills, and concepts in	Reading comprehension Vocabulary

reading, mathematics, language arts, social studies, science, etc.	Computational ability Problem-solving ability Critical thinking Work-study skills Trade knowledge and performance
Aptitude—art, music, language, mechanical	Rhythmical discrimination Tonal memory Manual dexterity Spatial relationships
Attitudes or beliefs[+]	Attitude toward minorities, the Church, etc. Civic beliefs Militarism-pacifism
Interests[+]	Vocational interests Reading interests Interest in extracurricular activities
Personality[+]	Ascendence-submission Neurotic tendencies

[+]Also referred to as scales, inventories, and questionnaires.

Classification of Objective Tests by Technical Features

In addition to the classification of tests by psychological characteristics, it may be valuable to summarize briefly the classification of objective tests by such technical features as formar and construction, standardization, use of results, and procedures for administration. Some of the major classifications according to this logic are presented in the chart on the next page.

Chart Illustrating

Classification of Tests by Technical Features

Individual	*Versus*	*Group*
Most individual tests require oral questioning and observattion of reactions of the individual to test exercises. *Example* Individual Binet Examination of Intelligence or Rorschach Test.		Most group tests permit many individuals to be tested at same time in a group situation. *Example*; Standford Achievement Battery or Kuder Preference Record.
Subjective		*Objective*
In subjective tests judgment and opinions of scores affect score assigned to test responses *Examples* : Essay examination or rating scale of personality.		In objective tests a standard and specific scoring key provides for assigning a uniform score by competent scores to test responses. *Examples* : california Reading Test or Differential Aptitude Battery.
Standardized		*Informal*
Require uniform test content and testing procedures; each usually has norms, permitting comparisions with scores of the normative population. *Examples*: Pintner. Otis. or or California Tests of Mental Ability.		Informal tests are usually teacher-made for particular unit of study and do not have norms.
Speed		*Power*
Speed tests require the individual to complete as many problems or tasks as he can		Power tests usually present a series of problems or tasks of increasing

at maximum speed. *Examples*: Purdue Peg-Board Test or Speed of Regarding Test.	difficulty, allowing reasonable time for individual to complete as many as he can. *Examples* : Cooperative Reading Test or Henmon-Nelson Test of Mental Ability.
Performance	*Pencil-and Paper*
Performance tests require demonstration of skill by manipulating objects or apparatus: *Examples*: From board tests or typewriting tests.	These tests require answering questions by drawing or writting: *Examples* : Interest Inventory, Mental. Ability Test, or Attitude Scale.
Survey	*Diagnostic*
In survey tests, emphasis is usually upon a general and undifferentiated measure of ability or skill. *Example* : Batteries of Achievement Test.	In diagnostic tests various subtests and interpretation of their results permit identification of more specific abilities and disabilities. *Examples* : Diagnostic Reading Test or Diagnostic Arithmetic Test.

Objective tests may be classified in a number of ways, in this brief introduction, tests have been classified in two categories, first, by the psychological characteristics they purport to measure second, by technical features. Specific tests will be described and illustrated in subsequent chapters of this volume. Brief descriptions of other evaluation techniques used in comprehensive programs of appraisal are presented in the following paragraphs.

Anecdotal Records and Observational Techniques

Anecdotal records and observational techniques are classified under the same category because of the similarity in the methods of obtaining data. Both methods depend chiefly upon an observer who records the activities, experiences, and expressions of individuals or groups.

Anecdotal records may be defined as cumulative notes or records which a teacher or observer makes of the representative behaviour of selected pupils. In compiling the anecdotal record for a pupil, the teacher makes notes of sample situations, activities, experiences, and expressions of the pupil selected for special study. The note or record made should be a concise description of the behaviour, *e.g.*, "John tore a page from Roy's book," and not the teacher's interpretation of this behaviour, *e.g.*, "John was angry was irritable." In order to keep the task of observing and recording from becoming too burdensome, the observations should be restricted to three or four important behaviour characteristics and to only a few pupils. The anecdotal record illustrates an informal method of teacher evaluation of personal and social characteristics of selected pupils. It is one of the practical methods available to the teacher for studying pupil adjustment.

Observational techniques may be defined as systematic methods of analyzing and recording behaviour by directly perceiving the individual or group. The method is generally characterized by observing what the individual actually does and making an objective record of that which is observed. The method may use special techniques and tools, such as specially prepared charts or checklists for recording the behaviour. Observational techniques may be roughly classified under those involving structured or controlled observation and those involving unstructured observation. Under structured observation, the observer may record the occurrence of simple expressive behaviour, such as smiling, laughing, physical or verbal contact with another individual, or complex behaviour and occurrence of acts, such as cooperation and initiative. Observation is also used in performance tests involving structured work samples, such as performance on a form board test or performance on a series of operations on an auto-mechanics test, including changing a tire, checking a battery, and aligning a wheel. Informal unstructured observations of individuals at work occur daily in a classroom, as when the teacher watches the pupil performing operations in arithmetic exercises or participating in an informal social group.

Oral and Essay Examinations

Oral and essay examinations are frequently used by the classroom teachers as informal methods of assessing and diagnosing the day-by-day growth and development of pupils. Both the oral and essay examination, however, have also been designed for use in more formal and structured types of exercises.

Structured types of oral tests include a standardized test of oral reading and oral trade tests. Employment agencies and others involved with industrial personal use the oral type of trade test frequency, such tests consist of a series of questions which it is believed can be answered only by those who know and understand the particular trade or occupation for which the test of designed. A test for general automobile mechanics, for instance, includes such questions as the following:

What are steel power bushings made of?

What joint is there between the differential and the transmission?

Unstructured oral tests include those commonly used by teachers in the classroom wherein an individual or a group is asked oral questions to which they may respond either orally or in writing, thus permitting the teacher to assess their mastery of subject matter or their attitudes, interests, or powers of thinking. In a like manner, the teacher may ask a pupil to read orally a selection from a book or text in order to determine his proficiency in oral reading.

The essay type of examination may be defined as a relatively free written response to a problem situation or situations in which the written answer, intentionally or unintentionally, reveals evidence regarding the functioning of the pupil's mental powers as they have been modified by a particular set of learning experiences. This type of test is widely used by classroom teachers, especially in secondary schools.

Questionnaires, Inventories, and Interviews

Questionnaires and inventories are methods designed to obtain information from individuals by means of a series of questions to which the responses are written. The interview is designed to obtain data in a face-to-face relationship.

The *questionnaire* may be defined as a list of planned written questions that are related to a particular topic or series of topics. Space is provided for indicating the response to each question. The questionnaire is intended for submission to a number of persons for reply. It is commonly used in obtaining specific facts and data and in measurement of attitudes and opinions. The structured type of questionnaire is prepared in such a manner that the answers may be checked or underlined by the respondent. The unstructured type of questionnaire is sometimes called the "open-end" questionnaire. The individual makes a free response to the question rather than selecting one of several answers which have been presented. The *inventory* is similar to the questionnaire, except that it has, in actual practice, been defined as a structured test or checklist used to determine the examinee's attitudes, opinions, or feelings.

The *interview* is a method for obtaining data by face-to-face conference with an individual. The interviewer may employ observation checklists and rating techniques as a part of the interview. Interviews may be classified into three general types. The first type is the diagnostic interview to discover detailed and related facts, opinions, attitudes, and personal experiences about the individual being interviewed. The second type is the survey interview in which the interest is not primarily in the person except as he can contribute an opinion or fact about a problem. A good example of this type is the interview used in connection with the public opinion poll in which the interest is to obtain data about a social, political, economic, or educational problem from a sampling of a population. The third type of interview may be called a treatment interview. This type is used mainly to help an individual to adjust to some particular problem or situation.

Checklists and Rating Scales

The *checklist* may be defined as a prepared list of items that may relate to a person, procedure, institution, building, or similar object. The list is used for the purpose of observation and evaluation by which the observer may show by check marks the presence, absence, or frequency of occurrence of each item being investigated. The diagnostic checklist, for example, is a device used in the classroom or clinic to aid in determining the deficiency of a pupil in reading, in arithmetic, or other fundamental skills. The major difference between checklists and rating scales is that the checklist requires the checking of specific items rather than the judgment of the degree to which a characteristic or the behaviour item is present.

Rating scales or rating methods are devices for the systematic recording of observations and judgments on a scale of units of values given to objects such as school building, textbooks, speciments of handwriting, or to persons, such as pupils or teachers, or to personality traits and attitudes. There are five major types of rating scales as follows:

(*a*) The descriptive rating scale, which contains a number of phrases defining varying degrees of a trait or characteristic;

(*b*) The graphic rating scale, in which a scale of units is indicated on a line and the observer records his rating by checking a point on the line.

(*c*) The product scale, consisting of a series of products, for example, specimens of handwriting arranged according to values determined by a jury. A product is rated by matching it with the scale products.

(*d*) The man-to-man rating scale consisting of descriptions of a number of persons, each of whom is known to the user of the scale, representing the highest lowest, and intermediate degree of merit for rating other individuals; and

(*e*) The numerical rating scale, frequently called a score, card, consisting of a number of items or characteristics each of which has been assigned a numerical value. Score cards have been constructed for rating school buildings, elementary-school practices, teaching ability, and courses of study.

Checklists and rating scales are discussed in more detail in Nine

Personal Reports and Projective Techniques

Personal reports and projective techniques have been used very widely to study the personality of pupils *Personal reports* are essentially self-ratings and are frequently called personality tests or inventories. An example of a self-descriptive personal report is the California Test of Personality. On such an inventory, the pupil answers or checks "yes" or "no" to such items as "Do you day dream?" or "Do you have many friends?"

Variations of the personal report include autobiographies or interviews, in which the individual reports on his personal history, likes, dislikes, goals, and problems.

In recent years, *projective methods* have been used increasingly to assess the personality of individuals. A projective method for the study of personality involves the presentation of a stimulus situation designed to elicit responses which will reveal the personal aims and projections of the examinee. The

Rorschach, one of the most widely known and used projective methods, uses ink blots as the stimulus for eliciting responses or projections of the examinee. Pictures, such as those devised by Murray in his Thematic Appereception Test, are used in a similar manner. In addition to these methods, other projective techniques include analysis of handwriting, painting, or drawing, completion of sentences or stories, role-playing, and the use of toys or puppets.

These methods are discussed in more detail in Chapter Ten.

Sociometric Methods

Sociometric methods may be defined as devices for revealing the preferences, likes, or dislikes that exist among the members of a group. This technique is characterized by the procedure of obtaining from individuals in a social unit a statement as to which group members would be preferred as cooperating participants in various activities or relationships. An individual may be asked, for example, to name the person that he would wish as a workmate, as a seatmate, or as a teammate in a school situation. This technique may be used for revealing the group structure of a social unit and identifying subdivisions of the group. It permits an analysis of various types of group members as, for example, leaders, isolates and those in rival factions or cliques. This technique is discussed in Chapter Eleven.

Case Study

The *case study* or case method may be defined as the use of comprehensive data about an individual as the basis for diagnosing and interpreting his conduct or behavior. It is a method of investigation that concerns itself with the careful examination of factors that are significant in the life of the person under study. Emphasis is placed on discovering what is unique in the case rather than what is characteristic of large numbers of individuals. The findings are especially related to the treatment of maladjustments displayed by the individual. It is a diagnostic and remedial procedure based on a thorough investigation of a person in order to acquire knowledge of his history, his home conditions, and all of the things that may have contributed to his behavior difficulties.

The ultimate aim of the case method is to diagnose and evaluate the total behavior of the individual in order that appropriate remedial measures may be applied. The case study generally contains a description of the behavior indicative of maladjustment, a physical and health report based on an examination, family background and history, early childhod history, mental capacity and educational achievements as revealed by tests and observational methods, a report on the child's personality, and a description of previous efforts to improve the adjustments.

Cumulative Record

The *cumulative record* is an individual record, usually of a permanent nature that is kept up to date by the teacher or other school personnel. It may be in the form of a card, folder, or packet A cumulative record, regardless of its format, is an educational history containing fairly complete information about the pupil's school achievement, course of study, attendance, health, and similar pertinent data. The record folder or record packet is frequently used as a convenient filing device for accumulating data over a period of time. This may contain some actual samples of the pupil's writing, drawing, and school work, as well as anecdotal records and other recorded observations made by teachers and school personnel. This technique is discussed in Chapter Thirteen.

USES OF EVALUATION DATA

The proper use of data from evaluation techniques requires that one or more important and desirable purposes shall be served. Intelligent planning is basic to the wise use of information obtained from various methods of evaluation. One way of classifying the uses of various measures is according to the functions of various school officers or personnel, namely, the administrator, the supervisor, the teacher, the guidance conselor, and the research worker. Several purposes may be satisfied by the same data. Thus, the data from an intelligence test, an achievement test battery, an interest inventory, or a sociometric technique may be used by school personnel for different purposes, as illustrated in the following paragraphs.

Administrative Uses

The administrator may use results of evaluation methods to provide records of pupil adjustment, interests, aptitudes, and achievement. The data may be entered upon the pupil's cumulative record card or in the cumulative folder and become a basis for the evaluation of the individual's growth and progress or that of the class group. Another used by the administrator is to provide reports to parents. Frequently, the principal may find it necessary and desirable to supplement his opinions or the teacher's opinions about a pupil by documentary evidence gathered by means of tests, questionnaires, interviews, or anecdotal records. Such evidence may frequently be used in reports to or in conferences with parents. A third use is to make available more systematic and objective records when a pupil is iransferred to another school Such records permit a better interpretation of a pupil's status and facilitate placement in a congenial classroom in the new school.

The administrator may also use evaluation data to provide periodic reports of school progress to the patrons in a community. Frequently, also, the data from sociometric, personality, aptitude, and achievement tests may be consulted in the classification of pupils for instructional purposes. Although learning is mainly an individual matter, the usual classroom situation demands that each pupil learn as part of a group. Data from evaluatian techniques are especially valuable in educational and vocational guidance to help counsel and assign pupils to such different curricula as college preparatory, trade, business, and general courses.

Instructional Uses

The supervisor, likewise, may use evaiuation results for a variety of purposes. His major task is to help the teacher do a better teaching job. This responsibility can best be realized if both the teacher and the supervisor have evidence about the status of the pupil as well as about his needs and interests. One of the uses that a supervisor may have for evaluation data is to determine the status of a class or a pupil in some of the major objectives of the curriculum. This will permit him to evaluate teaching methods and instructional materials, and to indicate desirable changes in instructional procedures and pupil-teacher relationships. Again this may be accomplished by obtaining evidence of the relative contribution which a particular teaching method or particular instructional materials make to the pupil's growth and development.

The teacher uses test and other evaluation data for a variety of purposes, many of which are similar to those of the administrator and supervisor. The teacher and supervisor often discuss quantitative and qualitative data in order to arrive at an agreement on various instructional and learning problems. The teacher may use the results of tests and measures:

1. to determine the status of each pupil in various subjects and in various objectives of the curriculum,

2. to identity the gifted pupil, "normal" pupil, and show-learning pupil,

3. to group pupils for instructional purposes within the class,

4. to analyze or diagnose an individual pupil's difficulties and rate of growth, and

5. to determine the status of the individual or class at the beginning and at the end of the term.

Such evaluation tehniques as anecdotal records, observations, rating scales, personal reports, interviews, and sociometric methods aid the teacher to assess and to guide more wisely the growth and development of pupils. If anecdotal records, observations, rating scales, and interview methods have been systematically used to collect data on personal and social adaptabilty, the teacher may use the results :

1. to identify pupils who are well adjusted and those who are poorly adjusted.

2. to diagnose the probable causes or contributing factors for maladjustment, and

3. to set up inividual and group conditions and situations to aid, whenever possible, growth toward better adjustment.

In a like manner, sociometric methods may be used as an aid to identity "leaders" and "is lates" among a pupil group and to establish social relationships in the classroom that will contribute to the maximum social development of each pupil. Interest inventories may be used to identify pupil interests in reading or other educational and vocational activities, thus permiting the teacher to counsel the pupils and adapt the curriculum to their needs. Attitude scales may be used to discern individual or group attitudes toward minority group. Although the case study is usually reserved for application to the seriously maladjusted pupil, the cumulative record should be studied as a method for evaluating and guiding the growth and development of every pupil.

Educational and Vocational Guidance

Educational guidance is now considered an integral part of the educational program. Skilled guidance has become a part of each teacher's responsibility to his pupils, as well as the responsibility of the guidance counselor. Individual needs and abilities are the bases of guidance. The teacher or counselor uses all pertinent data to advise or guide the pupil in his physical, mental, emotional, and social growth and development. This guidance aids the pupil in selecting appropriate courses of study changing his program of studies, motivating him to complete high school, selecting a college, understanding his interests and abilities, and improving his personal adjustment.

Vocational guidance is especially important in the modern secondary school. Advice is offered to an individual about whether or not to undertake certain vocations. Pertinent data can be obtained in part through intelligence, achievement, and aptitude tests, recorded observations, anecdotal records interest inventories, and the cumulative record. Based on this information, the pupil can be guided toward occupational choices adapted to his interests, aptitudes, and abilities. By using the data collected by means of various techniques, the teacher or counselor will have a more secure foundation for helping the pupil to plan for successful adjustment in an occupation.

Research Uses

Data gathered by means of various evaluation techniques are also used for research purposes. Carefully designed studies are sometimes made, for example, of the effectiveness of different methods of teaching reading or teaching arithmetic or or meeting the personal social needs of pupils. Occasionally, more ambitions studies are designed and conducted to judge the effectiveness of a curriculum experiment, such as a core curriculum. These studies may be conducted by a research bureau of a city school system or of a college or university. On the other hand, individuals interested in advanced graduate work may also undertake such studies. Other variations of research uses of evaluation techniques are diagnostic studies of learning difficulties, age or grade placement of subject matter, curves of learning for various curricular materials, correlations among various measures of aptitude, ability, and personal characteristics, and case studies of particular pupils.

Misuses of Results

Evaluation results may sometimes be misused. If the design of the appraisal program is narrow and limited, the testing program may tend to determine the emphasis upon specific objectives of the curriculum to the detriment of others and to the detriment of desirable trends in pupil growth. Sometimes, test results of a very partial nature are used to estimate or to rate the teacher's teaching ability. While such evidence may serve as a part of the data to be considered in rating teachers, few educators would defend a rating made solely upon this basis. Some administrators, however, misuse test results by employing them for purposes such as this. Reliable and valid instruments are, by their very nature, restricted to an appraisal of limited aspects of pupil behavior or growth. It is impossible to measure the whole result of an educative experience by any one test or battery of tests and measures. The fact remains, however, that, by evaluating many important and vital aspects of experience, appraisals may be obtained of the relative merits of diverse educational practices.

QUALITIES OF JUDGING AN EVALUATIVE TECHNIQUE

A test or evaluative technique is judged for its adequacy, efficiency, and consistency as a measuring device on the basis of commonly accepted qualities. These qualities are *validity*, *reliability*, *objectivity*, *norms*, and *practicability*. Validity is that quality which indicates the relationship of a measure or diagnosis with meanigful criteria of learning or behavior. Some criteria may be selected to show effectiveness to predict future performance, other criteria to indicate immediate status, other criteria to establish the representative nature and scope of content or behavior, and still other criteria to provide data for supporting or rejecting some psychological theory. 'Reliability' is that quality which indicates the consistency, equivalence, or stability of a measure that is obtained. 'Objectivity' is that quality which indicates the identity or similarity of the scores or diagnosis obtained from the same data by equally competent scorers. A 'norm' provides an average or typical value for a measure or diagnosis obtained by thr administration of a measuring instrument to a specific population so that subsequent scores or measures for ae individual or a group may be compared with the typical values of the normative population. 'Practicability' is that quality which indicates the feasibility for the general use of a test or evaluative technique on such bases as cost, time required for administration, case of administration, case of scoring and ease of interpretation of the results.

Validity

In a test or other evaluative instrument, validity is that characteristic which indicates the degree to which the instrument measures or provides a diagnosis of the psychological characteristics that it purports to measure. Validity is judged by the relationship between the measure or diagnosis and such meaningful criteria as ratings by teachers or performance of specific tasks. Cronbach (2) has indicated that the basic question in validity is how well a test or evaluative technique does the job that it is employed to do. Validity is not an absolute characteristic of an evaluative technique ; it is relative to the purpose of the test user. The same technique may be used for several different purposes, and its validity may vary from high to low depending upon the purpose. In a test of arithmetic computation, for example, the validity of the test may be high for determining the present status of pupils in skills of arithmetic computation. Its validity may be moderate for judging aptitudes of pupils for business arithmetic. Its validity may be low for predicting success in the mathematical aspects of a subsequent course of study in physics. Validity, therefore, must be defined in terms of the purpose that is to be served by the particular instrument or technique employed.

Various methods are employed to validate tests or other techniques of measurement, but all methods require meaningful criteria. These criteria may include future achievement, school marks, ratings by teachers or experts on pupils' abilities, skills, interests, attitudes, or personal-social adjustment, and content analysis of courses of study or an area of behavior which is the goal of training and guidance, in addition to these methods, some measures are validated by correlation with other known measures or by comparison between the accomplishments of widely spaced groups in the psychological function, or characteristic, under consideration.

The definition of a meaningful criterion and its reliable measurement present difficulties. In some instances, the translation of success or performance into o measurable and unambiguous score raises a number of serious problems. Frequently, teachers' grades are used as a criterion for validating educational tests and techniques, but these grades include nat only an evaluation of the pupil's mastery of subject matter but also a rating of the pupil's effort, verbal efficiency, work habits, sociability, and other aspects of his personality.

For the teachers purposes in grading, perhaps, all of these factors and others may reasonably be included in an evaluations of the pupil. In validation however the complexity of factor-affecting teachers grades tends to obscure many of the relationl ships which exist between this, criterion and the psychologica characteristic measured by a test or technique. In addition, when grades over a period or several years are combined, the comparability of ratings by different teachers raises another problem of defining the criterion with reasonable precision. This example illustrates how difficult it is to obtain a meaningful criterion and to obtain a reliable rating for the criterion. Despite these limitations, criteria are defined and rated as carefully as possible.

Kinds of Validity

Since validity is not an absolute characteristic, several kinds of validity may be identified, depending upon the purpose for which the evaluate method is to be used. According to a report (1) prepared by a joint committee of the American

Psychological Association. American Educational Research Association, and National Council on Measurements Used in Education, four categories of validity may be distinguished. These are *Predictive validity, concurrent validity, content validity,* and *construct validity.*

Predictive Validity

Predictive validity is judged or estimated by the degree of the relationship between a measure and subsequent criterion measures of judgments. This type of validity is required in such measures as tests of intelligence or academic aptitudes used for predicting later scholastic success ; in tests of aptitudes used for predicting later success in some field of study or work such as music, art, or stenography ; in vocational interest inventories used to aid in the choice of a vocation ; and in projective techniques or similar measures which are used to predict the future personal-social adjustment of an individual. Questionnaires and interviews designed to elicit opinions and beliefs and which are used for predicting future behavior of individuals or groups must also satisfy this type of validity.

Concurrent Validity

Concurrent, or status validity indicates the correspondence, or relationship, between a measure and the more or less immediate behavior or performance of identifiable groups. The difference between concurrent validity and predictive validity is solely a matter of time. Predictive validity requires correspondence with a future criterion whereas concurrent validity requires correspondence with the criterion at the time of testing or diagnosis. If the Thematic Apperception Test provides a relatively successful diagnosis of some personality difficulties of an individual at the time of testing, the degree of concurrent, or status, validity in doing so may thus be established. In a like manner, a personal report or personality test which gives a reasonably accurate measure of diagnosis of personal adjustment or maladjustment at the time of administration has a degree of concurrent validity. An opinion questionnaire or interview for immediate and not for future use is another example of a situation in which the need for concurrent validity applies. If the results of checklists of reading or arithmetic disabilities, a sociometric analysis of a class, an observational method, or an interview are to be used for immediate diagnosis, these techniques must be judged for their effectiveness in terms of concurrent validity—how well they measure present behavior or performance.

Content Validity

Content validity is judged by the degree of relationship or correspondence between a measure or diagnostic technique and achievement in the specific course or curriculum. In a technical sense, the test or technique will sample a universe of possible behaviors, content, or activities of a course or curriculum. An academic achievement test in history, science, or literature is examined frequently for content validity by checking the test items against courses of study and textbooks or curriculum guides. Performance tests for trade or industrial arts courses may be examined for content validity by checking them against a detailed job analysis.

Construct Validity

Construct validity may be established by indicating the correspondence or relationship between the results of a technique of measurement and other indicators of the characteristic or characteristics that are measured or assessed. This type of validation is often used for tests or measures of a psychological characteristic that is assumed to exist by empirical or theoretical deduction.

Briefly defined, a psychological construct is an ability, aptitude, characteristic, or trait that is assumed to exist to explain some aspect of human behavior. For example, it may be assumed that general mental ability comprises such fairly independent factors as verbal ability, number ability, perceptual ability, space ability. reasoning, and memory. In order to establish the construct validity of a test of ***number factor***, it may be necessary for an investigator to correlate the results of a test of *number factor* with results of other tests involving not only number reasoning and manipulation, but also other types of mental factors or abilities, to make systematic observations of persons having known scores on the test, and to show that the test discriminates between groups widely spaced in ability to manipulate and reason with numbers.

The same approach might be used to judge the validity of interpretations of personality characteristics that are assumed to be measured or diagnosed in a projective technique, such as the Rorschach ink blots. It may be assumed that individual who perceive forms on the Rorschach are better able to resist emotional stress. Validation would call for evidence that scores or results vary from person to person or from occasion to occasion as the theory would require.

Often construct validity is established by considering together many different kinds of incomplete but complementary evidence. Thus, it may rely on correlation of the test or technique with other tests, on systematic observation of persons having known scores or results, and on evidence that the test discriminates between widely spaced groups. If it is assumed that a score on "neuroticism" from a personality measure is associated positively or negatively with persons having certain defined physiques and with their total temperamental pattern, including their adjustment to certain occupations, the proof can best be established by the construct validity methods just cited.

Establishing the Validity of Various Techniques

Observational techniques, including rating scales, check-lists, and anecdotal records, will use one or more of these methods of establishing validity depending upon its purposes. This is true for the interview, the case study, and cumulative records when these are used as methods for assessing an individual's behavior.

It should be noted, however, that in predictive and concurrent validity the criterion of future performance or immediate performance is of major concern, and the test or measure is of interest only as an indirect estimate of the criterion behavior. In measures of achievement and performance where content validity is established, the test behavior, as a sample of the universe of appropriate content or behaviors, is the characteristic with which the examiner is chiefly concerned. Construct validity is ordinarily studied when several indirect measures of some characteristic are available and it is desired to show that the test or instrument measures a theoretical characteristic or construct. None of the indirect measures may be a good measure of the theoreticai characteristic or construct. yet each measure supports or complements others. The charaeteristic is of central importance rather than the test behavior itself.

This survey of validity indicates the central importance of a meaningful criterion, and clearly indicates the complex and difficult nature of establishing validity. Satisfactory criterion measures are difficult to achieve. Criteria for judging proficiency in a job, a course of study, or in personal-social adjustment require an immense investment of time and professional skill, despite which the results are often limited in scope and of low reliability. The limitations which these difficulties represent lead to the conclusion that obtaining satisfactory criterion data is perhaps the most difficult and costly aspect of measurement and evaluation.

Reliability

Reliability provides an index of the accuracy with which a test or instrument measures. Reliability is commonly defined as an estimate of the degree of consistency or constancy among repeated measurements of individuals with the same instrument. Whenever any physical object or psychological characteristic is measured, that measurement contains some degree of chance error. If the chance errors are small relative to the variation, or range, of measures of the object or characteristic measured, the reliability or consistency of measures is high. Thus, the reliability of a measure of height of adults is high when the majority of chance errors are less than 1/4 inch relative to a range from 60 to 78 inches.

Reliability is usually expressed as a *coefficient of reliability*, but is sometimes expressed as the *standard error of measurement*. The standard error of measurement may be termed absolute consistency. This degree of absolute consistency may be observed in the actual amount of variation which results when a particular measuring instrument is applied more than once to the same individual. It is to be noted that the standard deviation of such a distribution of repeated measurement is also referred to as the standard error of measurement.

Relative consistency, expressed by the reliability coefficient, is more frequently used in psychological measures. It is impossible to measure the same individual repeatedly by means of psychological tests without directly affecting the psychological characteristic. For example, repeated administration of a reading test will directly affect the reading ability of the individual tested. In order to meet this difficulty in measuring psychological characteristics, methods of estimating the reliability coefficient have been established.

The major procedures for estimating coefficients may be briefly summarized as follows :

(*a*) Administration of two equivalent tests and correlation of the resulting scores.

(*b*) Repeated administration of the same test or testing procedures and correlation of the resulting scores.

(*c*) Subdivision of a single test into two presumably equivalent halves, each scored separately, and the correlation of the resulting two scores.

(*d*) Analysis of variance among individual items and determination of the error variance from this statistic.

Reliability may thus be considered as the degree to which a true or perfect measurement of each individual is obtained when a measure is applied. It is impossible, however, to obtain a perfect measure in the physical sciences or in the biological sciences. The measure is always contaminated or made impure by chance factors which affect the accuracy of the measurement. Some possible sources of variation in psychological measurement are indicated in the following :

1. Actual difference among individuals in the psychological characteristic being assessed or measured. This applies to both general and specific characteristics, abilities, and skills.

2. Differences in abilities to take a specific test, such as : ability to comprehend directions or instructions, effects of practice in taking previous tests, and facility in dealing with specific test exercises.

3. Differences associated with chance factors, such as fluctuations in performance, memory, or reasoning, fortunate selection of answers by guessing, and unique possession of particular fact, knowledge, or opinion in an exercise.

4. Differences of a personal but temporary nature affecting the performance of the individual, such as : health. energy, fatigue, motivation, and emotional tension.

5. Differences associated with external conditions, such as : heat, light, ventilation. noise, broken pencil, and interference.

Types of Reliability Coefficients

Reliability is a general term and refers to several types of evidence regarding the consistency of measurement. Different types of reliability coefficients answer different questions and permit different inferences regarding the evidence. Three major types of reliability coefficients are generally used in describing consistency of measurement for psychological tests and techniques. These are :

(*a*) coefficient of internal consistency,

(*b*) coefficient of equivalence, and

(*c*) coefficient of stability.

Coefficient of Internal Consistency

The coefficient of internal consistency is the estimate obtained from the single administration of a test or instrument to a representative group of individuals. It indicates how accurately or consistently the test or instrument measures the individual's performance at a particular moment. It provides an estimate of the probable variability in his score or result if a different sample of questions, activities, or behaviors were examined or observed. Two methods are generally used to estimate this coefficient. They are :

(*a*) split-half method and

(*b*) Kuder-Richardson method.

In both of these methods the same general trait, ability, or characteristic of a homogeneous nature should be measured and the test should not be speeded.

The method of estimating reliability for a test by the split-half method may be described briefly as follows. The test is divided into two halves as equivalent in difficulty of items and in content as is possible. Each individual's test is scored so as to obtain a score for the first half, a score for the second half, and a score for the total test. The agreement or correlation between the halves is determined, and the Spearman-Brown formula (4 ; 40-41) or Guttman formula (3) is used to estimate the reliability of the test.

In the Kuder-Richardson formula (5) the coefficient is estimated by determining the variance of the individual items, namely. multiplying the percentage passing by the percentage failing each item and finding the sum for all items. This is divided by the variance of the total test, namely, the standard deviatian of the total scores squared. The resulting ratio is subtracted from unity and adjusted for the number of items in the test.

In the split-half method, the resulting coefficient is a serious under-estimate if the halves of the test are not closely equivalent in difficulty and content. In the Kuder-Richardson formula, the resulting coefficient is an under-estimate if the test does not measure a homogeneous ability or characteristic. In both methods, the coefficient is spuriously high if the test is speeded.

Coefficient of Equivalence

The coefficient of equivalence, as in the case of the coefficient of consistency, may be defined as an index of how consistently the test measures the individual's performance at a particular moment. It measures fluctuations from day-to-day in the individual and fluctuations in the sampling of content of the test or measure. The preferred method of determining this coefficient is to administer on two occasions to the same individuals two parallel forms of the test or measure, each form containtaining different questions or content but which can reasonably be assumed or proved to be equivalent. The correlation between the scores on the two parallel forms is called the coefficient of equivalence because it measures the relationship between equivalent forms of the test.

A less precise method of obtaining the coefficient of equivalence is to use the split-half coefficient based on equated parts of a test, provided the equated parts of the test are carefully documented for equality in difficulty of the items and equality of content of the characteristics or abilities that are being assessed.

To the extent that parallel forms of the test are not equivalent in difficulty and content, or split halves of the test are not equivalent in difficulty and content, the correlation coefficient will not provide a true estimate of the reliability of the test. Here again it is assumed that proper precautions will be observed regarding the homogeneity of the characteristic measured.

Coefficient of Stability

The coefficient of stability indicates the degree to which the scores on a particular test or measure are stable over a given period of time. It indicates whether a sample of behavior observed or assessed at one time is typical of behavior at subsequent times. This coefficient is estimated by the test and retest method. The same test is administered to the same individuals after an intervening period of time. A somewhat imilar coefficient is obtained when two highly equivalent orms of the test are administered with an intervening period of time. The correlations between the scores on the two tests or measures is computed in order to obtain the coefficient.

Factors Related to Reliability Coefficient

From the brief descriptions that have been provided and by inference from the method of obtaining reliability coefficients, the following generalizations may be made :

(*a*) The reliability coefficient depends on the length of the test or instrument.

(*b*) The reliability coefficint, since it deals with the variance of item performance as a ratio to variance on total test performance, is closely related to the spread or range of scores in the group studied.

Application to Various Types of Evaluative Instruments

Although reliability coefficients have been most widely

used among the objective types of tests and measures, they may be applied to various other evaluative methods. In data obtained by direct observational methods, for example, the results are often analyzed in terms of sampling error or reliability and observer error or reliability.

The sampling error answers the question : Is the cross section of behavior obtained by observation typical or characteristic of the individual or group ? This may be determined by splitting the observations into halves and finding the relationship between the halves. Observer error or reliability answers the question : What is the consistency of observations among independeut observers, or to what degree do the observers allow conscious or unconscious biases to influence their report ? This may be determined by correlating the results for two independent observers, who observed the same situations at the same times.

In rating methods experience has shown that the reliability of ratings may be increased by pooling the judgments of a number of persons. The number of judgments that should be pooled or averaged varies according to the degree of reliability sought and the nature of the trait rated. For many traits three or more independent ratings should be obtained and pooled. The reliability of ratings may be increased, also, by analyzing a trait into a number of subtraits and asking each judge to rate the sub-divisions. The reliability of the structured interview may be studied by techniques similar to those used for rating methods.

The reliability of the Rorschach and similar projective techniques has been examined by the test and retest method. In sociometric methods, questionnaires, and inventories the test and retest method has also been used to determine reliability.

Objectivity

Objectivity is an attribute of a test or instrument so constructed that identical or very closely similar scores are assigned by different but equally competent scores. In a highly objective instrument the scores assigned are not affected by the judgment, personal opinion, or bias of the scores.

In general, tests or instruments that possess the quality of objectivity are to be preferred to those in which the opinion of the scorer unduly influences the results. The administration of group tests of intelligence, achievement, and aptitude to large groups generally requires that the answers be scorable with high objectivity. On the other hand, flexibility with regard to objectivity is sometimes advantageous, especially in diagnostic and clinical work. Thus, the type of instrument, the purpose of the evaluation, and the technical competence of the examiner require relative degrees of objectivity rather than a fixed standard.

Techniques with High Objectivity

Standardized group tests of intelligence, achievement, aptitude, attitudes, and interests have high objectivity because they are provided with a scoring key which permits a competent scorer to determine without exercise of much judgment or personal opinion the right or wrong answers to the items of the test. All of those instruments are so designed in their structure that they permit the examinee certain choices of standard answers and the answer selected has an unequivocal standard value to contribute to the total score.

Techniques with Moderate Objectivity

Tests of intelligence such as the Binet and Wechsler-Bellevue, which are administered individually and orally by a clinically trained person, have moderate objectivity. Included in this category, also, are the projective techniques such as the Rorschach and the Thematic Apperception Test. In measures of this type the scoring and interpretation of the test or technique, while it has a high degree of standardization and uniformity, permits the examiner to use his judgment in assessing certain of the values and making interpretations of the responses of the examinee. Closely associated with these are the performance tests in which the examinee manipulates apparatus and in which the examiner, by observation, makes judgments regarding the performance of the individual and translates the judgment into the score or rating to be assigned. The checklist depends upon observation and judgment and therefore is classified as an instrument with moderate objectivity. Essentially the same factors of judgment operate when teachers use rating scales of products such as a handwriting scale or drawing scale. Direct observation, with categories of behavior to be observed defined in advance, also requires a moderate degree of judgment on the part of the observer in assessing the value or score to be assigned to the individual under observation.

Techniques with Flexible Objectivity

Flexible objectivity is especially desirable where the approach is clinical or pseudo-clinical. The major evaluation methods to be classified under this category are the unstructured interview, the open-end questionnaire, the anecdotal record, a running account of behavior by direct observation, and interpretation of data from projective techniques involving analysis of drawings, handwriting, and similar stimuli.

Norms

The results obtained from a test or other evaluative technique require interpretation. These results take on added meaning as they are compared or contrasted with those obtained from different kinds of persons, or populations, to whom the tests or techniques have been administered. The raw score, or number of items correct, on a standardized test becomes much more meaningful when compared with the average score obtained by reference groups arranged according to age, grade, years of study, or type of person.

A standardized test, for example, should have norms which will aid in the interpretation of the raw score obtained.

For this reason, authors and philosophers provide such norms as the following :

(*a*) Age norms for converting a raw score into a mental age, reading age, arithmetic age, etc.

(*b*) Grade norms for converting a raw score into the performance on the test of the average pupil at a given grade level.

(*c*) Percentile norms for converting a raw score into a comparison with the percentage of pupils of a given age or grade who obtained that raw score.

(*d*) Standard score norms for converting the raw score into a standard deviation from the mean, or average, for a given age, grade, or other reference group.

These basic norms are defined and described in more detail in Chapter Four. Such norms are called derived scores and help in the interpretation of test results. Variations of these types of norms have been devised by different test authors and publishers.

Among the recommendations of various committees which are attempting to establish standards for tests and diagnostic techniques, the following are included.

(*a*) Tables or scales used to report scores should be designed to permit easy and accurate interpretation by the test user.

(*b*) Norms should refer to clearly defined and described populations, or reference groups, such as grade, age, curriculum, or occupational group. These populations should be the groups to whom users of the test will usually wish to compare the individual or group tested.

(*c*) Norms should be based upon a representative cross section, or sample, of the defined population or reference group.

(*d*) Although norms may be reported in terms of grade or age groups, it is desirable, also, to provide percentile equivalents or standard scores into which raw scores may be converted.

(*e*) For some uses of tests, local norms are more appropriate and important than national, regional, or other group norms. In such cases, the test manual should suggest appropriate use of local norms.

These criteria, or standards, may well be applied by the test user in the evaluation and selection of specific tests. Unless a test can meet these desirable standards in the reporting of norms, its use may be of doubtful value.

Qualitative Norms

As in the case of objectivity, so in the case of norms, flexibility of interpretation is desirable in diagnostic and clinical types of instruments. Under the categories of evaluative methods for which flexibility in norms and interpretations is desirable are the following :

(*a*) Sociometric techniques, in which the qualitative and descriptive relationships among individuals and cliques can be more adequately communicated by qualitative rather than quantitative terms.

(*b*) Interview, especially the unstructured interview, in which the purpose is to diagnose and to provide treatment for some behaviour disorder or maladjustment.

(*c*) The open-end questionnaire, in which the various degrees of response are better expressed in qualitative and descriptive terms than in qualitative terms.

(*d*) Anecdotal records, in which the major purpose is to obtain a descriptive and diagnostic picture of the individual's typical behaviour in various situations.

Practicability

The qualities of practicability in a test or evaluative technique involve consideration of such factors as cost, ease of administration, ease of scoring, ease of interpretation, time requirements, and availability of comparable forms of tests or techniques. In addition, the test or technique must be reasonably acceptable to the persoes to whom it is administered and to the persons who use the results. This means that the test or technique must inspire a feeling of reality and purpose in the sense that some direct relationship may be observed between the exercises or content of the test or technique and the psychological characteristic that is to be appraised. Furthermore, the typographical and physical appearance of the test or technique should be as attractive and interesting as is feasible.

Cost

The cost of tests or techniques which measure the same psychological characteristic may vary from publisher to publisher. When a school system is testing a large number of pupils, a difference in the cost of a test or other evaluative technique may be an important consideration. It is wise, therefore, for teachers and supervisors to examine tests and techniques for measuring various psychological characteristics and to obtain the test or technique of highest quality that may be obtained within the budget provided by the school system.

Ease of Administration

Another practical consideration is the ease of administering a test. Some tests require the services of expertly trained examiners. Unless such speciaily trained personnel are available, it is impossible to use the tests and to insure validity and reliability of the results. The use of any test or technique should be judged in terms of the related competencies of the personnel available for administering the test and the degree of expertness that is required for obtaining accurate results.

Ease of Scoring

Ease of scoring or analyzing primary data is an equally important consideration. Some techniques, such as the individual Binet examination for intelligence and the Rorschach projective technique for personality appraisal, require expertly trained scorers. Some group tests use multiple and time-consuming scoring methods in order to arrive at differential scores for different psychological characteristics. A test or technique should be reviewed carefully to determine how practicable it may be in a specific school situation in terms of the degree of expertness, as well as the time, required for scoring.

Ease of Interpretation

Ease of interpretation of the results from various tests and techniques is another quality that must be judged. Some tests of personality, attitudes, aptitudes, and interests, for example, may require specially trained personnel in order that the results may be interpreted validly. When it is proposed to use techniques in which the interpretation of results appears rather complex, the technique should be studied carefully to determine whether or not it is feasible to interpret the results with the competencies of school personnel available for this purpose.

Time

Time requirements are frequently an important consideration. In many schools, as well as in business and industry, a limited time may be available to administer a test or technique.

A short test rather than a longer and more comprehensive one which would give more valid and reliable results. On the other hand, it may be more feasible to arrange for the administration of several short tests or techniques that will give a more complete description of the individual than a single longer test or technique. In addition to these administrative factors, the length of a test or technique has an important effect upon the cooperation, interest, and effort of the individual who is examined.

Comparable Forms

Parallel or comparable forms of a test or technique are especially valuable when these are used for research purposes or for measuring the effects of teaching or of therapy. When such purposes are to be served, it is essential that parallel forms of the test be available for administration before and after a particular course or a particular period of therapy. A parallel form is frequently valuable to confirm a test score which may be inaccurate because of some interference, either physical or emotional, when the first form of the test was administered.

SUMMARY

In this chapter, types, uses, and qualities of major evaluative techniqucs have been surveyed. The objective type tests, as one of the major techniques of evaluation, may be classified according to such psychological characteristics as intelligence, achievement, aptitude, attitude, interest, and personality. These tests may be classified, also, according to such technical features as individual versus informal norms, speed versus power, performance versus pencil-and-paper situations, and survey versus diagnostic purposes.

Other major evaluation techniques which were introduced include : anecdotal records and observational techniques; oral and essay examinations; questionnaires. inventories, and interviews; checklists and rating scales; personal reports and projective techniques; sociometric methods; case studies; and cumulative records. All of these techniques are explained and illustrated in more detail in subsequent chapters of this volume.

Uses of evaluation data were discussed according to the functions they serve for such school personnel as the administrator, research worker, supervisor, teacher, and guidance counselor. The administrator, for instance, uses evaluation data for official records, reports to parents, transfer and placement of pupils.

The research worker uses evaluation data to make analytical and comparative studies of pupil learning and adjustment. In direct instruction the teacher and supervisor use the data from evaluation techniques to adapt school activities and curricula to promote mental, physical, social, and emotional growth and development of pupils. In a like manner, the psychologist or counseler uses results from evaluative techniques for educational and vocational guidance. Along with the desirable uses of evaluation data, it is wise to guard against the misuse of data.

The qualities for judging an evaluative technique include validity, reliability, objectivity, norms, and practibility. *Validity* is that quality which indicates the degree to which the evaluative instrument measures or diagnoses the psychological characteristics that it purports to measure. Predictive validity is judged by the degree of the relationship between a measure and a subsequent measure of judgment of the performance or behaviour, such as predicting aptitude for educational or occupational activities. Concurrent validity is judged by the relationship between a measure and an immediate criterion of behavior or performance. Content validity is judged by the relationship between a measure or diagnostic technique and achievement in an activity or course of study which is the goal of training or guidance. Construct validity is established by the correspondence between the results of a technique and other direct or indirect indicates of the characteristic or characteristics that the assumed to exist through empirical or theoretical deduction.

Reliability is that quality which is judged by the degree of accuracy, consistency, or constancy of the measure obtained. Reliability may be expressed as the standard error of measure, or the actual amount of variation in scores which results when an individual is measured repeatedly with the same instrument. Reliability may be expressed, also, as a coefficient of reliability. Since the same psychological test cannot be applied repeatedly to an individual without altering the psychological characteristics measured, the coefficient of reliability is employed for tests.

Three major types of reliability coefficients are : coefficient of internal consistency, coefficient of equivalence, and coefficient of stability.

The coefficient of internal consistency estimates how accurately an instrument measures the individual's performance at a particular moment. It is obtained by dividing a test into equivalent halves and correlating the scores or by determining the variance of individual items and comparing the sum of this variance with the variance of the total test score. The coefficient of equivalence is obtained from the correlation between scares on two parallel forms of a test or measure administered on two occasions to the same individuals. The coefficient of of stability is obtained from the correlation between scores on the same test or instrument anministered to the same individuals at an earlier and later date, thus measuring the stability of the behaviour assessed over a given period of time.

Objectivity is that quality of a test or instrument which permits equally competent scorers to obtain identical or very closely similar scores on the same test or instrument administered to an individual. Techniques with high objectivity include standardized group tests of intelligence, achievement, aptitude, attitude, and interests. Techniques with moderate objectivity include individually administered tests of intelligence and projective techniques, such as the Rorschach and the Thematic Apperception Test, as well as performance tests, rating scales of products, checklists, and rating scales. Techuiques with flexible objectivity include the unstructured interview, the open-end questionnaire, anecdotal records, and running accounts of behaviour obtained by direct observation.

Norms are usually expressed as the average or typical score obtained on a test or instrument for individuals of a specified age or grade. Qualitative or descriptive norms are sometimes more appropriate and meaningful in summarizing results from such techniques as sociometric methods, interviews, open-end questionnaires, and anecdotal records.

The quality of *practicability* in a test or evaluative technique involves consideration of such factors as cost, ease of administration, of scoring, and of interpretation, as well as time requirements and availability of comparable forms of tests or techniques.

PROBLEMS FOR CLASS DISCUSSION

1. By interview and observation in a specific school, determine the uses made of intelligence and achievement test data by :

   (*a*) the school administrator,

   (*b*) the teacher,

   (*c*) the guidance or other special school personnel.

2. Examine carefully the manual or other related publication explaining the validity, reliability, objectivity, and norms of two standardized tests in a subject you teach or are planning to teach. For each of these qualities, indicate briefly the kind of data provided by the author and publishers of the tests you have chosen. Give your judgment about the adequacy of such data as are reported.

5

Administrative Aspects of Evaluation

Many obstacles stand in the way of realizing a comprehensive program of evaluation in a school or a department of a school. These obstacles include lack of sufficient personnel, lack of sufficicnt materials, lack of clerical assitance, and lack of budgetary appropriations for the purchase of tests and measures. Within these limitations, however, it is possible to introduce and to continue the administration of a comprehensive evaluation program.

Basically the leadership of a principal or supervisor will influence widely the type of evaluation program in a local school. The principal or supervisor must provide the leadership as well as manage effectively the personnel and materials that will be necessary to carry out the program that is planned. The administrator or supervisor must plan teachers' meetings and in-service programs on evaluation. He should guide the committee work of teachers in the selection and administration of standardized tests or in the construction of informal tests and should have available important reference books of handbooks on tests and related statistics.

The classroom teacher plays a major part in an evaluation program. If he is to use the results for guiding the growth and development of individual pupils and the class, then the use and interpretation of evaluation results become the ultimate responsibility of the classromm teacher who deals directly with the pupil. The teacher will use the results of formal and informal evaluation to plan the curriculum or course so that instruction is based on the needs of the pupils. The teacher also will participate directly or indirectly in the coustruction, criticism, and revision of any informal tests that are developed. The teacher and administrator or supervisor must work as a team in undertaking an evaluation program.

INTRODUCING THE EVALUATION PROGRAM

A comprehensive evaluation program should be initiated gradually so that the teachers will not be over burdened by too many new tests and techniques – all introduced at the same time. Even though it may seem desirable to evaluate a wide range of major objectives, it is wise to introduce the measurement techniques only as rapidly as they can readily be assimilated and used by the teachers.

Several considerations will determine the rapidly with which an evaluation program can be introduced. The design of the current testing or evaluation practices and its acceptance by school personnel is of major importance. Schools with more advanced practices can proceed more rapidly than others. The background and the interests of teachers will vary from school to school, and these individual differences must be considered in the formulation of an evaluation program.

In some schools teachers will have been introduced to more extensive evaluation programs than in other schools. The formulation of an evaluation program must provide opportunities for discussion and for in-service education of teachers on newer trends in evaluation and measurement, especially the application of results of measurement to the instructional program. This is a part of the responsibility of the principal or supervisor who is leading the program.

Local School Needs

The scope and nature of an evaluation program designed to meet local school needs will vary from school to school. The type of pupil personnel in the school, the type of curriculum or course offered and the adaptations of these to fit the pupil personnel are factors which must be considered. The major objectives to be emphasized – attitudes, thinking, information and skills, personal and social adjustment – must be determined. These major objectives should be determined by the teachers and supervisor in the school or in the department involved. In some schools or departments, the major objectives that are selected will involve mainly the measurement of skills, information, concepts, and knowledges. In others, the objectives may include not only skills, information and concepts, but also attitudes, interests, critical thinking, and the personal and social adjustment of pupils. Each school or department must determine or select the major objectives which it wishes to emphasize as the goals as a curriculum or a course.

The objectives selected for emphasis influence the tests and appraisal technique to be used. The first question is : What formal or standardized tests can be used to measure the major objectives and what will be their cost ? The answer will involve a survey of published test materials and consultaions with test experts in order that a wise selection of published tests can be made. A second question is : What informal or teacher-made tests and techniques can be used ? Standardized tests are valuable for a periodic check, probably once each term or each year, but informal or teacher-made tests may be required to measure growth and progress over shorter periods of time, especially for objectives for which published tests are not available. Another function of informal or teacher-made tests is their use for instructional purposes in order to locate strengths and weaknesses in the teaching and learning of specific units of work. The scope and nature of the informal tests must be be determined by the teacher in eonsultation with the supervisor.

Organizing Personnel and Materials

The operation of an evaluation program in a local schools calls for a wide measure of administrative efficiency. First, in an elementary school or in the departments of a secondary school, it is essential to delegate to selected teacher personnel various responsibilities in an evaluation program. Key personnel should be chosen from those who have interests and abilities in developing a more comprehensive evaluation program. In larger school, this may involve the selection of committees and charimen of committees to put the program into operation. Another basic consideration is the organization of materials. Principals and supervisors can help provide suitable materials and equipment needed by the teaching staff for testing. These materials should be readily available and up-to-date, and would include :

1. Books, articles, and pamphlets pertaining to the measurement of the objectives or courses.
2. A file of selected standardized tests indexed by objectives.
3. Equipment needed for construction of any formal test ; for example, stencils, mimeograph and hectograph materials.
3. Provision for filing informal teacher-made tests systematically so they are readily available when needed.

USING TESTS IN AN EVALUATION PROGRAM

The modern school committed to a program of evaluation will use many approaches to appraisal. However, the objective test will constitute a major aspect of the program the school will ultimately adopt.

When a school decides to give a test, whether it is one which will be specially constructed by the school or one which will be purchased from a commercial publisher, the school is actually setting a four-fold task for itself :

1. Constructing or selecting the test to be used.
2. Administering the test.
3. Scoring the test.
4. Interpreting the results obtained through testing.

The remainder of this chapter considers each of these four aspects of the administrative program.

CONSTRUCTING OR SELECTING TESTS

In many school situations, considerable attention is paid to the first of these four aspects of testing. The teacher or group of teachers charged with the responsibility of formulating a test for use in a given class, grade, or school subject will often spend a good deal of time in selecting the specific items which will be used. The analysis of the course of study and the identification of pupil knowledges, skills, and appreciations call for a considerable investment in teacher time and effort. (See Chapter Five and Six for a more complete discussion of the process of test construction.)

When a standardized test is to be purchased, the group may evaluate many possible choices before recommending that a specific test be selected. The various qualities characterizing an evaluative instrument, which were discussed in the preceding chapter—validity, reliability, objectivity, norms, and practicability—must be considered. Members of the group might find test, and utilize some rating device to quantify their subjective impressions. To this end, a scale such as that prepared by Rinsland (4) may be of value. The selection of a standardized test must be given great care.

Too often, however, the construction or selection of the test to be used is looked upon as the completion of the task,

The many important issues in the administration and scoring of tests are frequently afforded only casual attention by school personnel. Yet, if the time and expense involved in constructing or purchasing tests are not to be vitiated, test administration and scoring must be approach with as much care as that given to the writing of test items or to judging the relative adequacy of standardized tests.

Who Should Administer Tests

In general, tests should be administered to a class by the teacher of that class. It is rather surprising that no one question the ability of the teacher to administer tests which are teacher-made, yet many authorities feel that standardized test must be administered by specially trained examiners. It almost seems as if the teacher made test is looked upon as a relatively unimportant measure of pupil achievement compared to the standardized test which has been constructed by experts.

There is no reason, however, for relegating teacher-made measures to a secondary position in the evaluative process, or for feeling that teachers are generally incompetent test administrators. If the administration of a standardized test calls for special skills which cannot be mastered by average teachers, it should not be selected for use in the school's testing program.

Before a standardized test is administered by classroom teachers, it would be wise to biref the group. An excellent approach is to have the group take the test themelves, using the directions specified by the test manual and shortened time intervals. In instances where test directions are complicated, or when the test is to be administrated to a very young group of pupils, a demonstration of test administration to an actual class should be scheduled, and a discussion of procedures be led by an experienced examiner. When such training practices are utilized, there is no reason why classroom teachers cannot administer standardized group tests and obtain valid test scores.

There are definite advantages associated with having the teacher administer a test to his own group. The introduction of a strange examiner places entirely too much emphasis upon the fact that the test is a departure from normal school routine, that it is particularly important, and that there is something "special" about the whole business. The presence of the classroom teacher in the room during the test may be a reassuring factor, but it is difficult to eliminate completely the added tension which accompanies the unfamiliar examiner.

Moreover, the classroom teacher knows his pupils. He has learned, in the course of his work with the class, that Mary will need a smile or two of encouragement during the course of the test, that David will break at least two pencil points, and that Alan will need special help with the test directions. He can gauge pupil functioning in the test situation far more adequately than can a special examiner.

This role of the teacher is important so that care given to selecting the test shall not be negated by unfortunate administration of it.

What Procedure Should be Followed ?

As a first step, the teacher should study the direction for the administration of the test. This involves more than cursory reading of the directions, particularly when a standardized test is to be administered. Rather, each specific direction given in the test manual should be checked against the test booklet and, if necessary, appropriate notations should be made on a specimen copy of the test booklets.

Prior to the day testing, the teacher should assemble the materials needed ; test booklets, answer sheets, scrap paper, an adequate supply of pencils or crayons, a copy of the test manual, a watch or clock, and a sign – "Testing—Do Not Enter". The test should be administered in a comfortable, familiar setting. The children's own classroom should be used unless that room is very noisy. If warranted, arrangements should be made for a shift in rooms prior to the date of testing. If any children in the group are not be tested at the scheduled time, provision for their care during the testing period should also be made in advance.

During the testing session, the following precautions should be observed :

(*a*) In the lower grades, take the children to the toilet immediately before the test.

(*b*) The prepared sign should be placed on the classroom door before testing begins.

(*c*) The children should be seated as far apart as possible to prevent copying. Special attention should be given to seating handicapped children.

(*d*) Tht teacher should make sure that each child has the right page before beginning work. He should move about the room during the course of the test in order to note whether directions are being followed without error.

(*e*) The children should be encouraged to keep working at maximum effect. This should be done by gestures rather than by words.

(*f*) Children who disrupt the testing procedure should be removed from the room. The teacher should note on the test booklet or answer sheet observations of unusual reactions or any other information about the child that may serve to make the test results more meaningful.

(*g*) The teacher should make certain that all pupils stop work promptly when time is called. Test booklets or answer sheets should be collected immediately, and then other materials should be called for.

There are two requisites for successful test administration. *First*, the directions given in the test manual for administering the test must be followed without deviation. Even slight modification of the directions destroys the standardized nature of the test situation. If, for example, the pupil asks for the meaning of a word during a test, the examiner must avoid a direct answer to the question, unless the manual specifically permits such help. Without such permission, the teacher should indicate that the information cannot be given and that the pupil should go on to the next item.

In most test situations, the role of the examiner is limited to making certain that the pupil continues working at as high a level as possible : "Go on to the next page" ; "Look over your work to make sure that you have made no errors" ; "Use the side of the test booklet instead of scratch paper." However, the instructions given in the test manual should constitute the basis for determining whether even such limited assistance may be given to the pupil. Accuracy of administration depends upon adherence to these instructions.

The *second* requisite is accurate timing. The examiner must be very careful that all pupils begin work at the same time and that they all stop when the allotted time has elapsed. A teacher giving a test should follow the practice of recording the beginning time of a test immediately after giving the pupils the signal to begin work. A stop watch or a regular watch with a second hand should be used for timing. The examiner will find it of value to keep before him a personal copy of the test and to mark on it the exact time of starting, the time limit of the test, and the exact time at which the test is to end. For example, if the class is ready to start the test at 20 seconds after 9 : 30, the notation would be as follows :

Time of starting	9 : 30 – 20
Time limit (minutes)	40
Time of ending	10 : 10 – 20

Thus, the test would end at 20 seconds past 10 : 10. If a stop watch is used, the time for the test is measured from zero.

When a test is composed of several subtests, it is helpful to prepare a form for recording time intervals which can be filled out by the examiner during the course of the testing session. There are various ways in which this form may be prepared, though it is essential that it be accurate. An example of such a form, used by a large school system in the administration of the Pintner Intermediate Intelligence Test, is reproduced on the next page.

TEST SCORING

Accurate test scoring is fully as important as accurate test administration. No matter how carefully an examiner has followed the directions for administration given in the test manual, the results obtained will be misleading if inaccuracies are permitted in test scoring. If the scores are not accurately obtained in the exact fashion set forth in the test manual, they cannot be compared with the test norms, and the values obtained from testing will have been lost.

Who Should Score Tests ?

Certain teachers look upon the scoring of tests as a disagreeable task. Certainly, test scoring is not the most satisfying way to spend a pleasant May afternoon. However, few

For Examiner's Use

Time of Starting		———	———
Subtest	*Time Limit*	*Finishing Time*	*Finishing Time*
Test 1	4 minutes	———	———
Test 2	4 minutes	———	———
Test 3	8 minutes	———	———
Test 4	5 minutes	———	———
Test 5	4 minutes	———	———
Test 6	4 minutes	———	———
Test 7	7 minutes	———	———
Test 8	9 minutes	———	———
		Check	*Check*
Starting time....................		———	———
+45 min.		+45 min.	+45 min.
———		———	———
End of Test...		———	———

school systems have the facilities to provide test-scoring services through a central office. Even when such facilities are available, experience has indicated that considerable time elapses before the results of the test are available to the classroom teacher.

In most instances, there are decided advantages in having the teacher score the test papers of pupils in his own class. Not only will the results be available at an early date, but the teacher will gain valuable information concerning pupil errors and gain a better under-standing of the meaning of the test scores.

One should not assume, however, that because a teacher, rather than a clerk in a central office, is scoring the test, protection against errors in scoring has been assured. Early in the history of the testing movement, studies (1, 3) indicated that teacher scoring is not errorless. Good procedure will not eliminate errors completely, but will reduce errors to a minimum.

What Procedures should be Followed ?

When a teacher scores the papers of the pupils in his own class, he should exert every effort to make the process as mechanical as possible. The teacher should avoid noting to whom the test booklet belongs and should concentrate only on the answers to the test items. An impersonal approach decreases the likelihood of inaccurate scoring. The total task, too, should be divided into smaller units which can be handled efficiently and learned easily. It is generally inadvisable, for example, to score the entire test booklet for one pupil before going on to the next. Rather, it is preferable to score one or two subtests (or pages) for all pupils in the class at one time, and then go on to a second set of subtests. As the teacher becomes familiar with the scoring key, speed increases rapidly.

The school situations where the same test is administered to a number of classes, it is advisable to have a group of teachers cooperate in test scoring. Each teacher, in such instances, would assume responsibility for scoring a portion of the test booklet. All teachers should use the same symbols for checking right and wrong answers.

Provision must be made, of course, for making equitable assignments and for providing some means of rotating the test booklets from teacher to teacher. Ordinarily, this is done by placing the tests for each class in a separate envelope, and attaching a label in the form of a control sheet indicating the teacher's assignment and providing space for keeping track of completed assignments. Group scoring in this fashion is much more economical of teacher time and effort and has the additional advantage of eliminating the inequalities resulting fr m differences in class size.

All scoring should be checked systematically. This does not mean that every test booklet must be rescored, but that a random sample be checked. The World Book Company, publishers of many standardized tests, suggests that the following procedure be used in checking the scoring of the Metropolitan Achievement Test Battery (2) :

> "A recommended method of check scoring is that of selecting five papers at random and rescoring all tests in the battery for these five pupils. If no errors are found on any of the tests in the battery, it is not necessary to rescore any more papers. If one or more errors are found in a subtest, five more papers should be rescored for that particular subtest. If more than two errors are found in these ten papers, then all the papers should be rescored for this subtest. If in the first five papers there were three or more errors, it is then necessary to score the whole package of tests for this particular subtest.
>
> "The ideal plan for check scoring is to have one person or, at the most, a small number of persons on the staff do all the check scoring. If a teacher must check his own work, he should go back to his papers after the scoring job has been completed and use the same sampling system."

Most standardized tests provide that scores on subtests be transferred to the face sheet of the test booklet. The need for accuracy in this process is as great as that needed in scoring. Whenever data are transferred in this fashion, provision must be made for checking the accuracy of the record which is transferred. When groups of teachers participate in check scoring, the control sheet used in scoring should provide space for recording progress made in checking both original scoring and recording of scores.

INTERPRETING TEST RESULTS

Once the test has been administered and scored, the teacher is faced with the problem of interpreting the obtained results. The raw score which a pupil attains on a test has meaning only when some method of comparing his performance with that of other pupils is utilized. There are several methods of comparing scores, each of which is of value for a particular purpose. These derived scores are called norms.

Norms

A norm is usually the average or typical value of a particular psychological characteristic measured in a specified homogeneous population. For example, it may be the average reading comprehension level of a representative sample of all 12-years-old children or all fifth-grade children ; it may be the median achievement on a particular science test of a representative sample of all eleventh-grade pupils taking the science course. A norm is a statement of present achievement of the group and not a universal standard of accomplishment. In most cases the average, either the mean or median, achievement of a group is taken as the norm, but sometimes other points such as percentiles or points on the standard deviation scale are used. Most norms on widely used standardized instruments are based upon the scores of a fairly large cross section of pupils who live in widely scattered parts of the nation. In addition to such national norms, however, local norms for particular states, cities, or regions are sometimes used.

Grade Norm

A grade norm may be defined as the mean or median achievement of pupils in a given school grade on a given standardized test. It may also be defined as the average status of pupils in a given grade in regard to a single factor such as spelling ability, reading comprehension, or arithmetic ability. Grade norms are ordinarily based upon the assumption that a school system contains twelve grades. Suppose the average score obtained by sixth-grade pupils tested at the end of January on a reading test is 35 items correct. This is translated into a grade score of 6.5, which represents achievement of the average pupil in sixth grade, fifth month. Directness of interpretation and apparent simplicity have caused grade norms to be used very widely at the elementary-school level.

In spite of their many limitations, they probably represent the best available method for making scores comparable for elementary-school achievement tests. They do have direct meaning which is a highly desirable feature in any system of derived scores. Many teachers, however, confuse a grade norm with a standard of work and consider that a given class is doing satisfactory work if the class is up to the norm, regardless of other relevant factors such as general intelligence level of the pupils, community background variables, curriculum deviations, and similar factors.

Age Norm

An age norm is a statement of the mean or median performance on an intelligence or achievement test by a group of pupils of a designated chronological age. Suppose pupils who are 11 years 8 months old have an average of 35 items correct on a reading test. The age score or norm for 35 items correct would then be 11.8. By disregarding grade placement, age norms make the tacit assumption that increase in chronological age is the important consideration, not the grade in which recent instruction was received. This factor becomes less important as promotion is more and more on the basis of chronological age, provided instruction is well suited to the needs of the individual child. Age norms prorate growth over a 12-month period which is an assumption contrary to that made in setting up grade norms, namely to prorate growth over a 10-month school year, which assumes that no growth or relatively little growth takes place during the summer period. Age norms are especially useful in the standardization of intelligence, or mental ability, tests.

Percentile Norm

A percentile norm may be defined as a point on a scale of measurement determined by the percentage of individuals in a given population that lies below this point. Percentile norms may be defined also as corresponding to the points which divide the total number of cases contained in a frequency distribution of a normative group into 100 equal parts. Each of the 100 parts is assumed to eontain the same number of cases. Although the more common method of reporting norms is in terms of the median, which is the same as the 50th percentile, this is frequently supplemented by a statement of other percentile points in the frequency distributiou for a given age or for a given grade. A tenth-grade pupil, for example, may obtain a raw score of 37 on a reading test. This raw score is equivalent to a percentile score of 63. This score means that this pupil achieves a score above 63 per cent of tenth-grade pupils. Percentile norms are widely used on readiness tests for first-grade children, on achievement tests in various subjects for high-school children, on interest inventories, personality inventories, and rating scales.

Standard Score

A standard score is expressed as a deviation of a score from the arithmetic average of the normative group in which the standard deviation of the normative groups is used as the unit of measurement. Thus, if the average raw score of the normative group is 50 and the raw score standard deviation is 10, a raw score of 60 would be exactly 1 standard deviation unit above the average, and the standard score would be 1.0.

The basic formula for determining the standard score is : Score minus mean score divided by standard deviation of the normative group. In standard scores all differences between individuals retain their same relative values. In the basic formula standard scores use a pair of constants which result in a mean of zero and a standard deviation of one for the group used as a standard because the mean raw score is subtracted from each score and then each difference is divided by the raw score standard deviation. In order to avoid the use of decimals and negative signs, standard scores are frequently converted to various relative scales. Some variations of the standard score technique use mean values such as 50, 100, or 500 instead of zero, with standard deviations of 10, 20, and 100 respectively instead of 1. Such scores simplify interpretation and increase comparability. Standard scores are generally more difficult for the average classroom teacher to understand than the other derived scores. For this reason the standard score has tended to be used most frequently among psychologists and research workers.

Analysis Errors

The determination of an individual pupil's standing in a group is only one of the ways in which a teacher uses the results obtained on a test. He is also concerned with determining which of the areas covered by the test presented the most difficulty to the pupil. A tabulation of incorrect responses serves to develop this information.

An analysis of this type is of great value to the teacher in determining individual and group needs for additional help. It indicates where additional stress must be placed for greater understanding and where a directed program of remedial teaching is needed. While it is true that the tabulation suggested involves considerable work on the part of the teacher the values gained generally justify the investment of time required.

SUMMARY

Only as constructive leadership is provided will a modern program of evaluation be realized. The evaluation program should be formulated jointly by the supervisors and teachers to meet local school needs. The evaluation program should be introduced gradually so that the teachers will not be overburdened by too many new tests and techniques, all introduced at the same time. An important aspect in the administration of an evaluation program is the organization of personnel and materials. Competent and experienced personnel should be selected for committees to put the program into operation. The administrator should provide suitable materials and equipment, such as books, files of tests, mimeograph equipment, and provisions for filing teacher-made tests. The role of the supervisor must be creative and democratic to gain rapport with the entire staff. The role of the classroom teachers, however, is central in using the results for guiding the growth and development of individual pupils.

There are four major administrative aspects of a program of testing:

(*a*) constructing or selecting the test to be used,

(*b*) administering the test,

(*c*) scoring the test, and

(*d*) interpreting the results.

Test construction involves an analysis of the course of study used and the identification of the pupil knowledges, skills, and appreciations which are the objectives of the instructional program. The selection of a suitable test calls for a consideration of such factors as validity, reliability, objectivity, norms, and practicability.

Test should generally be administered by the classroom teacher, who should have received some training prior to the administration of the test. Care should be taken to emphasize the need for following test directions exactly as given in the test manual and for accurate timing. Insofar as possibe, test scoring should be routinized. A systematic method of check scoring should be developed.

The interpretation of the results of testing ordinary involves comparing the performance of a given pupil with that of the group of which he is a member. Norms—grade norms, age norms, percentile norms, or standard scores—are ordinarily used for this purpose. A norm is usually the average or typical value of a particular psychological characteristic measured in a specified homogeneous population. An analysis of pupil errors is also of value in interpreting group performance.

PROBLEMS FOR CLASS DISCUSSION

1. Assume that you are the principal of an elementary school which has four sixth-grade classes. You decide to administer an intelligence test and a test of achievement in reading in these classes.

   (*a*) Prepare scales for rating the adequacy of an intelligence test and a test of reading ability; use as criteria such factors as validity, reliability, objectivity, norms, and ease of administration, scoring, and interpretation.

   (*b*) Examine three intelligence tests and three reading tests suitable for use on the sixth-grade level and use your rating scales to determine which of the tests in each area you would use.

   (*c*) Assuming that only one of the sixth-grade teachers in your school is experienced as an examiner, plan a two-day schedule for administering the two tests to the four classes on the grade.

   (*d*) Plan a program for scoring and check scoring the two tests.

6

Short-Answer Tests

Written tests used by teachers for measuring pupil achievement may be classified as essay examinations or short-answer examinations. The latter are often referred to as objective, or "new-type," tests. The essay examination, which generally asks the pupil to discuss, compare, give reasons, and the like, requires the formulation of an extended verbal answer to the question. Short-answer tests, on the other hand, consist of questions to which the pupil responds by the selection of one or more of several given alternatives, by giving or filling in a, word or a phrase, or by some other device which does not call for an extensive written response.

In recent year, the essay examination, once the mainstay of the classroom teacher's approach measurement of achievement, has been replaced to a considerable extent by the short-answer test. Lee and Segel (5), in a comprehensive study of classroom testing practices, found that only 16 per cent of high-school teachers use essay examinations extensively. In view of their widespread popularity, the present chapter consists the more common types of short-answer tests—completion, multiple-choice, true-false, and matching exercises.

VALUES AND LIMITATIONS OF SHORT-ANSWER TESTS

Values

Short-answer tests, in comparison with essay examinations, possess certain definite advantages.

Sampling

In an essay examination, the process of writing a response is extremely time-consuming. Use of a short-answer test, where the response is quickly given, makes it possible for the pupil to answer many more questions in the same amount of time. As a result, short-answer tests generally show much better coverage of total course content than do essay examinations. Even spotty preparation may result in high grades when a pupil happens to study just that material called for by a few essay questions. Such chance results operate to a far less degree when short-answer tests are employed. In the latter situation, the teacher may be more certain that the grades the pupil earns is a true measure of his achievement.

Reliability of Scoring

One of the most likely sources of inaccuracy in assigning grades to essay examinations is the lack of objectivity in grading pupil answers. Sources of the lack of reliability in scoring essay questions are discussed in Chapter Six. In view of the fact that questions on short-answer tests generally have only one acceptable response, objectivity of scoring is relatively high. Clerical errors, rather than errors of judgment, reduce reliability of scoring.

Ease of Scoring

Since the short-answer test may be scored by use of a key listing correct responses, little technical skill is involved. In the usual classroom situation, scoring of essay tests calls for a large expenditure of teacher time, much of which can be saved by employing the short-answer tests. Identification of pupil weaknesses is also an easier task when short-answer tests are used. By counting the number of errors made on each question or item of the short-answer test, the teacher can readily ascertain the particular elements of course content which show inadequate mastery, and arrange for reteaching. A similar analysis of responses to essay questions in an exceedingly laborious task.

Instructional Uses

The relatively better sampling and identification of pupil errors makes it possible to use a short-answer test as a pretest prior to embarking on a new unit of work. By analyzing pupil errors on a short-answer test given before the new unit is introduced, the teacher can determine the degree to which the new work represents material already mastered, or material completely foreign to the class. On the other hand, the instructional values of short-answer tests when used at the *end* of a unit of work should not be overlooked. The studied of Curtis and Woods (1) and of Plowman and Stroud (6) indicate that returning corrected papers to pupils or having them correct their own papers prior to a discussion errors results in better ultimate achievement.

Limitations

The limitations of short-answer tests grown out of the nature of the responses which are required of the pupil and other factors which are discussed in the following paragraphs.

Guessing

In short-answer tests where the pupil is called upon to select one of a number of possible alternative answers, a series of fortunate guesses will markedly increase the pupil's score. In a test calling for the recognition of the truth or falsity of 100 statements, for example, a group of pupils would answer correctly 50 times, on the average simply by following the dictates of a tossed coin. Statisticians have proposed several formulae for reducing the effect of guessing. In the ordinary course of classroom teaching, however, there is little to be gained through the application of any of the proposed corrections. When pupils respond to every item of a test (the usual classroom practice), it can be shown that the relative rank of pupils will be the same whether their scores are computed by simply counting their correct answerss or by the use of any of the common scoring formulae which correct for guessing (3).

Difficulty in Construction

The preparation of good short-answer tests generally requires considerably more time than the development of an essay examination. Not only is it necessary to prepare a "blue-print" for the short-answer test as a whole, but the selection of the most appropriate short-answer form and the application of the form to a given question usually calls for more resourcefulness than the formulation of a few simple essay questions. Fortunately, a teacher can maintain a file of short-answer questions which have been utilized in the past. In this way, he may not only reduce the time involved in test construction, but create a reservoir of test items for use in special situations.

Cost of Administration

The large number of items which are included on a short-answer test generally makes it necessary to employ some mechanical means for reproducing enough copies of the test for class use. In most schools, of course, equipment for duplicating test copies will be available. When reproduction is not possible the teacher may find it necessary to resort to oral presentation of the test, Several studies (4, 9, 10) have indicated that oral presentation does not significantly decrease the validity or reliability of short-answer tests.

Testing Complex Processes

In many classroom situations, the teasher is concerned not only with the correctness of the pupil's answer to a question, but with the correctness of the thought process involved in arriving at a correct answer. Some progress has been in developing short-answer tests which attempt to reveal thought processes. In one approach, for example, the pupil is asked to justify a given conclusion by selecting appropriate statements from a list which is presented to him. Even in this kind of question, however, space limitations restrict the number of possible ways of justifying the conclusion which may be included in the list of alternatives. In teacher-made tests, the essay type generally remains the better instrument for testing complex processes.

TYPES OF SHORT-ANSWER TEST ITEMS

Completion Items

The completion item requires the pupil to complete the thought of a sentence by filling in the word or words that have been omitted, or it directs him to respond to a question by writing his answer in the blank space provided. Because the pupil needs to decide upon his answer and then write it out, a test composed of completion items takes longer to administer than do other forms of objective tests. If the test is timed, moreover: the pupil who writes slowly is handicapped. The scoring of the answers is not as fully objective as that for other types of items and alternative correct responses need to be included in the scoring key. The scoring of the item :

> The chief law enforcement officer of the United States is ————————————————

is not as objective as the scoring of these items :

> The Chief Justice of the U.S. Supreme Court is————————————

Who is the Governor of California ? ——— ———

The completion item, however, offers a natural form of questioning. It can be used readily with material calling for specific information. With questions requiring considerable reasoning or organization on the part of the pupil it is useful where the answer can be expressed in a few words.

A somewhat more complicated type of completion item is commonly referred to as the *connected-discourse* type. Test items put in this form have the advantage of providing the respondent with additional cues to guide the response.

Example :

———should be used as a thinner for paint, while

——— should be used as a thinner for shellac.

Several cautions must be observed in constructing completion items.

1. The blank must call for a *simple* specific response. For example, a poorly worded item would be :

   Wundt established th first laboratory for the experimental study of psychology in———.

   This may be correctly answered by writing a date, a city, or a country in place of the blank.

   The following item is still more vague in intent :

   On a school fire drill, the teacher must make certain that her pupils observe ———, ———, and———.

2. Statements should never be taken directly from textbooks. Not only does dependence upon the

textbook lead to rote memorization on the part of the pupil, but the test constructor will find that verbatim statements tend to be ambiguous. unduly wordy, and to contain too many cues.

3. In the lower grades, use direct questions in preference, to incomplete declarative sentences, thus :

   Poor :——— —is the capital of New York State.

   Better : What is the capital of New York State ?————

True-False Items

The true-false items requires the pupil to express his judgment of a given statement by indicating True or False, Yes or No, or some similar response. It is adapted to the testing of simple facts, ideals, and concepts. Scoring of tests composed of true-false items is easy and objective. Such tests seem simple to construct, but this apparent advantage is not a real one. In practice, considerable care is needed in framing the statements so that the ability to be measured is actually revealed :

Example :

Litmus paper turns blue in an acid solution...True False

True-false questions have been the source of greater irritation to pupils than almost any other type of short-answer question. This irritation, too, is generally expressed by the superior student who may see one or more exceptions to a statement which would be acceptable to a somewhat less-informed person. The primary difficulty, particularly when dealing with concepts, is that of formulating a statement which is completely true—that is, true without exception. For pinpoint information, there are fewer difficulties. However, even in the statement, "Edison invented the phonograph," some students may be bothered about "phonograph" because the term came into common use *after* Edison's invention.

In constructing true-false items, care should be taken to avoid several common pitfalls :

1. Avoid broad generalizations. The attempt to develop generalizations in true-false items leads to the use of *sphcific determiners*, words which are usually associated with either a true or a false statement, This, the words "all," "only," "none," "never," and "always" are generally found in false, rather than true, items constructed by teachers; words such as "generally," "as a rule," "most," "some," and "often" are found much more frequently in the statements. Careful review of a series of true-false items to make certain that such determiners, if used at all, are evenly balanced between true and false statements, is a necessary step in constructing a true-false test.

2. Avoid testing minutiae. The statement :

   T F The Henmon-Nelson Test of Mental Ability contains 90 items arranged in spiral order.

   calls for information which the teacher should not expect the pupil to have at his fingers tips. Whether the test contains 90 items or 75 items is inconsequential.

3. Avoid double statements. Each true-false item should test a single concept. This item is confusing to students :

T F The Wechsler Adult Intelligence Scale is designed to replace the Wechsler-Bellevue Scale, the most widely used individual intelligence test.

It would be preferable to cover this material in two items, thus :

T F The Wechsler Adult Intelligence Scale is designed to replace the Wechsler-Bellevue Scale.

T F The Wechsler-Bellevue Scale is the most widely nsed individual intelligence test.

4. Avoid long, complicated statements. Pity the poor student who is asked to unravel a statement like this :

T F Beard, in his interpretation of the United States Constitution, advanced a thesis of economic determinism, pointing a direct relationship between holders of the government debt and their advocacy of a strong government to pay it off, although he later indicated that not only economic factors, but the interplay of political, cultural, and international forces is also important for the interpretation of historical events.

This item is a measure of reading comprehension. Moreover, the test-wise student would respond "True," since he has learned that most long, involved statements are true. Teachers find it easier to write brief and concise false statements. Therefore, an attempt should be made to include approximately the same number of words in both true and false statements.

Multiple-Choice Items

The multiple-choice item requires the pupil to recognize which of several suggested responses is the best or the correct way to answer a question or complete a statement. While the completion item requires the pupil to produce the correct response without suggestion, the multiple-choice item calls for recognition only. It is adapted to the testing of complex ideas and interpretations. The scoring of the multiple choice item tends to be more objeetive and simpler than that of the completion item. The multiple-choice item is superior to the true-false item, which presents only two alternatives, in that it reduces the opportunity for guessing the correct answer. The multiple-choice type of question is also relatively free from "absolutes" in that the "best" statement of several that are given is to be selected as the "correct" answer. The "correct" answer, therefore, is relative to several other given statements rather than to all possible "not given" statements, as in true-false questions.

Multiple-choice questions are found in several patterns. Probably the most common pattern is the use of a *stem*, which sets the questlon, followed by several alternative statements, one of which is assumed to be the best answer.

Examples :

Of the following, which is the most widely used form of city government in the United States ?

1. the city-manager type
2. the mayor-council type
3. the commission type
4. the council-manager type.

In which of the following fields has the cooperative movement in the United States been most successful ?

1. Manufacturing and credit
2. Marketing and credit
3. Consumption and marketing
4. Credit and consumption.

Incorrect or unacceptable alternatives in multiple-choice items are known as 'distractors' or 'foils'. The formulation of such alternatives requires considerable care. Distractors should represent misconceptions and common errors which actually do do grise in the students' thinking. Distractors which are implausible are not likely to be choosen, even by a poor student, and therefore will not contribute to the measurement of his achievement. Distractors, if properly developed, can serve as important a function in the question as the correct answer, in that they starting point for diagnosis of individual difficulties.

The following hints may be of value in constructing multiple-choice items :

1. The stem of the item should pose the central concept which is being tested. The following is a poor item :

   A good group intelligence test

   (*a*) is highly reliable

   (*b*) was dexeloped for the U.S. Army in World War I

   (*c*) will give the same average results when administered to unselected groups of boys and girls

   (*d*) should give both verbal and non-verbal IQ's

In this instance, the distractors refer to four widely disparate concepts. Each of these concepts – test reliability, history of testing, sex differences, types of derived scores—might well serve as the stem of an item.

2. Distractors should be as concise as possible. In the following item, only the italicized words in each distractor need be used :

The preferred basis for placing a child in a group for instruetion in reading in a fifth-grade class is

(*a*) The 'mental' age obtained by the child on a good intelligence test.

(*b*) The 'intelligence quotient' obtained by the child on a good intelligence test.

(*c*) The 'chronological age' of the child as compared to others in the class.

(*d*) The 'reading grade' obtained by the child on a good achiviement test.

3. Distractors should be of relatively uniform length. Inex-perienced test constructors often make the mistake of including the largest number of words in the correct answer.

4. Distractors should be grammatically consistent with the stem. The stem and each of the distractors should make a complete sentence. The following item is poorly phrased :

Enrollment in colleges and universities in the United States.

(*a*) is at its highest level since World War II

(*b*) is declining at an accelerated pace

(*c*) more women than men are attending colleges

(*d*) high financial costs have reduced enrollments,

Matching Items

The matching exercise consists of two parallel columns of words, phrases. or sentences ; the pupil is required to match or associate each item of one column with the item which corresponds to it in the other column. Each matehed pair is scored separately. Actually, however, the pairs are interdependent because an incorrect response may make an item unavailable for correct pairing. For this reason, one of the two columns should contain more items than the other. Also, it is better to have two short matching exercises than one long one. Some test experts recommend three items in one column and five in the other as being the best number for reliable results.

E*xample* :

A. Score card for rating standardized tests	1. Buros : *Mental Measurements Yearbook* ( )
B. Critical comments on Cooperative Science Test	2. Monroe (editor) : *Encyclopedia of Educational Research* ( )
C. Article summarizing research on "Evaluation"	3. *Review of Educational Research* ( )
D. Summary of research on anecdotal records over three-year pcriod	
E. Derivation of formula for rank-order correlation.	

Younger children may be asked to draw lines between the items which match. Older children may be directed to indicate the appropriate letter for the matching item. The matching exercise takes little space and time on a test, but its usefulness is limited. It is not adapted to the testing of complex ideas or concepts.

The reader will note that no attempt has been made to describe the many variations which have been developed of the basic types of short-answer test items presented above, nor have many suggestions for writing test items been advanced. Remmers and Gage (7) and Ross (8) present relatively complete discussions of the first topic. Ebel's (2) summary of the prineiples and pitfalls in writing short-answer test items will be of great help to the neophyte.

TESTING COMPLEX PROCESSES

The teacher will generally find that formulating short-answer questions which measure acquisition of facts is a far easier task than developing materials for use in testing other objectives of instruction. The examples given below have been selected as representative of appraches to the measurement of pupil achievement in several common objectives.

Recognizing Assumptions

In this objective the student, when given certain facts and a conclusion drawn from the facts but involing an assumption, is expected to recognize the assumption. Such recognition may be expected in problems of health, housing, communication, etc.

Example :

Statement of Facts :

Family Income	Per Cent of Family Members Who Received No Medical Attention During the Year

Under $ 1200	47
$ 1200 to $ 3000	40
$ 3000 to $ 5000	33
$ 5000 to $ 10,000	24
Over $ 10,000	14

Conclusion. Members of families with small incomes are healthier than members of families with large incomes.

The conclusion is not completely justified by the facts given. It may be justified, however, if an assumption is made; that is, if a factor not stated in the given facts is taken for granted. What is this factor? What must be assumed in addition to the facts given in order that the conclusion be true? A multiple-choice qnestion, in which the correct assumption is listed with several alternatives, is most appropriate in the instance, thus :

Assumption : (Select one)

———(1) Wealthly families had more money to spend for medical care.

———(2) All members of families who needed medical attention received it.

———(3) Many members of families with low incomes were not able to pay their doctory bills.

———(4) Members of families with low incomes offten did not receive medical attentoin.

Interpretation of Data

In this objective the student may be expected to recognize when an interpretation goes beyond the data and when an interpretation is within the data. Data are, therefore, presented for the student to consider, together with interpretations to be judged. The question then becomes "Is the interpretation completely justified by the data alone? Is it contradicted by the data or are the data insufficient to judge its truth or falsity ?" In this objective, the pupil may be aware (or not be aware) of the various ways in which interpretations go beyond the data—by extension (extrapolation), by imputing cause or effect, by not having enough cases to warrant the conclusion, etc. Thus, interpretations involving these ideas, as well as statements which essentially describe the data, may be listed for the student to judge. In this kind of question, the natural form of the short-answer question is one in which the student is asked to "key" the individual statements according to a code. Such a code may be :

Indicated by :

A. Any statement which is true on the basis of the facts stated

B. Any statement which is probably true on the basis of the facts stated

C. Any statement for which insufficient data are given to judge truth or falsity

D. Any statement that is probably false on the basis of the facts stated

E. Any statement which is false on the basis of the facts stated.

In a study of social studies achievement, several tests were administered to pairs of pdpils in four experimental and four control classes in the ninth grade. The pairs were matched on the basis of chrono-logical age, IQ, and socio-economic status. The following test results were obtained :

Test	Number of Matched Pairs	Average Percentils Scores	
		Experimental	*Control*
Information and Facts	178	56	56

Skills in Obtaining Facts	193	57	48
Skills in Organizing Facts	181	53	51
Interpreting Facts	182	58	47
Applying Generalizations	184	58	56
Social Attitudes	182	51	53

1. The result indicate that pupils in the experimental classes are as proficient in skills and information as pupils in control classes.
2. Test results show that pupils in the experimental class have better mental ability and character traits than pupils in control classes.
3. Pupils in experimental classes achieve higher test scores on most of the tests than pupils in control classes.
4. In information and attitudes in the social studies, pupils in control classes make better test scores than experimental class pupils.
5. Pupils in experimental classes achieve better on some tests because they have had more practive in taking such tests than pupils to control classes.
6. The tests results prove that exprimental classes are are superior to control classes in the objectives tested.
7. Except on the information test, the differences between the two types of classes is statistically significant.
8. Skills and abilities especially stressed in the curriculum of the experimental classes were obtaining facts and interpreting facts.

Recognition of Limitations

Educational objectives involving recognition of limitations are expressed in many different ways. The following examples are presented to illustrate ways in which this objective may be translated into short-answer questions.

In the research problem presented below, ten conditions that may or may not be necessary for its validity are listed. Check the 'three' conditions that are most important for the validity of each of the studies.

An investigator wishes to determine the value of homework for retarded children. To one class of retarded children, to be taught by teacher "A," he plans to give spelling homework daily for two months. During this period, no homework will be given to a group of equivalent mental status and IQ, to be taught by teacher "B", The two classes will study the same words. It is planned to compare the relative progress of the two groups on the basis of frequent class tests and a final standardized scale at the end of the experimental period.

His results will be valid if :

1. Bias introduced into the study by the fact that the two groups are to study the same words will be insignificant.
2. There are no important differences in teacher ability.
3. There is no carry-over between experimental factors.
4. The curve for learning spelling words is similar to the usual learning curve.
5. The groups are representative of the normal school population.
6. The weekly tests given to the two groups are similar only in minor points.

7. No homework in subject other than spelling is given to the control group.
8. The two groups are actually equivalent.
9. The tests measure all the important gains likely to result from the use of homework.
10. All the words to be studied during the experimental period will appear on the standardized test administered at the end.

All investigator is interested in determining the accuracy of treatment of World War II in certain history texts used in the ihgh schools. Rank, using 1 for best, 2 for next best, etc., the adequacy of the following techniques in solving the problem.

1. Compare the number of pages allowed to that topic in the text to the number of pages allowed to topics of similar importance.
2. Compare the treatment of World War II in that book with the point of view expressed in recognized advanced treaties on the subject.
3. Compare the treatment of the topic in this book with its treatment in other history texts in use in the city schools.
4. Secure the judgment of expert military figures who participated in World War II on the accuracy of the treatment in the text.
5. Determine the likely effects of the treatment in this text upon the character and personality of the child
6. Investigate the professional standing and political point of view of the another of the text in order to discover possible causes of bias.

Application of Principles

The behavior expected from students when applying principles is usually described as *making* a *prediction* or an *ex-*

planation in a situation in which a science or social science principle or generalization may validly be applied. Also important is the ability to state the principle employed in making the prediction or explanation, as well as the conditions must exist if the principle may be employed.

Example :

John prepared an aquarium as follows. He carefully cleaned a ten-gallon glass tank with salt solution and put in a few inches of fine washed sand. He rooted several stalks of weed (elodea) taken from a pond and then filled the aquarium with tap water. After waiting a week, he stocked the aquarium with two one-inch goldish and three snails. The aquarium was then left in a corner of the room. After a month the water had not become foul and the plants and animals were in good condition. Without moving the aquarium he sealed a glass top on it. The sealed aquarium will probably remain in good condition for several months.

Directions

If you are uncertain about the truth or falsity of the underlined conclusion either because the problem is inadequately stated or for and other reason, indicate your uncertainty by placing the letter "U" immediately after the underlined conclusion.

If you believe that the underlined conclusion is quite likely to be true, place a "T" immediately after the underlined conclusion.

If you disagree with the underlined conclusion, place a "D" after the underlined conclusion.

Reasons: If you were uncertain ("U") about the conclusion, select from the first 10 reasons given below all those which help you explain from the first 10 reason given below all those which help you explain why you were uncertain. Indicate each reason so chosen by placing a check mark in the parentheses in front of the reason.

If you believe the conclusion to be true ("T") or if you disagree ("D") with the conclusion, select from reasons No. 11 through No. 24 all those which help you to explain your thoroughly. Indicate which reasons you choose by placing a check in front of each.

Reasons to be used if you are uncertain:

( ) 1. Many people who keep fish in bowls change the water frequently.

( ) 2. It is difficult to know what is meant by the term "good condition."

( ) 3. Not all of the aquaria I have seen were sealed.

( ) 4. The amount of exposed water surface is in important factor in keeping a sufficient amount of oxygen in the water to support life.

( ) 5. Some water plants produce more oxygen than others.

( ) 6. Too few fish in a large aquarium will affect the condition of the plants in the aquarium.

( ) 7. The amount of direct sunlight the aquarium receives is an important factor in determining whether or not the aquarium will remain in condition.

( ) 8. Some fungi harmful to aquatic life develop more rapidly when the oxygen supply is cut off.

( ) 9. I do not know how sealing an aquarium would affect the plants and animals in it.

( ) 10. It is important to know the amount of harmful chemicals, such as chlorine, used in the tap water.

Reasons to be used if you agree or disagree:

( ) 11. The balance between plants and animal is attained in aquarium when each supplies the needs of the other.

( ) 12. The water plants and micro-organisms would not grow rapidly enough to supply sufficient food for the fish.

( ) 13. Aquaria in biology classrooms are also kept in balance for several months even though sealed.

( ) 14. Plants in a sealed aquarium continue to manufacture food that is utilized in their growth, and they in turn serve as food for animals.

( ) 15. Just as organisms live at great depths in the ocean where there is little oxygen, so can fish live in a sealed acqarium.

( ) 16. Clerks in pet shops say that a balanced aquarium can be maintained for a long time even if sealed.

( ) 17. In a sealed aquarium, sufficient oxygen cannot be absorbed from the enclosed air to supplement the oxygen given off by the plants.

( ) 18. A balance in an aquarium tends to be maintained as long as one of the interdependent factors does not beeome predominant.

( ) 19. It is possicle to maintain a balance between plants and animals in a region.

( ) 20. If undisturbed, nature will strive a balance between plants and animals in a region.

( ) 21. Just as one does not need to feed fish in a pond, so one does not need to supply food in an aquarium containing an abundance of plant and animal life.

( ) 22. Anyone who has studied biology should know that a sealed aquarium can be maintained in balance for several years if undisturbed.

( ) 23. The snails in an aquarium can devour the solid waste material and excess algae in the water.

( ) 24. The animals in the sealed aquarium can breathe disolved oxygen supplied by the plants.

PLANNING A SHORT-ANSWER TEST

Unless a short-answer test is well planned. the result is apt to be an inaccurate test, a waste of time, or both. The most significant factors to consider in planning are the educational objectives to be represented by the test, the nature of the individual questions in relation to such objectives, the extent to which different kinds of situations and information are probed or sampled by questions, and the ways the responses by students are to be summarized.

Educational Objectives as the Starting Point in Planning A Test

Such objectives, of course, are of several kinds. Some specify the acquisition of information; some indicate the application of information, including problem solving and the analysis of argument; others specify the ability to interpret new information; still others call for certain abilities or skills such as reading, writing, and arithmetic.

For a short-answer test (or any other test for that matter) to be valid, the specific questions of the test should require the student to do those things (recall information, apply information, interpret) specifically called for by the educational objectives for which the test is being developed. If this requirement is to be fulfiled, such educational objectives must be defined in terms of behavior. For example, "To understand certain principles or generalizations of science or social science" may bc an enucational objective of a particular teacher or of several grade levels in a school. If so, the question arises "What will students be able to do if they understand such principles or generalizations ? What behaviour will they be able to demonstrate?" One illustration of such behaviour is that they will be able to recall specific examples of such principles or generalizations. Another may be the ability to explain new examples in terms of such generalizations or to predict the outcomes in particular new problems or situations by the use of such principles.

Often exen this detailed definition of student behaviour is not adequate for proceeding with the construction of a test question. For example, if the student is to recall examples of a principle or a generalization, is he expected, when given a statement of the principle or generalization, to give or recognize illustrations of the principle? Is he to give or recognize the principle if given several illustrations of it? Is he expected to indicate the limitations of the principle? The conditions under which it is not valid? These are the kind of specific questions to be answered in planning the short-answer test. The clearer the answers to such questions, the more likely it is that a valid test will result.

A second major question to be answered in planning the test is "In what context or in what situations should the student be able to demonstrate the desired behaviour?" If the student is to apply known principles in explaining new situations or in making predictions in problems not dealt with in direct instruction, how complex should spch problems be and how similar should they be to problems which have been dealt with in instrument?

Outlining the Test

Once the objectives of the test have been drawn up, an outline of test content should be prepared. Unifortunately, the term "test contest" has generally been used to denote only the subject matter of the test. As a result, test outlines are often restricted to an analysis of specific content. In order to make sure that a test will sample those aspects of behaviour which are deemed important, a test outline should also indicate the type of behaviour to be elicited with respect to each subject matter or content area.

A convenient way of identifying both aspects of test content ls through the use of a two-way chart. The example on page 97 presents a sample test outline developed for a unit on learning in a first course in Educational Psychology and shows the way in which the outline may be translated into a two-way chart. This two way chart is by no means complete. Many spaces have not been filled, nor has the chart been extended to include all of the material normally covered in a unit on learning. The reader will find it of value to attempt to develop a more complete formulation of a similar test outline and chart. It is generall helpful, in preparing such two-way tables, to include an extra row and column in which allocations of weight are given to each major content field and to each objective. This should be done in terms of point values on the basis of an appropriate scale.

A Test is a Sample of Many Possible Questions

An important assumption in the construction and use of a short-answer test, just as in any other test, is that pupil achievement on the test is a true indlcator of achievement in the objectives of instruction for which the test has been developed. Implicit in this idea is the ossumption that the quality of the answers to specific questions is indicative of what the quality of answers would be to other questions involving the same objective and content. Thus, an objective may specify that students be able to recognize assumptions in scientific situations. If so, a test would contain questions which would give students an opportunity to recognize assumptions in scientific situations. Such a test would, of course, contain but a sample of many possible scientific situations, and the student's success in such a test would be taken as an indication of equal success in another sample of such situations. The student's success would not be taken as an indication of his ability to identify assumptions in social problems. If instructions has provided practice for the student to identify assumptions in the latter type of situation, such situations can validly be included as a part of an achievement test.

The adequacy of the sample of possible situations depends, of course, upon the purpose of the test. If the test is designed to estimate the achievement of individual pupils, the sampling must be more complete than when the test purports to measure the achievement of a group of pupils. A test for estimating group achievement can, in general, be shorter than a test for estimating individual achievement and still have comparable certainty of measurement.

SAMPLE TEST OUTLINE

Educational Psychology—Unit on Learning

Objectives

1. *Acquisition of facts* concerning the learning process.
2. Formation of *generalizations* about the learning process.
3. Application of knowledge gained to classroom situations.

Content (*Major topics covered*)

A. "Types" of learning

B. The learning curve

C. Forgetting

D. Theoretical explanations of the learning process

E. The hygiene of school learning

F. Transfer of training

Two-Way Chart for Course in Educational Psychology

Content	*Acquisition of Facts*	*Generalizations*	*Applications*
"Types" of learning	Meaning of: Trial-and-error learning		How can trial-and-error be reduced?
	Perceptual learning	Difference in perceptual responses of adults and children	
	Association of ideas	Role of drill in associative learning	Multiple sense appeal
	Concept formation		Role of experiential background
Learning curves	Characteristics: Initial spurt	Causative factors	
	Plateau		How can the teacher help a pupil who is on a plateau?
	Short-time fluctuations		How can short-time fluctuations be handled?
	Limits		

Forgetting	Characteristics of forgetting curve	Role of : Whole Vs. part learning; Spaced Vs. massed practice; Recitation; Social participation	Teacher use of each of these in reducing forgetting

Summarizing Pupil Responses

Short-answer tests, more than any other, are constructed so that pupil responses may be summarized in part scores, or subscores. Since any pupil's achievement varies in different objectives or instruction, part scores are helpful in guiding the teacher's remedial or instructional work and in aiding the pupil in his self-evaluation.

Part scores on a test may be determined for different dimensions of a subject. For example, in arithmetic part scores may be developed for achievement in addition, subtraction, fractions, multiplication, etc. Part scores may also be utilized in measuring different types of response to the same set of questions. For example, on a test on interpretation of data, in addition to a "rights" score, the student's responses may be analyzed in terms of the per cent of total opportunities to go beyond the data, to be over-cautious, and to make crude errors in judgment.

Short-answer tests lend themselves to part score analysis more than do other types because of the greater number of specific responses obtained in the short-answer test. The test constructor and user should be aware, however, of the fact that part scores are almost always less reliable, subject to greater uncertainty of measurement, than are total scores.

SUMMARY

Short-answer tests, which include completion, true-false, multiple-choice, and matching items as basic types, are widely used in measuring pupil achievement. Such tests are generally superior to essay examinations in their sampling of course content, reliability of scoring, and ease of scoring. They also lend themselves to a number of instructional uses.

The limitations of short-answer tests include difficulty of construction, failure to eliminate guessing, and greater cost of administration. Efforts to provide short-answer tests which will measure complex processes have not yet been completely successful. To insure maximum validity in short-answer tests, they should stem from an analysis of objectives of instruction, be expressed in terms of expected pupil behavior, and should be based upon a test outline which identifies both course content and the type of behavior to be elicited.

PROBLEMS FOR CLASS DISCUSSION

1. Prepare ten true-false questions and five multiple-choice questions designed to test pupil understanding of the major concepts presented in this chapter. For each item you construct, indicate the objective to which the item is directed.

2. Obtain a copy of the course of study in social studies used in your community. Prepare a two-fold chart, similar to that on page 97, which would serve as the base for building a test for one of the units outlined in the course of study.

7

Essay and Oral Examinations

In spite of the widespread use of "new-type," "objective," or "short-answer" tests, examinations calling for responses in the form of an essay and classroom situations which require oral responses to questions still constitute an important aspect of the evaluation of pupil performance. Proponents of more "modern" forms of testing have been prone to give the more traditional techniques but slight regard. Airy dismissal of the old, without consideration of the values which might thereby be discarded, obviously does not constitute sound practice. This chapter analyzes both the values and the limitations of essay and oral examinations.

THE ESSAY EXAMINATION

The Essay Examination is still Popular

The essay examination calls for a relatively free written response to a problem situation, in which the written answer, when properly analyzed by the scorer, reveals information regarding selected aspects of the organization and functioning of the pupil's mental life. The essay examination has survived the continued criticism of experts in educational measurement, and remains an approach widely used by classroom teachers in achievement testing (11).

The relative popularity of the essay examination is not difficult to understand. The most widely used tests are those which are prepared, administered, scored, and interpreted by the classroom teacher. They are generally constructed for use only with those pupils enrolled in the course taught by the teacher who prepares the test. He may have many purposes in mind in administering the test—to motivate his pupils, to determine the success with which he has taught a unit of subject matter, to encourage additional study. The preparation of valid objective-type testing materials not only requires more time, but calls for training and experience which the classroom teacher seldom has had an opportunity to obtain. Nearly every teacher, however, looks upon himself as expert enough to construct a suitable essay test in his own subject, and to arrive at a satisfactory grade for a pupil. Technicalities such as adequate sampling of content, test validity, and test reliability are too often dismissed or ignored.

Objectives Measured by Essay Examinations

Valid educational otcomes exist which do not readily lend themselves to testing via so-called objective techniques. Many of these objectives may be subsumed under the general term "higher mental processes." At best-answer test of the multiple-choice type, for example, can serve only as a means for collecting evidence concerning how well the pupil can judge the best of several alternative hypotheses which are *presented to him*. Does this constitute the same kind of judgment which is involved in the formulation of a hypothesis in a problem? While the research evidence which is available does not permit a definitive answer to this question at the present time, it appears obvious that the use of short-answer questions makes it extremely difficult to "follow the students thinking" in such a higher mental process as formulating hypotheses.

The student's ability to organize and express his ideas effectively is another objective which lends itself to measurement via the essay examination. Although many attempts have been made to develop valid-answer devices for appraising a pupil's achievement in this objective, the results obtained have not been sufficiently convicing to merit their acceptance. In this connection. it should be noted that the use of the essay examination makes it possible for the teacher to direct the attention of the pupil to large segments and integrated units of subject matter. A question such as Compare the accomplishment of the F.D. Roosevelt and the Eisenhower administrations in the field of domestic affairs during their first year of office," forces the pupil to consider the available facts, select-those which are pertinent, and express his conclusions in his own words.

One must be careful, however, not to claim too much for the essay examination. Many writers, for example, maintain that the essay examination may be used to arrive at an estimate of the creative ability of the pupil. While it it is true, of course, that the ability to organize materials and the ability to formulate hypotheses are, in part, creative in character, an exact definition of "creatives," and an analysis of the extent to wnich this trait is actually operative in the testing situation, have yet to be presented. Until a more precise concept of creative ability is advanced, it appears to be unwise to place too great stress upon this value for the essay examination.

The pupil's response to an essay examination has also been looked upon as a. source from which the teacher could gleam some insight into the pupil's personality. Sims (9), in emphasizing the value of essay questions as a projective device, points out that test responses can furnish clues to the dynamics of the pupil's mental functioning. Unfortunately, the number of instances in which a pupil's responses to the usual essay question lend themselves to interpretation in terms of psychological adjustment is very small. While the teacher may, in isolated instances, uncover and unexpected manifestation of a personality characteristic, it is well to look upon the essay test as a measure of the pupil's achievement, rather than as a device from which to draw inferences concerning personality structure.

Criticisms of the Essay Examination

One of the most important characteristics of any test is the consistency with which competent examiners evaluate the responses of the examinee. The principal criticism of the essay examination has been directed to this point – the evaluation of answers to essay questions is unreliable. A very large number of studies have dealt with this factor of "reader reliability". From the early studies of Starch and Elliot (15) down to those conducted in recent years, research workers have consistently found marked variability in the marks or grades assigned to the same paper by two or more readers.

Several factors operate to make the marks assigned to essay questions unreliable. Often, different scorers disagree concerning the objective which is being measured—is the question stressing selection of facts, interpretation, or use of English? Scorers may disagree, too, in the weight which is assigned to the several elements of a response, in standards of grading responses of varying quality, or even in interpretation of the purpose of the question.

Extraneous elements may enter into the evaluation of pupil responses. Every experienced teacher is familiar with the student who says nothing, but who says it very well. Too often, he receives a grade based more upon his ability to express himself than upon his understanding of the subject. Comparison of one paper with others graded by the teacher may result in an improper mark – a mediocre paper looks very good to a teacher who has just read a series of poor papers; an average presentation seems very weak when preceded by a series of excellent papers. The teacher must also guard against a tendency to grade not only the answer which is before him, but also the work of the pupil in his class during the course of the school year.

The essay examination has also been criticized on the grounds that the sampling of content, or range of information tested, is narrower than it is in objective examinations. When the teacher administers a 100-item multiple-choice test, the pupil is called upon to make 100 independent responces. Rarely are an equivalent number of independent responses to be found in a pupil's reaction to the limited number of essay questions which can be asked in the same period of time.

The limited scope, in terms of sampling, of the essay examination, places a disproportionate emphasis upon correct interpretation of each question by the puyil. Failure to understand what the teacher has in mind on one essay question penalizes the pupil severely. The pupil who misinterprets two or three objective questions does not suffer such serious damage.

Another criticism leveled against essay examinations constructed by teachers is that emphasis is placed upon the recall of more or less specific information. In spite of the fact that teachers maintain that their courses are designed to guide the pupil to think critically, to interpret facts, and to organize materials, Sims (8) found in his study of a group of essay questions that over 35 per cent called for no more than simple recall of memorized information. While recognition and recall of information are important, such outcomes can be more validly and reliably measured by objective fixed-answer test items than by a free response essay examination.

Improving the Essay Examination

Much of the criticism of the essay examination is due to poorly constructed tests made by teachers for use in their classes. Many studies (7, 12, 14, 17) have indieated, however, that when appropriate care is taken in constructing and grading essay examinations, consistently good results may be obtained in appraising a pupil's performance. Suggestions for improving the essay examination are summarized below :

1. Each question in an essay test should be planned to measure one defined objective of instruction for which no valid or reliable short-answer test is available.

2. Essay questions should be formulated to require a definite, restricted answer for the objective tested. Questions should avoid being vague—"Discuss the following . . ," "What does the above show ?", or even "Write a half page on the following topic." To formulate essay questions of this kind is to play a

"cat and mouse game" with the student. Sometimes this procedure is rationalized by the teacher who "wants to see what the student can do." Such questions force the pupil to put his primary attention on making shrewd guesses concerning what it is that the teacher desires, rather than on the real problem of giving those specific responses which will demonstrate his achievement. Another reason why questions are often stated in general terms is that the teacher feels that by framing specific questions he is "giving away the answer."

The real point is probably that the formulation of questions definite enough for the student to know exactly what he is expected to do is not an easy process, With a little thought, however, questions can be developed with sufficient specificity without revealing the answer to the student. For example, the question, "Compare the League of Nations and the United Nations," may be improved by giving the pupil some help in framing his respodse as follows :

"Compare the League of Nations and the United Nationswith

(*a*) aims and purposes,

(*b*) administrative structure, and

(*c*) success in settling disputes among member nations."

The more elaborate form not only gives the pupil a clearer difinition of the intent of the question, but it allows for the development of a more reliable grade.

3. The pupil should not be allowed to make a choice among several questions. The use of optinal questions makes it almost impossible to arrive at comparable scores for pupils who have answered different questions, since the equating of two or more questions for difficulty constitutes a complex problem (13). Moreover, the judgment of the pupil concerning which

question he can answer to best advantage may be wrong, as Meyer (6) has demonstrated.

4. In grading essay examinations, a standard answer should be formulated in which a specific number of credits is allotted to each significant point which the pupil is expected to make. A sampling of pupil responses should then be read, in order to determine whether the respondents have interpreted the question correctly, and whether any changes in the standard answer are necessary. The following illustrations and saggestations, adapted from those nsed by the agency responsible for the selection of teachers for a large city school system, will serve to clarify the process of developing standard answers and allotting credit values.

(*a*) When there is a *limited* range of choice among acceptable answers or parts of answers, all or most of such possible choices should be included in the standard answer.

Example

Question : What are five of the most common and most reprehensible ways in which time is wasted by inefficient teachers during an arithmetic lesson ? In each case state what measures an efficient teacher should adopt to prevent such loss of time. (15)

Standard Answer : Three points were given for each of any five of seventeen listed instances of wasted time together with the appropriate preventive measure or measures.

Time may be wasted :

1. In taking too much time for the distribution of material. (For full credit an adequate means of mechanizing the routine was expected.)

2. In ruling paper and preparing heads with too great elaboration. (For full credit the proper preparation of the papers was to be indicated.)
3. In dictating problems when they may be presented in a shorter or easier way. (Acceptable means of correcting above : use of mimeographed sheets, use of textbooks, problems written on blackboard before the arithmetic period.)
16. In over-rationalization in the presentation of a new topic. (For full credit an illustration of proper use of rationalization was expected.)
17. In failure to grade difficulties in the presentation of a new topic. (An illustration of proper grading was expected.)

(*b*) As in the preceding example, a question may call for a specified number of "values," "examples," "reason," "instance," etc. When, however, the number is not specified in the question, the standard answer should definitely state how many of these should be required for a maximum rating. In such case, it is usually fair to provide for a degree of flexibility by taking into consideration the fullness and clarity of treatment given by the applicant to each of the separate values, examples, reasons, etc., adduced by him. Not all points for which credit is allowed need be given equal value ; obviously, the weight given to an item should be in proportion to its significance or its importance.

Example

Question : In a paragraph of about fifty to seventy-five words, state, with reasons, the value and the limitation of the use of model compositions in instructing children to write English well. (15)

Standard Answer : It is reasonable to expect that at least ONE important "value" and ONE important "limitation" shall be EFFECTIVELY developed for a maximum answers. In lieu of a thoroughly effective development of ONE point, a less convincing treatment of two or three important points may be accepted a worth the maximum rating.

(*c*) If the possible range of answers is very wide, it may not be practical to do more than to suggest one or more typical answers and to lay down certain general principles that should govern the rating.

Example

Question : State, with reasons, six measures or precautions which a teacher should take in order to safeguard the eyesight of the children in his class. (12)

Standard Answers : There are a very large number of possible acceptable answers. These may be drawn from considerations involving care.

in schoolroom lighting,

in use of the blackboard,

in adjustment of furniture,

in furnishing books and paper in accordance with hygienic requirements for children,

in teaching them to break or to avoid deleterious eye habits,

in identifying pupils with visual defects,

in getting such pupils under treatment,

in seeing to it that they wear their eye-glasses. etc.

Any six acceptable points with suitable "reason" should be given maximum rating. "Reasons" are likely in most cases to be rather general, but should be accepted if correct ; medical technicalities should not be required.

The points should, of course, be mutually exclusive. If an applicant says, first, that the teacher should discover which children have defective vision, and, later, that a teacher should periodically examine the eyes of children, these two partial reasons should receive only two points credit, not four.

(*d*) Answers of the type referred to in the three preceding sections usually range in quality from altogether acceptable answers worthy of maximum rating, through answers worthy of partial credit, to altogether unacceptable answers. An answer or a subdivision of an answer may deserve only partial credit because it is only partially true‘ because it is too general, because it is true only in a limited number of instances, because it represents too minute a subdivision of the thought, because it is in the nature of a repetition or overlapping of some other part of the answer, or because of other faults. The standard answer should, when practicable, give typical instances of answers for which partial credit may be given. In each case the amount of credit permissible should be stated.

Example :

Question : Describe how a first-grade teacher may develop in the minds of her pupils a clear conception of the magnitude of a quart (4).

Standard Answer : For maximum credit an applicant should give two superior devices or three acceptable devices. Scale accordingly, one superior device being worth two points ; one acceptable device, 1.3 points : one inferior device, 0,7 points or less to 0.

Superior

1. Teacher brings to school land allows children to SEE AND HANDLE common forms of quart measures in commercial use, as quart-sized milk bottle, quart oil measure used in garages, quart measures used by housewives, quart berry box, etc.

2. Children estimate the number of quarts in vessels such as pitcher, aquarium, etc., and then verify their guesses by actual measurement.

Acceptable

3. Teacher shows children quart measure.
4. Teacher compares quart measure with pint and gallon by actual measurement of liquids. (Not superior because pint and gallon are taught in second grade.)

Inferior

5. Teacher reminds children of quart measures they have seen.
6. Teacher compares dry with liquid quart measures.
7. Children tell what they have bought by the quart.

(*e*) The standard answer should subdivide the point allowance for the question and clearly state how many points should be allowed for each subdivision and each "sub-subdivision" of the question.

Example

Question : Explain and illustrate the following : "There is a tendency away from class or mass teaching in our schools of today." (10)

Standard Answer : The ten credits were subdivided, allowing four (4) for the explanation and six (6) for the illustration.

Under the explanation the following were expected :

	Allowance
1. Statement of historical background	1/2 point

2.	Clear explanation of mass teaching versus individual teaching	1 point
3.	Appreciation of the influence of educational measurements, of intelligence and achievement tests	1½ points
4.	Influence of modern child study	1 point
	Total	4 points

(*f*) For a question for which the organization of the answer is not more or less indicated in the question itself, and especially one which explicitly calls for a well-organized answer, it may be desirable to allot a small portion of the total point allowance to a rating on organization.

Example

For excellent organization of the answer, allow a maximum of 3 points; for a reasonably good organization, allow 2 points; for fair organization, allow 1 point; for definitely poor organization, allow no credit. Intermediate ratings of 2.5, 1.5 or 0.5 may be used where appropriate.

Sims (7) recommends the use of a technique which involves the sorting of pupil papers into five groups : very superior, superior, average, inferior, and very inferior, on the basis of a rapid reading of the total examination. Careful reading follows in order to correct mistakes in the original evaluation based on the first nursory reading. Letter grades are then assigned to the total examination : A for very superior papers, B for superior, etc. Sims feels that approximately 10 per cent of all papers would be rated A, 20 per cent B, 40 per cent C, 20 per cent D, and 10 per cent F.

This approach deals largely with the general merit of the examination as a whole. When more than one question appears on the total test, variability in pupil respons from question to question makes a general appraisal rather difficult. The teacher, too, will find a model answer approach to grading single questions in essay examinations of greater value as a guide to pupil weaknesses. The use of a rating procedure, while of some value in quantifying a pupil's mark, does not reduce reader unreliability to the same degree as the use of a model answer.

Student Reactions to Essay Tests

Another important aspect of the essay examination is the mind set and related modes of study that students us in preparing for tests. Douglass and Tallmadge (2) found that students report that, in preparing for an essay examination, they reviewed and read generalities and trends, attempted to draw several important conclusions from tables, formulated personal opinions, and read notes on the texts and lectures carefully but without memorizing details.

The same students testified that they paid more attention to minute details and tried to remember the exact words of the book and other specific points when they prepared for short-answer tests. Meyer (5), in studies of the examination set which students have, concluded that the essay question is of fundamental importance in learning and retaining sense material. In effect, if the teacher wishes students to recall isolated facts, when specific cues are given, a new-type objective examination set may be used with profit. If the teacher wants students to recall material in an organized fashion and to know facts when cues are not given, the essay examination should be used in preference to any objective-type examination. It is important for the teacher to determine what sort of reaction he wishes to test and to adapt his methods toward the outcome he has in mind.

THE ORAL EXAMINATION

In the past, the classroom teacher relied very heavily on the oral work of his pupils in order to arrive at an estimate of the extent to which they mastered the work of his course. The modern teacher, of course, does not attempt to grade every oral contribution of every pupil, rarely does one find a present day classroom dominated to such a degree by the making book. The re-citation of a learned lesson, with the opportunity it provided for grading pupils, has given way to patterns of classroom procedure organized in terms of experiential activities. This change has been accompanied by a marked reduction in the opportunities provided for testing and marking the oral work of pupils.

Limitations of the Oral Examination

Even at its best, however, the oral quiz serves as a very poor basis for determining the grade which should be assigned to a pupil's work in a given course. Oral examinations take too much time to administer; like the essay test, they present the same difficulties of poor sampling and high subjectivity in marking; comparability of questions is difficult to obtain.

Values of the Oral Examination

The oral questioning of an individual pupil constitutes an excellent means of following the thought processes which he has used in solving certain problems, such as one in mathematics. Used in this manner, the oral quiz becomes a valuable tool for the diagnosis of pupil difficulties. Skillful questioning by the teacher, too, many help the pupil to apply known scientific information to a new situation or to see implications, such as those involved in adopting a given economic policy. The use of this Socratic-like approach should not, generally, be looked upon as a rod for measuring pupil achievement; rather, it represents a worthwhile instructional technique.

In some situations, an oral examination constitutes the only way in which a measure of pupil attainment can be obtained. When children have not yet mastered the intricacies of reading, an oral examination must be used. Reading readiness tests and intelligence tests given in the lower elementary-school grades, for example, generally call upon the pupil to follow a series of oral directions in making his responses on a printed page. Such tests, of course, require standardized administration and scoring.

The oral examination, used in the course of classroom work, does have the obvious advantage of saving the time and expense which is involved in reproducing copies of a test. As a result, oral administration of teacher-made tests of the short-answer type is frequently found. In a sense, oral presentation of such teacher-made tests eliminates some of the difficulties which are associated with the administration of mimeographed or printed tests. The relative informality of the oral test situation is far less frightening to the timid child. The pupil cannot ponder over an item which he finds difficult, losing so much time that he cannot complete the test. Moreover, the oral examination places a premium upon oral rather than reading comprehension. The relatively heavy emphasis which the school places upon the latter aspect of comprehension is thereby reduced.

The Reliability and Validity of Oral Examinations

In general, the research studies which have been conducted in this field indicate that short-answer tests which are administered orally yield appreciably the same results as printed tests. Briggs and Armacost (1), Lehman (4), and Stump (16), for example, have found that an oral true-false examination compared very favorably with such tests presented in visual form. In general, the correlation between the same true-false test administered orally and visually differs only slightly from the correlation between the old and even items of the test given orally. Much the same results were obtained when a five-alternative multiple-choice test was studied. In this instance, while oral presentation tended to increase the difficulty of the test slightly, no loss in reliability or validity was demonstrated (10). One may conclude, from the available evidence, that orally presented teacher-made short-answer tests yield results that are comparable to mimeographed or printed tests of similar length and construction.

Oral Trade Tests

One of the most recent applications of the oral examinations is seen in the development of the oral trade tests. Such tests are designed to gauge an individual's knowledge of a given trade or occupation. As such, they offer a ready means of screening applicants for a position when only a brief time is available for interviews. Oral trade tests were widely used by the armed forces during World War II as an aid in the proper classification of personnel.

In preparing oral trade tests, a number of general principles must be borne in mind. The wording used in questions must be clear; the language chosen must be that used by the worker on the job. The question must relate to an activity or to a task which is an important element of the trade and which represents common trade practice. The question must be specific, and call for a specific answer; general questions evoke generalities as responses. Most important, the questions must be able to distinguish between the various levels of trade knowledge. In a well-constructed oral trade test, apprentices will make lower scores than journeymen, who, in turn, will make lower scores than experts. Novices or persons working in related fields should show little or no knowledge of the given trade. In general, a total of fifteen questions proves to be all that are needed to arrive at an adequate estimate of the trade background of a worker. When these criteria are met, an oral trade test provides a valuable supplement to the other information which an employment interviewer needs in correctly classifying a job applicant.

Sample questions from oral trade tests developed by the Occupational Analysis Section of the United States Employment Service (3) will serve to make clear their general nature :

Automobile Mechanic

> Name the firing order on a six-cylinder motor. What clearance do you allow on crankshaft bearings with forced oiling system? What is the average limit of toe-in on automobiles without knee action ?

Pastry Cook

What percentage of shortening do you use in a good pie crust ? What ingredient do you put into biscuit dough that you do not put into pie dough? What do you use as leavening in angel-food cake ?

SUMMARY

Essay examinations, which still constitute a widely used approach to achievement testing utilized by the classroom teacher, are of greatest value in testing the higher mental processes, such as formulating hypotheses and organizing and expressing ideas. The criticisms which have been directed against the essay examination deal largely with reader unreliability, lack of objectivity, inadequacy of sampling, and stress upon recall of specific information. The research evidence in the field, however, indicates that the essay examination can be improved. Too, it appears that students preparing for essay examinations use techniques of study which stress the development of general conclusions.

The oral examination, like the essay test, is widely used by the classroom teacher, particularly as an informal device for evaluating pupil performance. Even at its best, however, the oral quiz is a poor basis for assigning pupil marks. It has value as a diagnostic tool, and in situations in which written tests cannot be used. The reliability and validity of teacher-made short-answer tests orally presented, compares favorably with that of mimeographed or printed tests of similar length and construction. The oral trade test is of particular value in evaluating the background of job applicant.

PROBLEMS FOR CLASS DISCUSSION

1. (*a*) Prepare an essay question designed to test student understanding of the major concepts presented in

this chapter. (*b*) Set up a model answer for use in grading the question, indicating the reasons for assigning the values you give to the several sections of the model answer.

2. Select a trade area about which you have some working knowledge. Prepare an oral test for administration to a hypothetical candidate for a position in the trade. Justify your choice of questions and the point value, if any, you would give to each questions.

8

Observation and Anecdotal Records

Direct observation of performance or behavior is the basis for collecting data for anecdotal records and observational teceniques. Both methods of evaluation require an observer who records the activities, experiences, and expressions of individuals or groups. When these methods are restricted to selected aspects of behavior and when records are made systematically and as objectively as possible, these techniques gain in reliability and validity.

Informal observation is employed daily by the classroom teacher who watches and notes such pupil performance as competence in oral reading or in solving an arithmetic exercise. Observation may be used, also, in making a running account of pupil conduct. Structured, or controlled, observational techniques, however, require making an objective record of the defined activities under study. For this purpose, the method may use special techniques or tools such as specially prepared charts or checklists for recording behavior.

Anecdotal records are cumulative notes of an individual's behavior observed in typical situations, activities, and experiences. The anecdotal record is a concise and objective description of the behavior, e.g., "Sue cried when she failed to solve an arithmetic problem." The interpretation of such behavior should be reserved until an adequate sample of such observations has been collected. The observations should be restricted to three or four defined characteristics and to a reasonable number of individuals so that the burden of observing and recording will not become excessive, contributing, thereby, to increased validity, reliability, and objectivity of the anecdotal records.

The role played by observational techniques in measurement and evaluation is somewhat different from that of anecdotal records. Systematic observational study, using predetermined units and time samples, is in the main carried out by research investigators in psychological and sociological studies of children and adults. Anecdotal records and informal observation, on the other hand, are used by the classroom teacher, counselar, or group worker to a greater extent than by professional psychologists and researchers. There is, however, no strict line of dermarcation between the methods and their use. The remarks on observational techniques are directed to teachers as well as to research persons.

Objectives Evaluated by Observation

It has been pointed out (2) that if a given objective is regarded as an important feature of the school program, provision should also be made to determine it is being achieved. Data on physical status, academic achievement, and study skills can be obtained more easily by evaluative instruments other than that of observation. Objectives for whose evaluation methods of observation are most valuable are generally in the areas of social adjustment or personal and emotional adjustment and growth. Observations on the physical and intellectual aspects of growth should be made by use of this technique only if they seem to have a marked bearing on the child's personality. It should be noted that the obsrvation of any objective requires that it be defined in terms of overt actions of individuals.

In the area of social adjustments and growth, observations on many forms of behavior can be made. For instance, in what situations does a child play alone of with other, follow or lead ? Does he fight with other children ? The personal and emotional adjustment of the child has to do with his growth in personal independence, in responsibility, and in initiative. Emotional reactions which may be observed are manifold. Does the child have nervous habits ? Does he strike or push others ? Does he exhibit frustration ? Methods of direct observation, however, have also been used to measure study habits, interests, kinesthetic movements, and other diverse problems.

OBSERVATIONAL TECHNIQUES

Place of Obsevation in Evaluations

Observation is a direct method of sampling behavior in social situations, and, as such, performs a vital service as a tool of evaluation. Through the use of observation, an objective description of individuals in their actual interrelationship with each other and with their environment may be secured. By catching the natural modes of their actions and expressions, observational techniques permit the process of measurement without disturbing the normal activities of groups or individuals observed. Data gathered by observation are amenable to treatment by conventional statistical techniques (9).

The types of social situations which may be explored through observation are extensive, ranging from a study of the physical, social, and emotional behavior of young children in nurseries, kindergartens, and classrooms, to a study of adult behavior in factory, office, discussion group, home, and other community situations.

Definition of Observational Technique

Goodenough (3) indicates that the technique

"... consists simply in the observation of the everyday behavior of an individual or a group of individuals for definite short periods of time and the recording of the

> occurrence or non occurrence of certain specified and objectively definnd forms of behavior during each of these periods. The number of periods in which the report is positive for a given individual is then treated as his score. Since the number and length of the observational periods are the same for all individuals, a direct comparison of the frequencies or scores is thus made possible. A further requirement is that all individuals be observed undet similar conditions, either during the performance of similar activities or when variation in activity is brought about only through the free choice of the subject himself."

Jersild and Meigs (4) make three distinctions among situations to which direct observation has been applied. They speak of "free situation," conceiving them as situations which contain no restrictions other than those inherent in the situations themselves, Second are "manipulated situations" situations to which the investigators have added special factors or introduced additional variables, such as frustrating taskes or planned interruptions, in order to precipitate given types of behavior. Third are "partially controlled" situations, a fusion of the two previous types.

The observer, before approaching the situation, decides which aspects of the behavior of the individuals involved he will select and record. Units of behavior or patterns that are to be recorded and scored should be defined in terms of overt action. Measurement of the objectivity of the definition used should be attempted. Both control of the observer and measurement of the reliability or fidelity of the observer is at least desirable. Other requirements include appropriate timing and distribution of observation periods, and observation periods sufficient in duration and number to give a reliable sampling. Quantitative results reported for observation carried on with these safeguards may be accepted with confidence.

Methods of Recording Observations

Two methods of recording observations may be described. In one, the units of behavior which are to be observed are defined in advance. These definitions, called categories, represent a summary of a particular form of action and behavior. A behavior category may describe a simple form of expressive behavior such as smiling or laughing, or it may indicate a more complex form of inter-personal behavior such as "being helpful." Categories are arrived at by exploratory observations and are refined in accordance with the emphasis of the study undertaken.

During the investigation a check or symbol is entered on the record each time an item of a given category occurs. An observer cannot see and record everything, though several observers may agree to concentrate on different units of behavior and pool their observations. Whether, however, the emphasis is on detailed desriptions of limited aspects of behavior or on a simple listing of the occurrence or non-occurrence of general patterns of activity, the principle of selectivity must be recognized. It is necessary to plan what will be recorded and what will be ignored, what will be noted in detail and what will be described in more general terms.

Scientific use of the direct observation method necessitates testing the objectivity of a set of categories. This can be done by having two or more investigators, independently of each other, develop categories for the systematic recording of the behavior under investigation. The investigations, of course, must previously be instructed regarding the purpose and emphases of the study. The categories are then compared and refined. Ambiguities are removed ; categories may be merged or subdivided. These operations are performed, of course, with the purposes of the study in mind. The guiding principle is the selection of categories which will best record the data needed for subsequent evaluation. In this way, the design of the observation is made explicit and makes repetition by other workers feasible. If the study is carried out by one individual and standards of scientific adequacy are a lesser consideration, the investigator may classify behavior at different times and compare the categories evolved.

This methods of using units defined in advance (predefined categories) has been found expedient when data of a quantitative nature are involved. This method is useful for comparing frequencies of clearly definable and psychologically distinguishable forms of behavior. For instance, the frequency of such things as the number of times a child talks to his neighbor per a given time unit may be tallied. An illustration may clarify this point (8) :

> "Each time a pupil engages in an activity which falls within the scope of any one of the defined categories, the observer writes the code or symbol next to the pupil's name. During the total period of observation a given pupil may engage in the acts five, twenty, or any number of times. This frequency is a quantitative value, and represents the frequency of occurrence per stated unit of time. If a class is observed for a total period of time amounting to 200 minutes, the score for the category of inititative for pupil A may be 5, for pupil B, 12, and for pupil C, 22.

A disadvantage of predefined categories lies in the fact that once units have been decided upon, the observer is not free to adapt his account to what he observes ; rather, he must fit what he observes to his categories. This sometimes means that he is compelled to project his own definitions on the behavior that he observes (4). Categories based on exploratory study and refined in terms of such study partially meet this criticism.

For many purposes, however, it is important to consider items of behavior in terms of their context and the patterns of which they are a part. This relatedness of acts is unique for each situation and thus is not accessible to previous categorization. This requires a second method of recordig observations, the "running account" method which enables the investigator to capture the context in which units of behavior occur. The observer using this method gives a fluid, running account. He records as fast as he can and as much as he can hear and see which he feels is relevant to the problem under study. This latter consideration is important. Running account observations are not planless observations. There must be understanding, before the observer begins to take second regarding the points of emphasis in the observation.

Measurement of observer reliability becomes more difficult when this method is used. However, comparisons can be made between the content of the records of independent observers, even though a decision as to the interpretation of a given item of behavior has not yet been made by the observer. This procedurs serves to make explicit to the observer the forms of behavioe he is likely to emphasize in his observations. Many studies combine checklists, containing predetermined categories, with space for supplementary running accounts.

Length of Observation Periods

Single observation periods may extend anywhere rfom several minutes to several hours. Total observation of behavior in studies of growth and development has been carried on for months and years (5). Two factors determine the length of the observation period : the nature of the phenomenon under study, and feasibility. There is also a limitation which is imposed upon the duration of observation by the division of school activity into class periods. Jersild and Meigs (4) advise a series of many short, rotated periods, ranging from five to fifteen minutes, when studying the behavior of young children, especially in "free" situations.

The use of shorter observation periods may mean a loss in sequence of observation, due to the chain of stimulus-response-stimulus behavior which exists in social situations. Activities may be initiated before the onset of an observation period, and behavior manifested during that period may be a part of a sequence of chain behavior reactions released by these activities. In shorter observation periods, important relationships may be missed or misunderstood by the observer.

If frequencies of specific behavior units are to be scored, it is necessary to divide the observation period into time units of observation. Whether or not such refined time units are needed depends entirely on the nature of the behavior studied and the degree of quantification desired. Time units ranging from five seconds to several minutes have been used. How often a given behavior is likely to occur and how best to discriminate beetween behavior units will enter into a decision regarding the scheduling of time units within observation periods. Similarly, a decision to time observations may be made if comparisons between observers are indicated for the refinement of categories or for a check of reliability, or if two observers are to serve supplementary functions in the recording of data.

Postion and Effect of Observer

The function of the observer makes it necessary for him to be in a favorable position for observation. It is advisable for him to take a position that enables him to see or hear the behavior which he intends to observer. But, as symonds has remarked, much that passes for observation is obtained only from fleeting glimpses, with obstructions to the view, and in the face of various distractions (5). The observer should be able to locate readily the object of his observation. A device available in classroom observation is the seating plan in which each child's name is inserted. In order to capture ceatain reactions it may be necessary for the observer to change position or to move rapidly. It is often not possible for the observer to assume a position most useful to him in observation. The better position may interfere with the natural development of the social situation under study. Thus any consideration of observer position is related to considerations of the effect of the observer upon the situation, Symonds writes :

"On the one hand there are those who would remove the examiner entirely from the situation. If he is present, it is agreed he should be a passive and unobtrusive visitor, but it would be better still if he could be invisible. The Yale Psycho-Clinic has devised a screen behind which the observer becomes invisible to children in the room, and is therefore eliminated as a stimulating factor in the situation. The writer became skillful in observing the study habits of boys through a technique of concentrating on a certain boy until the boy looked at him, whereupon he would turn his attention elsewhere. It is possible to disarm suspicion by apparently being unaware of what is going on. At the other extreme is the observer who actually takes an active part in the situation by asking questions, making suggestions, teaching and the like. The part an observer takes in the situation depends on the particular problem under investigation." (5)

It has been found that the presence of an observer distorts the behavior under study less than anticipated. Very young children tend to be less conscious of the presence of an observer than are older children or adults. The effect of the observer's presence, however, seems to vary with time. As the group observed gets to consider the observer as a part of their environment, the natural reaction and interactions between individuals resume and valid data can be obtained. The need for one-way vision screens would seem limited to situations where the investigators predict adverse effects from the introduction of an observer.

Cautions to the Observer

Investigators are cautioned to keep the following points in mind when employing the method of observation (1).

(*a*) The significance of observations depends upon the ability, understanding, and characteristics of the observer.

(*b*) The observer needs to be conscious of the danger of misinterpretation through the confusion of symptoms with underlying causes.

(*c*) Recording of observations should be made promptly, so that none of the important detatls will be forgotten.

(*d*) Generalizations from observation should be arrived at only after careful study. Such generalizations should be held to a minimum.

Interpreting the Data

Time spent in obtaining the data may be short in comparison with the time that subsequently must be spent in analyzing the data. Less time will be spent in analysis if the observations were made simply to compare frequencies of specific activities rather than if they were made to gain insight into fundamental behavior processes. In the latter event, the records will be interpreted in the light of other pertinent knowledge which the investigator may possess. If he is studying aggressive behavior, before interpreting the records gathered by observation, he will read related studies and base his interpretations on a framework of knowledge and theories developed by other workers in this area.

Advantages of Data from Observation

Some of the advantages of observational techniques for certain areas of evaluation are the following : In a relatively "free" situation—defined in terms of absence of outside pressure—observation may reveal important aspects of the personality and behavior of individuals studied (2). The individual does not feel "on the spot." He is not singled out for questioning or testing. He engages in his usual activities and interests with others spontaneously. As the child, for instance, meets frustrating or satisfying situations we observe his natural modes of reaction and response. The records gathered can be systematically treated and are subject to comparison.

Limitation of Data from Observation

Observation as a technique requires a considerable amount of skill. Observers must be conscious of the difference between *describing* behavior and *evaluating* behavior. The personality of the observer becomes an additional variable. The experiences, biases, and values of the observer cannot always be completely separated from the behavior he is recording. Similar behavior manifested by different individuals may not have the same meaning to different observers. Observation, of course, does not give the same insight into individual personality structure as do projective techniques. In addition, observational techniques are time consuming.

ANECDOTAL RECORDS

Definition of Anecdotal Records

Traxler (6) reports several definitions of anecdotal records which appear in the literature. Anecdotal records have been defined as "reports of significant episodes in the life of students," as "simple statements of incidents deemed by the observer to be significant with respect to a given pupil," and as "descriptions of actual behavior taking place in situations noted by the instructor," in contrast with rating scales which provide records only of the summary interpretation of the behavior observed.

In general, anecdotal records are a series of notes on exactly what a child said or did in concrete situations. As successive observations accumulate, the records contain a variety and continuity of evidence which yield a picture of the child's behavior patterns and growth, his interests and attitudes, his strengths and weaknesses, and problems. These records are not to be confused with case studies, which contain more extensive data, including developmental and family histories. Anecdotal records are reports of current observations of specific incidents which illustrate the child's reactions. Such observations are entered on these records frequently enough to give an adequate picture of the child's growth.

A few entries from the record of Bob, an eleven-year-old boy (7), will illustrate :

2/8/55 Before class period when children were all talking in small groups, B, stood alone.

2/14/55 Did not take part in discussion on what we would look for at the museum. Sat quietly.

2/15/55 Wrote about trip to museum but crumpled up his paper and threw it into basket.

2/17/55 Only child who did not volunteer to do something for the Mexican play which the children decided to produce.

2/23/55 In the yard at lunch time, asked B, what he liked to do best outside of school. He replied, "Play the violin. My mother is going to help me become a violinist." Said he had no friends because his mother does not allow him to play with the boys on the street. Asked him if he would play his violin at assembly. He accepted with a smile, agreed to rehearsal in class tomorrow.

2/24/55 Brought his violin and played well. Children applauded and congratulated him. He smiled and offered to play any time we wished. Then he said he knew some Mexican songs for the play. (This is the first time he has volunteered anything.)

Though anecdotal records are in some respects similar to other observational techniques, such as time sampling, they differ from them in method. Other observational techniques are characterized by a systematic recording of previously defined units of behavior described in terms of activity over definite time intervals. Anecdotal records are less carefully controlled than techniques utilizing time sampling. They approximate the "running account" method of observation though there still is an important distinction between the two, The requisite for the successful use of anecdotal procedures is that the anecdotes be written freely about all kinds of social situations where significant items of behavior are observed.

Anecdotal Records Help Teachers Understand Children

Anecdotal records help teachers understand and guide children. These records direct the observation of the teacher to the child's needs and so help in guiding his development. From his observations and his study of the records, the teacher gains greater understanding of the child's personality and his needs. This knowledge affects the teacher's procedures and attitudes and results in a relationship with the child which fosters his growth. As the teacher observes and learns to know one child well, he learns more about child behavior in general and is then better able to establish the understanding atmosphere in which children can best develop healthy personalities.

Anecdotal records are of value not only to the teacher who makes them, but also to subsequent teachers and to other staff or agency workers who are concerned with the child's development and adjustment. If these persons have this information available, they do not have to begin from scratch in accumulating data about a child, and, in dealing with him, they are able to avoid unnecessary mistakes caused by a lack of knowledge. Thus, the records make possible more effective guidance of the child's development throughout his school career.

The actual observations may seem much more important than the written records, but the record is also essential as concrete evidence both fort the person making the notations and for other school personnel interested in a particular child's adjustment. A systematic record to which one ean refer for an accurate account of the child's behavior is certainly preferable to memory. Almost any elementary psychology textbook will cite experimental evidence of how much people forget. Not only do we forget, but we tend to forget that which does not agree with our previous impressions and to remember that which confirms our ideas and attitudes. Consequently. without records interpretations of a child's behavior are likely to be impressionistic and subjective,

Objectives to be Evaluated by Anecdotal Records

If the teacher is not to become swamped by a mass of unrelated detailed observations, he must know where to focus his observations. It is desirable to concentrate on a few major aspects of child growth for which information cannot be obtained except by observation. Adequate data on physical status, academic achievement, and study skills can be obtained from tests, rating scales, and checklists using predetermined categories. Consequently, observations in these areas of physical and intellectual growth should be recorded only if they have a marked influence on the child's personality. Objectives for whose evaluation anecdotal records are most valuable are those in the areas of social adjustment and growth, personal and emotional adjustment and growth, as well as other factors which may have a major influence on a particular child's adjustment.

Social Adjustment and Growth

By social adjustment of the child is meant his relationships with other children and with adults. The school is committed to an improvement of inter-personal relations and to increasing the social adjustment of individual children. Anecdotal records can play a great part in helping the teacher and the outsider evaluate progress made in these directions.

The records include incidents that illustrate the child's relations with other children—*e.g.*, incidents that show whether and in what situations he plays alone or with others, with whom he plays, whether he works well with a group, leaves a group if he cannot get his own way, or fights with other children. Also included are entries illustrating how well he gets along with his teacher and other adults—*e.g.*, whether he requires much attention or affection from adults ; adjusts well with adults, but poorly with children ; is shy and fearful, of adults, or is antagonistic to them.

Personal and Emotional Adjustment and Growth

Attempts undertaken in promoting personal and emotional adjustment and growth are similarly subject to evaluation and clarification through the use of anecdotal records. Incidents illustrating the child's independence or dependence, his manner of meeting new situations, his assumption of responsibilities, and his demonstration of interests are included under this heading. Incidents illustrating his pattern of emotional reactions, showing whether he is cheerful, laughs readily, cries easily, worries, is fearful, is enthusiastic, is easily discouraged, has temper tantrums, or shows nervous mannerisms all should be reported. Sometimes physical manifestations like vomiting, headaches, and indigestion may be symptoms of emotional difficulties.

Other Factors

Since the school is concerned with the total adjustment of the child, anecdotal records may be kept dealing with any other factor which has a major influence on a particular child's adjustment.

These factors will vary for different children. An unusual event in a particular child's life may have a marked effect upon his adjustment– *e.g.*, birth of a new baby, illness of a parentor of the child himself, change in the economic status of the family, separation of parents, placement in a foster home, or moving to a new community. With another child it may be some constant home factors—*e.g.*, home standards in conflict with neighborhood standards, quarreling parents, or working mother. With still another it may be the discovery of a special talent, a strong interest, or a special disability.

Number of Children Observed

Records for just a few children are preferable at first. Since considerable practice is required to develop the techniques for recording and interpreting anecdotal records, and since a teacher's first efforts will necessarily include a period of experimentation and floundering with a new type of record, the most effective way to begin is by studying a few children only. It is suggested that, at first, no more than two children be observed. If the teacher who is just beginning to keep records studies a few children only, he has an opportunity to work out his techniques as well as to learn about the children's needs. If, instead, he attempts to keep records for the whole class, he will become swamped with the process and, as a result, the reports may become a chore that will not meet the needs of the individual child.

Experience in keeping cumulative records is necessary to develop techniques. To learn to use cumulative anecdotal records most effectively in obtaining a continuous picture of the child's growth, it is necessary to keep records of behavior over a period of time. As the teacher studies the child and makes his notes, his techniques of observation, recording, and interpretation will improve. He will become more expert in selecting events which are significant for the child and in writing objective reports of these incidents. His records will present an increasingly accurate picture of the quality of the child's behavior. Most teachers will probably need at least a year or more of experience in writing and interpreting anecdotal records for a few children before they have mastered the techniques.

Where Chidren are Observed

Observations for anecdotal records should be made in a variety of situations as children show different behavior under diÿerent circumstances. To obtain a fair sampling of the child's reactions, he should be observed incidentally in a variety of activities and situations : in plannting or other aesthetic expression, free play, athletic games, dramatic improvisation, and other learning situation ; on trips and in the classrom, the halls, the assembly, the lunchroom, and the yard. If the record is really to reflect the child's individuality, most observations should be made in situations in which he has freedom to display a variety of reactions. For an adequate picture of inter-personal relations, it is necessary to observe the child in flexible situations such as those just mentioned, wherever the child has an opportunity to choose his companions and to have social relations.

Information about the child's reactions at home is often vital in interpreting the child's behavior and should be obtained whenever possible by means of informal interviews with the parents. Often teachers have used the opportunity of interview a parent when she has come to school to attend a parent-teacher meeting or a class teacher, or when she has come to call for a younger child. Ideally, there should be a regular time set aside for conferences with mothers and fathers.

Criteria for Recording Anecdotes

Certain uniform stands should be observed in recording anecdotal material. The following list includes some of the essentials for any ancedotal record keeping.

1. Each entry should be dated, so that the sequence and lapse of time are clear when the record is reviewed for evidence of the child's development and growth. Incidents should be recorded on the day on which they occur before memory of them becomes distorted.

2. Each entry should contain some statement of the situation in which the incident occurred, so that it can be properly interpreted. A child's shouting excitedly during a ball game and his shouting in the midst of an arithmetic test would certainly be interpreted differently.

   Examples

   4/15/54 During class discussion - —- —

   4/22/54 While painting in class————

3. Each anecdotal entry should be a brief factual description of an incident complete enough so that it can be understood later, when an attempt is made to evaluate the child's behavior.

   Examples : Entry for a first-grade girl, Arlene :

   10/3/53 Came in crying this morning, "May dear, dear doggie was at the kennels and my daddy told me that he is not coming have again."

4. Entries should be objective reporting of facts insofar as possible. A generalized statement or tentative interpretation may be necessary to make the picture clearer, but should always be accompanied by reports of specific incidents and should be based upon adequate facts. Interpreations and generalizations shoulds be placed in parentheses to differentiate them from factual data.

Traxler points out that many teachers obscure the report of what they observe with subjective statements of opinion concerning interpretation and treatment (6). He giʌes the following example of such a "mixed" anecdote.

> "In a meeting of here club today, Alice showed her jealousy of the new president by firing questions at her whenever there was an opportunity. She tried to create difficultles by constant interruptions throughout the period The other students showed their resentment by calling for her to sit down. It is apparent that she is a natural trouble-maker, and I think her counselor should haue her in for a serious talk."

Traxler explains that the phrases "showed her jealousy." "showed their resentment and others are value statements and do not represent an objective description of what happened.

He objectifics the report in this manner :

Incident

> In a meeting of her club today, Alice fired questions at the new president at every opportunity. She interrupted many times during the period. On several occasions the other students called for her to sit down.

Interpretation of the incident may then be added to the objective deecription, to quote :

Interpretation

> Alice seemed to be jealous of the new president and desirous of creating difficulties. The other students appeared to resent her action. The girl seems to enjoy making trouble for others.

Sometimes observations which are fused with evaluative comments display good insights into the behavior observed. These in sights would stand out more clearly, however, if they were sparated from the descriptive material.

5. Entries of incidents showing desirable, passive, inconspicuous, or non-participating behavior are as important in giving a true picture of the child as incidents of undersirable or dramatic behavior.

6. Enter information about home attitudes when it is obtained, since it may contribute clues to the interpretation of the child's behavior which no amount of school observation will yield.

7. Have an adequate number and sequence of anecdotal entries upon which to base judgments and interpretation of behavior. For some children more entries are necessary than for others. A teacher just beginning to keep records should make only about one entry a week for each chosen child, more if necessary. With experience, fewer entries may be found suffieient

Common Errors in Recording Which Should be Avoided

1. A common error or beginners is to give generalized description or evaluations of behavior rather than specific incidents.

   Examples of generalization :

   Charters all the time.

   Is interested in art.

   Examples of evaluations :

   Is as lazy as two donkeys.

   Is very sensitive—a good child.

2. Another common error is to give the teacher's personal reactional to the child rather than the child's behavior.

Example

Isn't an interesting or colorful subject to report on. Gets in your hair. Shows no interest. Wish I could see what's behind the Iron Curtain she's set up.

This entry shows the teacher's reaction but gives us little information about the child's actual behavior.

A sweet, charming child.

This again indicates the teacher's reaction rather than the child's specific beyavior.

3. Beginners tend to interpret behavior before there are adequate data and to confuse such interpretations with facts.

4. Recording primarily negative or dramatic incidents is a tendency that must be guarded against. The record must not be allowed to become a report of a child's misdeeds and failure to conform. It should be a balanced, not a one-sided picture of the child.

5. There is no need to worry if a significant item is omitted. It is impossible and unnecessary to record everything. The record contains only samples of the child's behavior. If the behavior that has not been recorded is really important in the child's adjustment and growth, the same pattern of behavior will be repeated and there will be later opportunities to record it. If that pattern is uot repeated, the original incident was probably not important.

Methods of Recording Anecdotes

Anecdotal records may be kept on simple forms. The form for the original record may be plaoed on a small card (3" by 5", or 5" by 8"), a half sheet, a full sheet, or a page that will fit into a loose-leaf notebook. The size of the form will determine the number of anecdotes which can be written on each. A sample form is given here.

Anecdotal Record

Pupil—————————————Class———

Date	**Incident**	**Comment**
		Interpretation

Observer——————————

The advantages of using small cards is that a few cards may be carried in one's pocket and brief notes be made when there is occasion to do so. Original records for each child will be field together in chronological order to provide a cumulative picture of the child for later review.

Interpretation of Cumulative Anecdotal Records

Teachers often hesitate to summarize and interpret anecdotal records. In his daily work, the teacher is constantly called upon to make tentative interpretations upon which to base his decisions for handling children and he does so with assurance. However, when he is ready to interpret anecdotal records he becomes timid and doubtful of his abilitp, feels that the interpretation should be an elaborate psychological diagnosis to be made by experts. True, experts should be called in to help in interpreting some cases, but for most children the teacher can evaluate the record himself. His intimate contact with so many children of a particular age gives him a rich background of comparative data to help him evaluate an indivi dual child's behavior. Naturally, the broader the teacher's background in child study and psychology is, the more accurate and comprehensive will be his interpretations. As he gains experience in evaluating records, he will find it easier to make more intensive interpretations. It should be emphasized, however, that no elaborate ease study or diagnosis can be made solely on the basis of anecdotal records.

The following steps are involved in interpreting the records.

1. The notes are reviewed preriodically every month or two, to see what trends in behavior are revealed what suggestions for handling the child are implied, and to decide what further information should be obtained.

2. The facts are examined to see if there is sufficient information upon which to base conclusions for each aspect of growth. If the data are inadequate, further observations should be made and addition information sought. Conclusions should be drawn only on the basis of repeated instances.

3. At the end of each half year, the teacher writes a summary and interpretation of each record. This report is not a case history, but should help in planning for the child's social and emotional growth and adjustment. The report should include a

summary of repeated patterns of behavior and evidence of growth or regression shown in the record. If there is an adequate series of dated and classified facts, these major trend will stand out. If the data in any area are not sufficient to show a clear picture, this fact should be stated.

On the basis of the summary, the teacher makes a tentative interpretation of the child's motivations and of the his major problems and needs. This interpretation is based upon the teacher's knowledge of the particular child and of scientific principles of behavior. The child's behavior is interpreted in the light of his level of maturity, his home reletianships, the economic and cultural level of his family and neighborhood, and other related factors. As further work is done with the child, the interpretation may have to be changed. It is only an hypothesis. It is the best that can be done with the available information, but that information is always just a small sample of the child's total behavior. Only by seeing the outcome of attempts to help the child, based on these interpretations, is it possible to determine whether the evaluations are valid. Increasing confidence can be placed in these interpretations as a number of successive teachers give consistent reports over a period of years.

SUMMARY

Direct observation and recording of behavior is the basis for collecting data by means of observational techniques and anecdotat records. Obrervational techniques include the structured, or controlled, recording of observations by using defined catgories of activities in a running account of pupil conduct. Anecdotal records are cumulative notes of an individual's behavior observed in typical situations.

The types of social situations for which observations are made include nursery school, classrooms, factory, office, discussion group, home, and community activities. These may be free or natural situations, manipulated situations, or partially controlled situations. The objectives of observation usually emphasize social growth and adjustment, for example : solitary play, cooperative activity, personal independence, nervous habits, study habits' interests, kinesthetic movements, and o.her diverse activities.

Two major methods of recording observations are used. In one, the units of behavior to be observed are defined in advance and a record is made of those activities only which fit the defined categories. In the other, a running account of observations is made without the benefit of predefined categories. The first method is adapted to formal studies but the second method is beiter fitted to informal situations. Such factors as the length of the observation period, and the positon or effect of the observer are directly related to the purpose of a particular evaluation. Length of each observation must be determined by activity and objective, based upon an analysis of the situation. This may vary from one minute to fifteen or thirty minutes for each one of a series of observations. Generally, the presence of an observer distorts the behavior under study less than is anticipated.

Observations and their validity depend upon the ability, understanding, and characteristics of the observer. Recording of observations should be made promptly and objectively. The observer should be careful to discriminate between symptoms and underlying causes. Generalizations from observations should be cautiously made after extensive samples of activity have been recorded.

Anecdotal records are a series of notes on exactly what a child did or said in a specific situation. Objectives for which cumulative anecdotal records are most valuable include social adjustment and growth, personal and emotional adjustment, and related factors.

It is recommended that anecdotal records for only a few children be kept at first. As a teacher or observer gains experience, the number of children for whom anecdotal records are recorded may be increased as judgment indicates. The situations in which children's activities are recorded should emphasize flexible relationships on the playground, in the lunchroom, in committee work, in a play or club period, or wherever the child has a maximum of choice in expressing personal and social relationships with others.

Minimum standards for recording anecdotal records include : date of each entry, statement of situation in which incident occurred, a factual description of the incident, objective reporting of any related information, and an adequate number and sequences of anecdotal records upon which to base a judgment. Common errors to be avoided are : generalized evaluation of behavior rather than description of specific incident, observer's reactions but no objective facts on incident, recording of negative data only, generalizing before sufficient data are collected, and concern that a pattern of behavior will not occur after a previous observation. The method of recording should be kept as simple as possible.

So long as an adequate sample of observations is obtained, interpretation of the cumulative records is possible. For adequate interpretation of records, it is recommended that the notes be reviewed periodically to check trends in behavior, to determine if data are inadequate in any areas, and to prepare a summary and interpretation of the record to help in planning for the child's social and emotional growth and development.

PROBLEMS FOR CLASS DISCUSSION

1. Make a "running account" of the physical movements of each of ten children, allowing three minutes of observation for each child. Examine your "account" and organize the physical movements into tentative predefined categories for checklist observation.
2. Make anecdotal records of the nervous habits or mannerisms of three children over a period of a week. Keep your entries specific and objective. Interpret your records for each of the three children to make tentative generalizations about their nervous behavior.

9

Questionnaires, Inventories, and Interviews

Questionnaires, inventories, and interviews are similar techniques for gathering data by securing answers to questions. On the questionnaire, the respondent writes answers to a limited number of questions. The questions may refer to matters of fact or matters of opinion. On the inventory, one may write (or encircle "yes," "no," etc.) short responses to a rather complete set of questions. In the interview, one communicates verbally and directly, face to face with the questioner or counselor.

There is a rather arbitrary division between the questionnaire and the inventory ; however, there is no mistaking the differences between the questionnaire or inventory and the interview when one considers format, situation, and purpose. When the questionnaire. inventory, or interview is used for an evaluative or diagnostie purpose, it should have a reasonable and appropriate degree of reliability, validity, and objectivity, and should fit the practical situation.

Some confusion may arise in the mind of the teacher who feels that all questionnaires, or all inventories, or all interviews must be alike. As a matter of fact, there is no absolute or set pattern to which all questionnaires conform. There is no required number of questions, nor special types of questions, nor distinctive format for all questionnaires, inventories, and interviews.

Such devices are constructed in order to satisfy the requirements of a particular problem or study. These statements should not be interpreted to mean that questionnaires, inventories, and interviews do not contain typical sections or types of items. The main point to remember is that social scientists have not as yet structured these devices into any static set-up.

This chapter considers the nature and use of questionnaires and interviews in evaluation. Since the inventory is so similar to the questionnaire, it will not be treated separately.

THE QUESTIONNAIRE

Constructing the Questionnaire

The impression of many people is that a questionnaire is a very simple instrument which can be constructed quickly. Such individuals usually mimeograph a list of questions, with a space after each one where people can write their responses. They give little through to the many factors which make the difference between a poor and a good questionnaire.

For practical purposes, the individual who desires to construct a questionnaire should observe the following points :

(*a*) Use the questionnrire technique when it is most appropriate.

(*b*) Define general purposes and specific aims.

(*c*) Construct appropriate questions

(*d*) Arrange questions in appropriate groupings.

(*e*) Design the format with appeal.

(*f*) Check the questionnaire for adequacy.

What factors should be considered under each of these steps ?

Use the Questionnaire When Appropriate

There are a number of conditions under which the questionnaire is appropriate. A questionnaire may be useful to the teacher when answers to a series of important questions are needed from a number of students within a limited time. For instance, after a group of students returned from a two-month field trip as part of a regular sociology class, the evaluator administered a questionnaire in order to secure answers to many questions about aspects of the trip which could not be gathered in the time available through interviews. The classroom teacher may be faced with a similar situation at the beginning or end of a term, when student reactions prior to or subsequent to school experiences are desired for evaluation purposes. Here, too, the time element is important.

When there is insufficient time to interview or to contact each person or group of persons personally, the questionnaire may be a time-saver. Valuable class minutes can be saved by utilizing a questionnaire which can be filled out at home or outside of class. This is not an unmixed blessing, for some students may forget to bring their completed questionnaires to class.

The questionnaire is feasible when it is not possible to reach each person directly by telephons, or by personal visit. In such cases, individuals can be reached through questionnaires by mail or in class or interet groups in the school. In a class group, a teacher who wants the reactions of all students to a few questions must guard against suggestion and collaboration. If the teacher asks for a show of hands in class voting or polling, there is a tendency for students to watch each other and vote with the "crowd" or to follow certain "leaders." A major value of a written questionnaire in a class situation is the privacy accorded each response.

Questionnaires are appropriate also for securing data which are not readily available or not conveniently assembled. For instance, while data on high-school students may be available in personal records or cumulative files in the main office, a subject-matter teacher cannot conveniently obtain the specific data he desires and have such data at hand for reference purposes. Also, there are times when data on any given group of individuals are filed in four or five different places. For convenience, it may be advisable for the teacher to develop questionnaires for his student groups on the specific material he needs.

A pencil-and-paper technique such as the questionnaire is generally best suited for collecting impersonal or general data about the student. Many times the student hesitates to record on paper certain "unpopular" personal data.

However, it should not be stated with absolute certainty that because a matter is very personal, the interview rather than the questionnaire should be employed. It may be that some people, ashamed of speaking face to face about personal matters, are happier to record on paper what otherwise be difficult to discuss. As in so many cases or situations, the judgment of the teacher is significant in determining what technique is most appropriate to the material, the person, and the situation.

The questionnaire is frequently employed as a means of comparing persons or groups. For example, the teacher may desire to compare the responses of a class of boys with those of a class of girls on the same grade level on an interest questionnaire. The fact that both groups have been asked the same questions, in the same order, and at the same time, permits the teacher to draw appropriate conclusions.

In summary, then, the questionnaire may be used when :

(*a*) The group may soon break up because it is temporary.

(*b*) The group is together for the first or last time.

(*c*) There is insufficient time for individual interviews.

(*d*) There are too many to be interviewed.

(*e*) There are too many people who can't be reached personally.

(*f*) An independent response from each person is desired.

(*g*) Desired data are either non-existence or not conveniently available.

(*h*) Answers to a comparable set of questions are desired.

Define Purposes and Aims

One of the main weaknesses in questionnaire construction is the lack of clearly stated purposes and aims. Many individuals have a blind faith that, somehow, pulling together the answers to a number of questions will reveal valuable information. This is a misplaced faith in the process of "what comes naturally." Unless one formulates clear purposes, the process of constructing questions for the questionnaire becomes blind and inefficient. The teacher may find, after the responses are tabulated, that he forgot to include questions whose anwers are essential or that much of the data collected was irrelevant, tedious to tabulate, or a sheet waste of valuable time. The purposes of the questionnaire become the criteria, therefore, for the inclusion or exclusion of any question.

One of the most important reasons for administering a questionnaire is to secure background data on an individual (or group) which may be valuable in accounting for classroom behavior (6). To know that a boy is an orphan who is working part-time every day after school may illuminate the reasons why the boy is so reserved and serious in class. Also characteristics of a whole class may account for the level and type of work of the group. For instance, the fact that all the students reside in a well-to-do suburban area many account for their musical and artistic accomplishments and interests. The first important reason for using a questionnaire, therefore, is to gather data which bear directly or indirectly on the educational process.

The questionnaire may also be used to secure a pencil-and-paper aid in evaluating the extent to which educational objectives are being realized. An objective like "encouraging students to attend symphony concerts" may be said to have been achieved if the student who has never attended such a concert buys a subscription to a series or goes to one or two concerts. A questionnaire may contain questions, therefore, which will permit the student to reveal what new interests, skills, appreciations, knowledge, and attitudes he is developing as a result of classroom stimulation. Questions may be designed to secure either quantitative or qualitative data pertaining to the achievement of student, teacher, or class objectives.

A third purpose in using a questionnaire is to secure data which will be pertinent to planning the curriculum. A student teacher in one high school included the following questions in her physical and health education questionnaire in order to help her plan her work in accordance with student interest and needs :

Directions

If you agree with the following statements, circle the A ; if you disagree, circle the D ; if you are uncertain, circle the U.

A U D 1. I like team sports better than individual sports.

A U D 2. I would like to have bowling put in the physical education program.

A U D 3. Folk dancing is a good way to start boys and girls dancing together.

A U D 4. Ballroom dancing should be taught in school.

A U D 5. I would like to have modern dance taught in the ninth grade.

A U D 6. When learning ballroom dancing, I would like to be in a class that includes boys and girls.

A U D 7. I would like to play touch tackle instead of hockey.

A U D 8. Apparatus work is a waste of time.

A U D 9. Track is more fun than tennis.

A U D 10. I would like to learn to shoot a rifle.

A U D 11. I enjoy playing badminton.

A U D 12. I would rather have dancing than sports in gym classes.

A U D 13. I would like to learn to fence.

A U D 14. If I could get out of taking physical education, I would.

A U D 15. What I learn in gym class will not be of any use to me after I get out of school.

Directions

Under each season list the number of the activity would which you would like to have at that time. List as many as you wish under each season.

1. Apparatus work	8. Hockey	15. Soccer
2. Archery	9. Horseshoes	16. Softball
3. Badminton	10. Marching	17. Swimming
4. Basketball	11. Tumbling	18. Tennis
5. Bowling	12. Ping-pong	19. Touch Tackle
6. Dancing	13. Riflery	20. Track
7. Exercises	14. Shuffleboard	21. Volleyball

Fall (Sept., Oct., Nov.) *Winter (Dec., Jan., Feb.)*

Spring (Mar., Apr., May)

If there are any physical education activities that we do not have, but you would like to have added to our program, list them below.

1. 4.
2. 5.
3. 6.

An examination of these questions shows that the same information can be used in different ways. While this information is valuable for planning the work of the class, it can also be used to reveal background data about the student. Also, if the questionnaire were used at both the beginning and the end of a school term, the teacher might be able to draw some conclusions about the changes which have taken place for each person or for the whole class.

The fourth main purpose in using a questionnaire is to secure a picture of the status of an experience, a unit, a project, a study, or a group. For instance, the teacher may want to know how many boys and girls work after school, have home responsibilities, follow hobbies, attend the moves, view television, etc. Such a study of outside school activities would be a description of the status quo, conditions as they are, among the students. Another type of status study might involve questioning the groups on how far each one has progressed in various activities (in or out-of-school), the reactions of the students to each activity, and the plans the students have to continue or discontinue such activities. The questionnaire which follows was used to secure a picture of the status of the field experience of a group of freshman students preparing to each.

COMMUNITY-FIELD EXPERIENCE PROJECT—STATUS INVENTORY

Council of Social Agencies—Teachers College, University of Cincinnati (Volunteer)

1. Name——————Date——————
2. Education 1, Section No.——————Instructor's Name————————

3. For what agency did you volunteer ?– ————

4. Who was your immediate supervisor in this agency ?———-——

Y N 5. Will the second semester cause any change in your plans to volunteer in a social agency ? If yes, indicate nature of change.

6. How many times have you been to your agency ? (Encircle one)

1 2 3 4 5 6 7 8 9 10 11 12 13 14 15

Y N 7. Do you feel you have lost interest since you first volunteered ? If yes, why ?

Y N 8. Do you find you are speading more time than you should on the agency assignment? If yes, is it more than two or three hours per week?

Y N 9. Do you look forward to your agency experience each week?

Y N 10. Do you make any advance preparation for your agency experiences each week?

Y N 11. Do you feel as though you are needed in your job with the agency?

Y N 12. Dou you have the feeling you are a part of the agency staff?

Y N 13. Do you feel that the agency has helped you to become a part of the staff?

Y N 14. Do you feel that you are getting all the help and supervision you need to carry out your job successfully in the agency? Why?

Y N 15. Do you feel you are getting adequate cooperation from the agency people in carrying out your work? Explain.

Y N 16. Have you had any training while you were on your agency job? What type? Adequate?

Y N 17. Do you feel you need any additional training for your agency job? If yes, what kind? If not, why?

Y N 18. Are there any factors in your agency job; including agency policy, which you think need modification? Explain specifically and indicate what improvement you think is possible.

Y N 19. Do you feel that there are proper channels for offering criticisms and suggestions in your agency? Illustrate.

Y N 20. Do you feel that participation in the agency project has defiinitely helped you attain what you originally desired and needed? Explain you answer.

Y N 21. Do you feel that your agency experience is contributing to your preparation for teaching? Explain your answer.

Y N 22. Do you feel that you would like to continue your agency experience next year?

Y N 23. Do you feel after this experience that you would like to continue as a volunteer youth leader after you graduate from college?

On the back of this sheet please wrtie any suggestions which you have not mentioned already for improving the social agency field experience.

Construct Appropriate Questions

Since the main purpose of a question is to secure from the respondent a valid and reliable answer, factors which promote this goal should be carefully observed. Some of the typical kinds of errors made in question construction might be examined.

In the first place, a question which is not clear to the reader is unlikely to yield a proper response. Lack of clarity may be due to vocabulary difficulty, sentence complexity, the use of ambiguous terms, and blurred printing of questions. Stated positively, a clear question is one whose:

(a) vocabulary is understandable,

(*b*) phrasing is simple and straightforward,

(*c*) terms are nuequivocal, and

(*d*) print is readable.

In the second place, a question may not be vali l in a questionnaire when it is double-or triple-barreled. For instance, in response to a question "Do you enjoy playing Bridge, Poker, and Canasta?" the person who says "No" may mean that he enjoys one or two of the games but not all three. If each game had been listed separately, there might have been two "yes" aesponses aud one "no" response. The weakness in a double-item lies in the difficulty of interpreting the response to parts of the whole question. The illustrative question should be phrased "Do you enjoy playing Bridge ( ), Poker ( ), Canasta ( ) ? (Check)."

A third weakness in constructing questions is that of confining the responded to a choice, which does not describe his position. Suppose Many had to answer the question, "When you sew, do you prefer a sewing machine ( ) or a needle ( ) ? (Check one)." If Mary did not know how to sew, she really could not answer the question because the choices are not suitable for a non-sewer. Under such circumstances, one-would have to ask "Do you sew ? Yes ( ), No ( )." If the answer is "yes," one could be requested to answer the preference item "Do you prefer a sewing machine ( ) or a needle ( ) ?"

A fourth weakness is to include too many questions. A few well-constructed, important questions are superior to a large number of unimportant questions. There is always a temptation on the part of the person constructing a series of questions to include many "interesting" questions because there is space available. Such practices tend to disturb the respondent who, feeling perhaps tfiat too many unimportant questions are being asked, may fail to answer all items seriously. Research has shown, oowever, that interest and willingness to answer are more important than length in determining the number of replies which will be received to a questionnaire (5).

A fifth major weakness in question construction is the failure to consider how the item will be tabulated. For instance, to the item "How old are you ? ( )" the respondents might write in 8, 10, 12, 13, 14, 18, etc. When it is necessary to tabulate the answers to such a question, it may be advisable for one to group the ages, possibly 8-11, 12-15, 16-19. In that case, it would have been easier to have the individual respond to the item "check the age group to which you belong, 8-11 ( ), 12-15 ( ), 16-19 ( )." This question is both easier to tabulate than the previous one and subject to less error in classification and tabulation. When one knows or has decided how the data to any given question will be tabulated, the question can be fashioned accordingly. In the case just cited, if three age groups were going to be compared, it would be best to frame the age question in the latter form, which permits the tabulator to sort the three age groups from one another at a glance, without thinking about the individual age and the group to which it belongs. To summarize, questions should be clearly stated, simply constructed, worded to encourage valid free responses, selective as to importance and relevance to the purposes, and written to facilitate tabulation and presentation of findings.

In the process of constructing questions for the questionnaire, it is advisable to write each question on one side of a separate index card or sheet of paper. If one person is constructing the items, he can write whatever questions he can think of, without attempting to refine or polish phrases for grammar, and just wrire until he is out of relevant ideas. Then he can go over each of the items for editing and remove duplicates, etc. When two or more persons are cooperating in the construction of a questionnaire (something which should be encouraged because others can contribute more ideas and good criticism), each can jot down items separately and share them. Following this, each person might take those items which deal with an area in which he has special interest or knowledge and work those questions into polished form.

After the questions have been approved, each question should be numbered. This simple procedure is important for two reasons. First, when any individual (peer or respondent) wants to comment on the item, the number beside the question permits everyone to turn to the right item immediaiely. Second, there is less likelihood of confusing items in tabulation if each question is separately numbered. If there is a question 3 on page 1 and a question 3 on page 2, it is possible to confuse tabulated data—or in any event, it takes more trouble to avoid such confusion. Numbering all questions separately, therefore, is recommended for efficient and accurate criticism and tabulation.

Arrange Questions in Appropriate Groupings

There are three main reasons for grouping questions dealing with the same points or areas. It seems that when a respondent directs his attention to any question. he is mindful of factors relating to that question. Consequently, so long as one has a "mind-set" toward a particular group of facts, it would be in the interest of efficiency (time expended recalling answers to questions) to group similar items. The principle of similarity extends not only to the construction of the item as to type (multiple-choice, true-false, recall, etc.) but also to areas being sampled. A second reason for grouping items is to make the tabulation more systematic and interpretation of the question simpler. Finally, keeping similar items (or content) together permits one to see more readily whether any important points or questions are being omitted or whether unimportant questions have been retained.

Design the Format with Appeal

The design of the questionnaire is an important consideration, one which teachers tend to neglect because they are so concerned with the questions and their answers. Actually, poor design creates attitudes in the respondent which militate against the collection of valid and reliable data. A crowded-looking sheet of paper which lists question after question in monotonous style does not encourage the reader to respond willingly and completely. On the other hand, a well-printed, well-spaced, and attractive-looking questionnaire encourages the respondent to answer questions fully and with interest.

What comprises a well-designed questionnaire ? Without too much detail, the following recommendations are pertinent :

(*a*) Center the title of the questionnaire. Make the title look good and sound good. The title should be clear, concise, and descriptive of the project.

(*b*) If there is an interested group or class or committee administering the questionnaire, cenfer its name under the title.

(*c*) If there is special importance attached to the month (or season) or year of the study, include the date, etc., in the title.

(*d*) If there are no written instructions provided on a special sheet and if the questionnaire is being administered orally, there may be need for a few lines devoted to explaining the purpose and use of the questionnaire and its results.

(*e*) Usually, basic data of a descriptive nature are collec, ted first. One asks for name, age. class, standing, sex, address, etc., at the beginning of the questionnaire. The questions should all be grouped together. Plenty of space should be provided to allow for clearly-written answers.

(*f*) Adequate room for answers to questions should be provided. An important question which should stimulate the respondent to answer fully may need eight spaces, while a relatively unimportant question may need only two spaces. Sometimes the nature of the question rather than its imoortance may dictate the size of the open space. A common error is to provide too little or too much space for an answer to a question.

(*g*) To save time and to appeal to the eye, questions of a similar nature may be grouped together. (See items 9—14, and 15—17, of the illustrative questionnaire on page 142).

Check the Questionnaire for Adequacy

Since most human beings, including teachers and research investigators. are liable to make serious or simple mistakes, it is always advisable, before mimeographing or printing, to check the questionnaire for adequacy. Spelling, grammatical, and typographical errors should be eliminated. However, before cutting final stencils, or setting type, it is advisable to seek criticism from Interested colleagues and from a small group who are similar in most respects to the group which will respond to the final draft of the questionnaire. Encourage these persons to raise questions when they do not understand the vocabulary or the meaning of various questions. After passing this hurdle, it is generally advisable to engage in sample tabulations, so that any inadequacies will show up before the final draft of the questionnaire is administered to the main group, If a question is not eliciting the kind of information it was designed to collect, improvements can be made before final copy is approved.

Administering the Questionnaire

Although it would appear that administering a questionnaire is as simple as "handing it out and collecting it," there are a number of conditions which are necessary for good administration. These conditions are :

1. insuring a good climate for proper administration,
2. stating clear purposes, and
3. providing clear direcctions a good working situation.

Insufficient attention is generally paid to various intangibles, such as the attitude of the administrator and the atmosphere of the classroom. The teacher who indicates to the group that the answers to a questionnaire are important and possibly confidential (if they are to be so held) can expect students to respond to questions with a seriousness demanded by the device. If the teacher exclaims "Here is something we must collect, so let's get it over with as fast as possible," there is little likelihood that the results will be worth much. If the students trust the teacher, one can expect honest and complete responses; if not, there is little chance that students above the sixth grade will provide informatioa of a self-incriminating or self-revealing nature.

This leads to the second point, the atmosphere of the classroom. A "permissive" classroom is one in which the students feel that the teacher is functioning primarily as an interested and helpful guide. The students are free to ask the teacher questions which may seem irrelevant or which reveal personal inadequacies or ignorance; the teacher answers question patiently and pleasantly; the teacher and students share experiences and ideas and always look to each other's well-being without undue judgment or vindicativeness when things or people go "wrong."

It is probable that students who answer questionnaires in such a classroom will be more likely to provide valid and reliable responses than those in a classroom characterized by authoritarian controls and practices. The attitudes of both the instructor and student and the atmosphere of the classroom form the background into which the questionnaire is brought for administration. Attention to this backgroud should improve the results obtained through questionnaire administration.

Should questionnaires be signed or anonymous ? It is frequently stated that a person is more likely to be honest if he cannot be identified, but the research evidence on this point is not conclusive. The teacher, then, must deal with this problem according to the demands and nature of the situation. If honesty in response makes the student subject to recrimination, it seems unlikely that students in any large numbers would risk being honest, with or without signing their name to a questionnaire.

While no authoritative conclusion concerning unsigned Vs. signed questionnaires is available, the teacher is counseled to have signed questionnaires. If students do not trust the teacher or do not want a teacher to know something about them, it is unlikely that unsigned questionnaires will elicit such information. If students trust the teacher, they will be happy to tell him what he needs to know. It should be noted, too, that follow-up work with individual students is impossible when questionnaires are not signed.

Stating the purpose of the questionnaire also leads to better results. Administrators tend to overlook the importance of stimulating students to respond clearly, honestly, and fully. When students are told the reasons why a questionnaire is being given, assuming these reasons are important and therefore convincing, the students will be highly motivated.

Clear directions and good working conditions must provided for those taking the questionnaire. Whether the directions are oral, written, or a combination of both, the respondent must know how each question is to be answered.

Typical things to check in the administration of a questionnaire do not differ from ordinary requirements of a good physical set-up in a classroom : adequate lighting, proper temperature and ventilation, suitable chairs and desks, freedom from disturbances and noise, a sufficient supply of pencils and erasers, space for the proctor or teacher to walk around each student (to insure that directions are being followed or to answer any questions raised), and provision for students to leave without disturbing those who are not finished. When a student says he is finished, it is wise to check over the answers in the presence of the student so that if there are omissions, the student can answer the omitted questions immediately. Otherwise, one typically finds a situation where students have neglected to answer questions, and the tabulation, as a result, becomes incomplete or uneven.

THE INTERVIEW

The Nature of the Interview

The interview is an extremely valuable means of conducting evaluation in the school. Not only can the interview be used as an information-gathering device in the same manner as the questionnaire, but the teacher can employ the interview to diagnose student behavior and to appraise the achievement of an individual.

Probably the greatest advantage of the interview over the questionnaire is its flexibility. It allows the interviewee to ask for classification of a question and the interviewer to raise all kinds of follow-up questions to the answers of the respondent. Sometimes. the responses which are given may stimulate the interviewer to raise questions which he had not thought of at the start of the interview.

Another important characteristic and advantage of the interview is the opportunity it gives the interviewer to hear *how* an interview has said something as well as *what* he has said. The answers to a questionnaire may not include such important background information about a person as accent, fluency, tone of voice, meaning, and so on. The student who has said "I sure would hate it" might be saying "I'd love to do it" if the interviewer observed his wink, his smile, and the way he said it. These important aspects of the individual often can be obtained only by the interview method.

While it is true that the main function of evaluation is to appraise educational objectives, it should not be forgotten that the process itself, including the means employed, may be educative. Teachers and students are usually unaware of the benefits of interviews for teaching or learning purposes. An interview on how Johnny solves an arithmetic problem may reveal to the teacher what techniques of thinking Johnny employs, but at the same time Johnny may be learning more arithmetic. In this connection teachers need to be conscious of the fact that interviews are not necessarily "formal," with the trappings of appointments, special interviewing rooms, etc. The informal interview with a student in the classroom is a neglected means for diagnosing student behavior. Quietly chatting with a student at his seat. the teacher is in a position to gather valuable information about the pupil.

Many times the interviewer is so concerned with the answer to his questions that he fails to take advantage of the interview for its value along other lines. One college teacher required each member of his class to be interviewed at least three times during the term. During one of the interviews, the instructor noticed the student tearing off pieces of her finger-nails and fighting back tears. While there was no apparent relationship between the answers to the question on classroom progress and the emotional symptoms, an unplanned question about the evidences of tension brought forth an important story of familial difficulties. As in this case, one advantage of the interview is that confidential and personai materials can be handled so as to help students grow emotionally as well as intellectually.

This inter-relationship between the interviewer and the interviewee, while a great advantage, may also be a disadvant-age. There are always chances that time will be wasted, un-neeessary questions raised, irrelevant materials covered, or that a constructive person-to-perso relationship cannot be sustained because of the personality of either the interviewer or interviewee.

Types of Interviews

In recent years, the respective followers of Darley and Rogers have carried on a running controversy concerning the type of interview to be employed, particularly in the field of counseling Dariey (3) has stressed that the interviewer, being well informed, is in a better position to guide the interviewee than the relatively ignorant and confused interviewee himself. Consequently, Darley is considered the advocate of a *directed* interview. The directed interview is one in which the inter-viewer asks "directing" questions and makes suggestions to the interviewee.

Rogers (4) and his followers place stress on the *non-directive* technique of interviewing. Although the interviewer asks certain questions and, to that extent, guides the interview, stres is placed on helping the interviewee gain self-insight. The assumption is that if the interviewee faces his problems on his own, and develops intelligent answers or approaches during the interview, he gains independence and self-insight, In this sense, the interviewer does not "tell" the interviewee or counselee what to do.

For the elementary student in the field there may be no need to take sides. Which type of interview is more useful depends on the contents of the interview and on the maturity and understanding of the interviewee. As Wrenn (7) points out, most interviews are, in all probability, a combination of directive and non-directive techniques. At a time when people are becoming conscious of the meaning and implications of a democratic philosophy, it is not surprising to find educators sensitive to anything which seems to involve authoritarian techniques of imposing solutions on people without respecting their personalities and permitting them to arrive at their own decisions.

Techniques of Interviewing

There are at least three main aspects to the technique of interviewing. First, various parts of the interview involve different purposes. Second, there are certain mechanics related to the raising of questions. Third, there is the problem of recording results. Without going into too much detail on these three matters, what principles should be observed in interviewing ?

Parts of an Interview

Although interviews may be broken down in various ways, there is always a beginning, a middle, and an end. The main goals at the beginning entail establishing rapport and clarifying the purposes of the interview. For the former, depending on the time, place, and person, the interviewer may just smile pleasantly and greet the person by name or may offer some refreshment. The purposes of the interview, of course, are set by the person who initiates the interview. Sometimes the teacher and student decide together what is going to be taken up.

The second part of the interview involves carrying out the purposes of the interview. If the purpose is to gather background material on a person or to explore the various alternatives to solving a problem, this stage of the interview constitutes a question-and-answer session. If the purpose is to help a student gain personal insight, find out the kinds of books he should read, or the experiences he needs, then the gaining of such insights on the part of the interviewee is the goal of the middle of the interview.

The end of the interview involves terminating the face-to-face relationship. Toward the close of the interview, either the interviewer or interviewee may attempt to summarize what has been learned or what must be done, etc, The actual leave-taking may involve setting up an appointment for the next interview or any other condition appropriate to follow-up. Of course, the usual social amenities are followed to insure continued rapport between pupil and teacher.

Securing Responses

The interview may be conducted in a variety of ways. When there is an attempt to have a structured or controlled interview covering definite ground, schedules of questions are generally drawn up beforehand, and made available to the interviewer alone or to both the interviewer and interviewee. Under circumstances where the interview is less controlled or less structured, one may give the interviewee a list of topics only and ask questions about them. In an unstructured interview, conditions are least controlled. The interviewer will raise various questions orally with the interviewee and take advantage of the flexibility and informality of the situation.

Recording Results

When an interview lasts for approximately one half hour, many matters will have been discussed, and it is obvious that some type of record will be necessary. Attempts have been made to record interviews by using outside observers and by having the interviewer take notes. The main argument against taking notes during the interview is the adverse affect it may have on the interviewee. Writing notes tends to break down rapport and the continuity of the interview. It is, therefore, customary to find the interviewer summarizing the interview as soon as it is over by jotting down the most important points and re-creating the questions and answers. Covner (1), however, compared interviewers' reports written after the interview with phonograph recordings of the interview situation. He discovered that only 10 to 35 per cent of the material included in the recorded interviews was written up by interviewers who did not use some means of note-taking.

To be sure, the purpose and further use to which the interview materials will be put determine the nature of the records to be kept. It must be remembered that the ordinary teacher does not have the time to make intensive records or to utilize the results of such records when his classes are large. At the present time, it is likely that the teacher will take brief notes during the course of the interview and summarize the main points after the interviewee leaves.

Recording equipment is increasingly being used to put interviews in more permanent form for subsequent analysis or use (2). The use of record dises is not as economical as tape recordings, for the former are permanent while the latter can be crased and re-used. However, recorded interviews may be invalid because the interviewee may be under tension in the presence of a microphone. While using concealed microphones is ethically questionable, it is common practice to explain to the interviewee why a recording is being made and to secure his permission to record.

SUMMARY

Questionnaires, inventories, and interviews are techniques for gathering data by obtaining responses to questions, Questionnaires and inventories are similar in that they constitute paper-and-pencil approaches, embodying similar questions and purposes. The interview is a face-to-face personal relationship in which greater flexibility in questioning is possible. The interview also lends itself to dealing with confidential and personal material which cannot be obtained through the questionnaire.

In constructing questionnaires, and inventories, several important points should be observed. These are:

1. use the questionnaire when it is most appropriate,
2. define the purposes and aims,
3. construct appropriate questions.
4. arrange questions into appropriate groupings,
5. design the format with appeal, and
6. check the questionnaire for adequacy. In the administration of a questionnaire or inventory, one should insure proper condition. state clear purposes to the students, and provide them with clear directions.

Although the interview may be conducted in several ways, depending upon the degree of flexibility which is desired, every interview has a beginning, a middle, and an end. The beginning of the interview is given over to establishing rapport and clarifying the purposes of the interview; the middle to data-gathering or exploration of alternative solutions to a problem; the end to termination of the interview. In most instances, the interviewer will find that a written summary of the main points, based upon notes taken during the course of the interview, will serve as an adequate record.

PROBLEMS FOR CLASS DISCUSSION

1. Below you will find a questionnaire used in a survey of certain interests of sixth-grade pupils. What are

the major weaknesses of this questionnaire ? How would you reframe the puestionnaire in order to eliminate these weaknesses ?

A NEWSPAPER. RADIO, TELEVISION, MOVIE AND MAGAZINE QUESTIONNAIRE

Roosevelt School—Sixth Grade Survey

Television programs, movies, and magazines are enjoyed by students in our sixth grade. Your marks will not be affected by your answer, so please be frank. Follow directions given for each item below by circling Y (Yes) or N (No) or by writing in answers to questions as fully as possible. The results will be shared with all 210 students in the seven different sixth-grade groups in order to reveal our favorite reading matter or recreational program.

Name——————————————Date ———————————

Address——————————————————————

Sex—————Age —————Homeroom Teacher——————————

Y N 1. (*a*) Do you enjoy reading a newspaper regularly ?

(*b*) Which newspaper do you enjoy reading regularly ? (Check one or more)

( ) Chicago Tribune

( ) Chicago Daily News

Y N 2. (*a*) Do you enjoy listening to the radio?

(*b*) Name your three favorite radio programs

1. ————
2. ————
3. ————

Y N 3. (*a*) Do you enjoy watching television programs ?

( ) Chicago Herald-American

( ) (Add others)

(*b*) Name your three favorite television programs.

1. ————
2. ————
3. ————

Y N 4. (*a*) Do you enjoy going to the movies ?

(*b*) Name the three movies you enjoyed most in the past year.

1. ————
2. ————
3. ————

Y N 5. (*a*) Do you enjoy reading magazines ?

(*b*) What three magazines are your favorite ?

1. ————
2. ————
3. ————

6. If you could have only one of these five activities (newspaper, radio, television, movie, and magazine) which one would be hardest for you to give up ?

————

7. Write a few reasons why you can least do without the activity mentioned in your answer to question 6.

2. Construct a questionnaire designed to elicit information concerning the extent to which a junior-high-school group is aware of and utilizes available resources in your local community.

3. Assume that your local school system wishes to undertake a study of the careers of its former students for a five-year period after their graduation from high school. Prepare a schedule of questions which might be used as a basis for a controlled interview with each graduate.

10

Checklists and Rating Scales

Checklists and rating scales are similar types of evaluative instruments. The checklist, as the name literally indicates, is a selected list of worlds, phrases, sentences, or paragraphs following which an observer records a check (—) to denote the presence or absence of whatever is being observed, The checklist may include items which represent expected desirable or undersirable forms of behavior, a sequence of skills associated with a given operation, or a group of ideas. The rating scale is a selected list of words, perases, sentences, or paragraphs following which an observer records a value or rating based upon some objecrive scale of values. The fundamental difference between the checklist and the rating scale, there fore, lies in the use of the latter as a means for quantifying judgments about obseravations.

This chapter, after a discussion of the school uses of these instrument, considers various types of checklists and rating scales and ways of constructing them.

USES OF CHECKLISTS AND RATING SCALE

Checklists and rating scales are commonly used in schools for a variety of reasons. Among the more important values associated with the use of these instruments are :

(1) promotion of good teaching,

(2) assistance in curriculum planning, and

(3) improvement in administration.

Promotion of Good Teaching

There are numerous ways in which the intelligent use of checklists and rating scales can promote good teaching. Both teachers and pupil are interested in the degree of achievement attained, not only in the final product (an essay, a painting, a wooden tie-rack, etc.), but also in the degree to which methods of working (process values) have been mastered. Checklists and rating scales can be used in evaluating the work process and products of individuals or groups of children in school. These techniques help diagnose strengths and weaknesses in the ways in which a student goes about his work and in the quality of the completed work. (An excellent illustration of these use may be found in the checklist on microscope techniques shown on pages 160-162). Checklists of common faults, used as a basis for prevention or correction, may help students overcome barriers to their continued school progress.

Another important value in using such tools is that pupils come to learn what is expected of them. Cooperative teacher-pupil planning should result in the devevlopment of goals to be attained by individual pupils and by groups. A checklist of such goals can serve both as a guide to learning and as a means of determining what has been accomplished at the end of the school year. The development of a checklist of purposes thus can foster educational values associated with cooperative work and self-group discipline based upon common understanding and agreement.

Pupil formulation of checklists and rating scales may serve as a means of encouraging the development of the ability of discriminate and of fostering good habits. By rating books, movies, comics, radio and television programs, trips, and other interests, pupils practice the art of selection. Individual charts for recording progress in mastering skills in health, speech, social manners, etc., kept up to date by the pupil under teacher guidance, help the student learn what constitutes acceptable behavior. Ofcourse, the great pitfall for the teacher to aviod is the rote learning of the items on a checklist in formal drill style.

Assistance in Curriculum Planning

Checklists and rating scales may be used profitably in curriculum planning and evaluation. It may be desirable to have classes and teachers who follow common curricula indicate what they enjoyed or learned most about in the way of content, and what methods of teaching were most successful. Those responsible for curriculum planning might then use such faculty and student opinions and judgments as the basis for making improvements.

Checklists or rating scales (in the form of a score card) are sometimes used to rate such things as books, pamphlets, and magazines, when these are to be selected for the new school year, Since limited school budgets necessitate careful selection of school materials, the use of such devices is of great value.

Improvement in Administration

Administrators can use checklists and rating scales in two ways. First, some of the material which ultimately is recorded on the cumulative record card for the individual student may haves as its origin a teacher or pupil checklist used in the classroom. Second, checklists can be used to rate various aspects of a school. Illustrating this approach are the Evaluative Criteria employed in the Cooperative Study of Secondary Scnools (1).

TYPES OF CHECKLISTS

Checklists and rating scales take many different forms. A few illustrations at various school levels of the innumerable varieties of such instruments are given below as suggestive models for the teacher.

The following is a portion of a checklist which was used for teaching and research purposes in a study carried on cooperatively by the Rochester, N. Y., school system and the staff of the Evaluation of School Broadcasts, Ohio State University.

Radio Checklist

Boy———————

Name————————————————————Girl——————

(print) Last First (check one)

Age————Birthday———————Grade———Teacher———

Month Day

School——————————City——————————State————

————————————————————————————————

————————————————————————————————

Directions

Most boys and girls like to listen to radio programs at home. Do you listen to any of the programs in the following list ? Mark those programs.

1. if you like the program so much you don't want to miss it.
2. if you like to listen to the program sometimes.
3. if you listen the program when you have nothing else to do.

Write in the names of other you think should be included in this list, and mark them also with n 1, 2, or 3 to how much you like them.

Mixed Programs	Dramatic Programs	
—Jack Beny	—Silver Theatre	—Jack Armstrong
—Charlie Mc-Carthy	—Screen Guild Theatre	—Little Orphan Annie
—Johnny Presents	—Camphell Playhouse	—Scattergood Baines
—Bob Hope	—Lux Radio Theatre	—Amos and Andy
—Al Pearce	—Texaco Star Theatre	—Lum and Abner
—Fred Allen	—Hollywood Playhouse	—Blondie
—Major Bowes	—Columbia Workshop	—Lone Ranger
—Avalon Time	—First Nighter	————————
—Burns and Allen	—Grand Central Station	————————
————————	————————	
————————	————————	

Crime and Mysteries	Quiz Programs	Commentators
—The Shadow	—True or False	—Walter Winchell
—Ellery Queen	—Doctor I.Q.	—Paul Sullivan
—Sherlock Holmes	—Information Please	—Edwin C. Hill
—I Love a Mystery	—Battle of Sexes	—Elmer Davis
—Mr. Keen	—Kay Kyser	—H.V. Kal-tenborn

—Big Town	—Professor Quiz	—Raymond Gram Swing
—Gang Busters	—Don't Forget	—Fulton Lewis
———————	———————	———————
———————	———————	———————

People Places, Events	**Classical Music**	**Dance Music**
—Pilgrimage of Poetry	—Ford Sunday Eve. Hour	—Henry Busse
—The World is Yours	—Voice of Firestone	—Guy Lombardo
—Hobby Lobby	—Rochester Civic	—Benny Goodman
—Vox Pop	—NBC Sym. Orch.	—Eddy Duchin
—Americans at Work	—New York Philharmonic	—Horace Heidt
—What Price America	—Metropolitan Operator	—Hal Kemp
—Democraey in Action	—Cities Service Concert	———————
———————	———————	———————
———————	———————	

The sequence type of checklist is illustrated by the following, which was used for diagnostic purposes in college botany classes (9). The entire checklist is given in order to illustrate the degree of completeness which may be achieved in evaluating both process and product.

Checklist of Student Reactions in Finding an Object Under The Microscope

Student's Name————————Time Begun———————

Section——————————Time Finished————————

Date———————————Time Consumed———————

Directions

On the microscope table are a microscope, yeast culture, or other sutable material, slides, covers, cloth, and lens paper. Direct the student to find a cell or other object under the microscope and show it to you. Time him in seconds from the time he receives the directions. Trace his action by placing a figure 1 after his first action, a figure 2 after his second action, and so on in the order of his performance. Characterize his behavior and his mount by checking appropriate terms frnm the lists given below.

Add any additional comments in the blank on this page. In summarizing the student's actions the instructor may wish to ruggest skills in which the student should receive additional fraining by checking the appropriate items in the list of skills in which student needs further training.

Student's Actions	*Sequence of Actions*	*Student's Actions*	*Sequence of Actions*
a. Takes slide	—	e. Moves bottle of culture along the table	—
b. Wipes slide with lens paper	—	f. Places drop or two of culture on slide	—
c. Wipes slide with cloth	—	g. Adds more culture	—
d. Wipes slide with finger	—	h. Adds few drops of water	—

i. Hunts for cover glasses	—	s. Turns to lowr power objectivc	—
j. Wipes cover glass with lens paper	—	t. Turns to high-power objective	—
k. Wipes cover with cloth			
l. Wipes cover with finger	—	u. Holds one eye closed	—
m. Adjusts cover with finger	—	v. Looks for light	—
n. Wipes off surplus fluid	—		
o. Places slide on stage	—	w. Adjusts concave mirror	—
		x. Adjusts plane mirror	—
p. Looks through eyepiece with right eye	—	y. Adjusts diaphragm	—
q. Looks through eyepiece with left eye	—	z. Does not touch diaphragm	—
r. Turns to objective of lowest power	—		
aa. With eye at eyepiece turns down coarse adjutment	—	ay. Says he cannot do it	—
ab. Breaks cover glass	—	az. Told to start a new mount	—
ac. Breaks slide	—	aaa. Directed to find object under low power	—

ad.	With eye away from eyepiece turns down coarse adjustment	—	aab.	Directed to find object under high power	—
ae.	Turns up coarse adjustment a great distance	—		**Noticeable Characteristics of Student's Behaviour**	
af.	With cye at eye-piece turns down fine adjustment a great distance	—	a.	Awkward in movements	—
			b.	Obviously dexterous in movements	
ag.	With eye away from eyepiece turns down fine adjustment a great	—	c.	Slow and deliberate	—
			d.	Very rapid	
ah.	Turns up fine adjustment screw a great distance	—	e.	Finger tremble	—
			f.	Obviously perturbed	—
ai.	Turns fine adjustment screw a few turns	—	g.	Does not take work seriously	—
aj.	Removes slide from stage	—	h.	Obviously angry	—
ak.	Wipes objective with lens paper	—	i.	Unable to work without specific directions	—
al.	Wipes objective with cloth	—	j.	Obviously satisfied with his unsuccessful efforts	—
am.	Wipes objective with finger	—			

an. Wipes eyepiece with lens paper —

ao. Wipes eyepiece with cloth —

ap. Wipes eyepiece with finger —

aq. Makes another mount —

ar. Takes another microscope —

as. Finds object —

at. Pauses for an interval —

au. Asks, What do you want me to do ?" —

av. Asks whether to use high power —

aw. Says, "I' m satisfied" —

ax. Says that the mount is all right for his eye —

Skills in which Student Needs Further Training

a. In cleaning objective —

Characterizations of the Student's Mount

a. Poor light —

b. Poor focus —

c. Excellent mount —

d. Good mount —

e. Fair mount —

f. Poor mount —

g. Very poor mount —

h. Northing in view but a thread in his eyepiece —

i. Something on objective —

j. Smeared lens —

k. Unable to find object —

Skills in which Student Needs Further Training

f. In using diaphragm —

b. In cleaning eyepiece	—	g.	In keeping both eyes open	—
c. In focusing low power	—	h.	In protecting slide and objective from breaking by careless	—
d. In focusing high power	—			
e. In adjusting mirror	—			

Additional Comments

In a course in Home Mechanics for junior-high-school boys and girls, this checklist was used to evaluate the final products of student work.

BULB SOCKETS AND PLUGS ANALYSIS CHART

Name———————————————Date————————

1. Insulation :

Ragged ends	—	Clean cut	—
Particles left	—	All removed	—

2. Wire :

Strands cut	—	Intact	—
Corroded	—	Clean	—
Too long	—	Correct length	—
Too short	—	Twisted	—
Spread	—		

3. Terminals :

Direct to terminal	—	Wrapped around prong to terminal	—

Wire counter-clockwise	—	Clockwise	—
Loose	—	Tight	—

4. **Operation :**

No results	—	Bulb lights	—
Fuse blown	—		

Comment :—————————————————————

Checked by——————————

Simple illustrations of abbreviated checklists containing a group of "expected desirable forms of behavior" in the area of health habits are reproduced on the opposite page.

Check whether the pupil has good health habits for each of the following :

Word Type	*Phrase Type*	*Sentence Type*
Teeth	Brushed Teeth	He brushes his teeth each morning.
Hair	Combed Hair	He combs his hair each morning.
Nose	Cleaned Nose	He has a clean nose each morning.
Eyes	Cleaned Eyes	He has clean eyes each morning.
Ears	Washed Ears	He washes his ears each morning.
Face	Washed Face	He washes his face each morning.

An illustration of a portion of a checklist containing a group of ideas, to be used in checking the answer to an essay question dealing with the probable results of unemployment may take the following ;

Directions : Check whether the pupil has seen relationship between unemployment and the following ;

Effect on human beings

M—aterially *—Psychologically*

—Socially *—Emotionally*

—Politically

Effect on social institutions

—Industries *—Church*

—Unions *—Political Parties*

—Schools *—Press, radio, movies, TV*

Govenment

The following checklist, which is to be completed by the student, includes items which involve a series of steps in finiding out about a new people, in this instance, the Hindus :

Directions : *Check only the steps you have taken* :

—Consulted an encyclopedia —Consulted Cumulative Book Index

—Consulted the dictionary —Consulted New York Times Index

—Referred to card file on Hindus in school library

—Consulted Readers Guide to Periodical Literature

—Wrote to Indian Embassy in Washington, D.C.

TYPES OF RATING SCALES

1. The Descriptive Rating Scale

The checklist may be converted into a descriptive rating scale with little difficulty by the addition of a scale for noting the degree to which a given aspect of behavior is in evidence; The following rating scale was drawn up by a scout leader to evaluate his group. The scale can be further quantified by assigning the values 3, 2, 1, and 0 to "all the time," "most of the time," "occasionally," and "never," respectively.

DESCRIPTIVE RATING SCALE

Name——————— *Date*—————

	All the Time	*Most of the Time*	*Occasionally*	*Never*
1. Waits his turn to talk.				
2. Talks to the point.				
3. Tries to see the other fellow's point.				
4. Listens to suggestions of others.				
5. Offers suggestions to group.*				
6. Abides by majority decisions.				
7. Doesn't get "sore" if his suggestions aren't carried out				
8. Takes his share of responsibility.				
9. Carries to completion the tasks he accepts.				
10. Doesn't "play around," but gets down to business,				

11. Can work without specific instructions.
12. Looks out for interest of group.
13. Works well with most of the boys in the group.
14. Is liked by most of the group.*
15. Doesn't try to be "boss."
16. Doesn't feel that others are "picking" on him.
17. Takes responsibility for some leadership.
18. Accepts leadership of boys his age.
19. Doesn't take petty group difficulties to leader.
20. Considers leader's suggestion.

---

*Many—Average No.—Few—None.

2. The Graphic Rating Scale

The graphic rating scale represents a variation of this approach. The rater's evaluation is indicated by placing a check or cross on a line to indicate presence or absence of a given trait. The instrument on page 166, constructed by Dr.

H.C. Raye of Southern Illinois University, and used in classes in stenography, is typical of the graphic rating scale. The scale values which are used to quantify ratings, instead of being restricted to 1, 2, 3, 4, 5, may also run from 100 to 0, thus embodying the familiar per cent concept.

3. The Forced-Choice Technique

One of the major disadvantages of both the descriptive and the graphic rating scale is in the rater's ability to control the final result of his ratings. In recent years, the staff of the Personnel Research Section of the Adjutant General's office (5) has developed a forced-choice technique to offset this difficulty, In essence, the technique forces the rather to choose between paired alternatives, both of which rates in general are equally willing to use in describing a person. The two alternatives, however, differ in the extent to which they discriminate between two groups—for example, successful and unsuccessful supervisors.

The examples given below are drawn from a scale now being used experimentally in rating school supervisors in a large city system. In each instance, the paired items are approximately equal in "preference" value, in that they are equally acceptable to persons who are used as raters. One of each pair, however, is the better as a description of the good or poor supervisor.

A. An effective speaker.

B. Has maintained or built a fine parents association.

A. Has no sense of values : cannot distinguish the good from the bad.

B. His instructions are indefinite or hard to follow.

A. Conducts a continuous evaluation of teaching procedures.

A. Continues to be a student.

B. Seems neurotic.

B. Uses the school for the advancement of pet theories and projects.

4. The Rank Order Method

One rating approach has attempted to eliminate the use of a published scale altogether. Rather, persons being rated are placed in serial or rank order in accordance with the rater's judgment of the degree to which they possess the quality or attribute under consideration. Ratings made by a number of judges may then be combined into a composite or average rank. The statistical treatment of rank order data, which has been described by Guilford (2) and Thurstone (7), is relatively simple.

RATING SCALE OF FACTORS THAT DETERMINE SUCCESS IN LEARNING SHORTHAND

I. Desire to Improve—Attitude

1	2	3	4	5
Evidences intense desire and interest at all times.		Usually shows normal desire to gain skill.		Definite lack of interest and motive.

II. Home Work

1	2	3	4	5
Usually exceeds assignment. Neat. Always on time.		Normally well done and prompt.		Often incomplete. Messy. Late.

III. Class Attendance

1	2	3	4	5
Always present and prompt.		For absences; justifiable.		Frequently absent—many unexcused.

IV. Materials and Supplies

1	2	3	4	5
Always has good pen and note paper.		Usually supplied with satisfactory tools and supplies.		Bad pen ; dull pencil. Low grade paper.

V. Relaxation

1	2	3	4	5
Always comfortably relaxed. No tenseness.		Usually holds pen lightly ; does not bear down.		Tense, "Pinches" pen. Musciles of hand, arm, and body are tight.

VI. Vocabulary

1	2	3	4	5
High-frequency words automatic. Readily builds others.		Normal ability to write common and new words.		Even brief forms hazy. No word-building ability.

VII. Word-Carrying Capacity

1	2	3	4	5
"Gets it" even though 20--30 words behind.		Usually writes okay when gap is not too large.		Always loses out when dictator gets ahead.

VIII. Penmanship

1	2	3	4	5
Legible and beautiful. Uniform size and slant.		Normally readable and good looking. Fluent motion.		Illegible - bad looking. Tends to draw outlines.

IX. Reading of Notes

1	2	3	4	5
Always reads accurately, rapidly, with meaning.		Usually able to read satisfactorily.		Frequently unable to read.

5. The Paired-Comparison Method

The paired-comparison approach also obviates the use of a scale. In this approach, each individual, in turn, is judged as better or worse than every other individual in the group. The results of these paired comparisons are then handled statistically to arrive at relative ratings. The statistical analysis which is required (8) is extremely time-consuming. When twenty individuals are compared, for example, a total of 190 judgments, which involve computing 190 proportions and looking up 190 scale values in a set of tables, must be made. Although it gives more reliable results than rank order or rating scale methods, even the labor-saving statistical techniques suggested by Guilford (2) do not seem to make the paired-comparison method effective for teacher use.

CONSTRUCTING AND USING CHECKLISTS AND RATING SCALES

Sources of Material

The teacher who wishes to construct a checklist or rating scale for classroom use has several possible sources of material which can be utilized. As a first resource, there is the teacher himself. No matter what the level or subject matter, the teacher usually has some specific goals and sub-goals for particular attitudes, information, and skills in which he feels his students should grow. The teacher himself, therefore, can list the kinds of things he wants his students to achieve by any given time. The teacher, by utilizing his own resources, can develop a checklist very rapidly.

While this approach may obviate the arguments and bickerings which sometimes accompany a cooperative enterprise, using just one's own ideas has serious shortcomings. First, the teacher may have some biases or pet prejudices of which he is unaware and which may creep into his checklist. Second, the work of one person may be narrower in scope than the outcome of a cooperative effort involving other interested teachers and pupils. Third, when a cooperative approach is utilized in constructing a checklist or rating scale, those who help realize its purposes and values more readily. Consequently, other teachers and pupils will participate more willingly in its administration.

In the light of the relative strengths and weaknesses of an individualistic approach, one might well make it a practice to use other teachers and pupils as a source of material for checklists and rating scales. Not only are a number of sound educational objectives promoted in such cooperative work, but there would also be the advantages of :

1. a wider range of ideas and suggestions,
2. increased objectivity because of the corrective influences of others,
3. increased likelihood of the device applying to all the groups who are supposed to take it,
4. increased probability of getting valid responses from pupils who accept and favor the device because they have had a hand in constructing it,
5. likelihood of more intelligent use of the results, and
6. less likelihood of errors in typography and English.

A third source of items for the checklist is the expert or group of experts. When it is urgent to get a job done quickly and when money is available, the school can gain many suggestions from capable consultants. The expert may be a member of a liberal arts or teachers college in a local or nearby university. Sometimes, state supervisory personnel are available for such tasks. For more elaborate evaluations, a short workshop may be set up under public or private auspices.

A fourth source of checklist items is the numerous types of "job analyses" which have been made on various reading, writing, arithmetic, and citizenship skills and appreciations. Information concerning such valuable analyses of various attitudes, information, and skills in all fields is contained in the yearbooks of the National Society for the Study of Education and publications of subject matter specialists in mathematics, social studies, English, music, etc. In addition, standard text-books, in the teaching of various subjects at both elementary and secondary levels are rich sources for checklist material. Research studies are also valuable sources of materials. The checklists reported in such studies may serve as the bases for modified devices which suit local purposes and local situations.

Courses of study and curriculum bulletins constitute still another source of material. Large city and state systems publish courses of study which can be purchased or examined in reference libraries of local universities.

Common Errors in Construction

Several faults generally appear in constructing checklists and rating scales. Among the more common faults are: unclear headings, use of too many items, overlapping items, and inclusion of extreme items. In part, some of these faults arise from the fact that certain traits are more amenable to rating than others. Thus, Shen (4) found that it was possible to rate such traits as scholarship, leadership, and intelligence more adequately than judicial sense and tact. The development of a rating scale or checklist, then, demands an adequate des-cription of what is being rated in such terms that the person using the instrument has a clear picture of the behavioral characteristic involved.

To some degree, such weakness may be minimized by preparing a manual of directions which contains specific details about the meaning of each quality or characteristic included on the instrument. It is important, too, to try out the instrument, using several raters and a few subjects, to check for possible weaknesses. Judges should be encouraged to raise questions when any doubts raise.

Another common error which one finds on rating scales is the use of too many or too few units on the scale which is employed. The use of too many units or steps makes it difficult for the rater to discriminate between one unit and the next ; too few steps make for coarse ratings, since the rater is not given an opportunity to exercise discrimination to the extent to which he is capable. While on rule can be given for the exact number of steps which should be included on a rating scale, in most instances the use of seven units will yield optimal reliability (6).

Errors in Use

A very common error in using checklists and rating scales in school situations grows out of the failure to employ enough judges, with consequent loss of reliability. While experts diffier in their recommendations concerning the number of persons whose judgments should be pooled, at least three independent ratings should be obtained in most instances in which human traits are being evaluated (3).

Individual judges may also make errors which tend to reduce the reliability of checklists and rating scales. Frequently, personal bias may result in ratings which are too high or too low, or in failure to check favorable or unfavorable items on a checklist. When scale values are employed on a rating scale, many judges feel constrained to avoid extreme ratings and tend to use only the central values of the scale. The rater's general mental attitude or general impression of a person being rated also results in a systematic error. Rugg (3) has pointed out that this "halo" effect leads the rather to attribute the general impression or attitude to particular qualities. Ratings of character and personality traits are most likely to be subject to this halo effect.

SUMMARY

Checklists and rating scales are similar types of evaluative devices. The former is a list of words, phrases, sentences, or paragraphs following which an observer records a check to denote presence or absence of that which is being observed. The rating scale is a list of qualities set down on a continuum upon which a rater indicates a value or rating. There are various kinds of checklists and rating scales which may be used to evaluate both technique and product. Using these devices may:

1. promote good teaching,
2. aid in curriculum planning, and
3. improve school administration.

Sources of items for checklists and rating scales may be found through self-analysis, by consultation with others, by studying job analyses, and by examining texts, courses of study, curriculum bulletins, and standardized scales and checklists. Common faults to avoid in constructing checklists and rating scales are unclear headings, use of too many items, overlapping items, inclusion of extreme items, and use of too many or too few steps on the scale which is employed. Common errors in the use of checklists and rating scales grow out of failure to employ enough rates, personal bias, failure to use extremes of the scale, and halo effect.

PROBLEMS FOR CLASS DISCUSSION

1. (*a*) Construct a checklist designed to elicit the favorite television programs of a group of upper-elementary-school children. Arrange for the administration of the checklist to a class,

(*b*) Convert the checklist into a rating scale by the inclusion of an appropriate rating device, and administer this scale to the same group.

(*c*) To what extent do similarities or differences appear when the results are compared ?

2. Construct a sequence checklist which would enable you to evaluate the technique and product of a vocational-school pupil called upon to :

(*a*) change a tire, or

(*b*) give a finger wave, or

(*c*) sew a French seam.

3. Construct a rating scale designed to porvide a measure of the effectiveness of a teacher. Ask a number of pupils in a high school to apply the scale to their teacher. To what extent do the pupils agree in their ratings ? To what factors may differences in ratings be attributed ?

11

Personal Reports and Projective Techniques

Probably no other psychological characteristics are so difficult to measure as the intangible and complex qualities involved in personality. In recent decades an increasing variety of personal reports and projective techniques have been devised to aid in the analysis and evaluation of personal and social characteristics. The attempts to devise more adequate measures have provided a variety of methods, from self-descriptive tests with the standarized questions and problem checklists to tests or techniques ink blots or pictures. In addition to these techniques, other methods include analysis of handwriting, analysis of paintings or drawings, completion of unfinished sentences or stories, dramatic play, and situational tests using toys or puppets. The experimentation and research in this field continues unabated. Significant progress in the evaluation of personality has been achieved, but many problems still require comprehensive and rigorous study before satisfactory solutions will be achieved.

SCOPE AND NATURE OF PERSONAL REPORTS AND PROJECTIVE TECHNIQUES

Personal reports are instruments of evaluation which rely upon the individual to be evaluated for opinions regarding his own behavior, feelings, and traits. In personality tests, inventories, problem checklists, and autobiography, the individual describes or rates himself and reports his likes, dislikes, conflicts, and problems. Personal reports usually consist of verbal responses to a list of standardized questions.

Projective techniques are intended to go beyond testimony and self diagnosis by the individual. They make possible a qualitative, comprehensive, and intensive study of the personality. Projective methods include all the devices—ink blots, cloud pictures, thematic pictures, play materials--that enable the subject to project himself into a situation outside of himself. Through reacting to unstructured stimuli, the subject supposedly expresses his own way of organizing experience. He expresses his way of seeing life, its significance and patterns, and his own own meaning and feelings (6). As Murphy (10) says: "He sees in it (the stimulus situation of the ink blot, the picture (what he personally is diposed to see or does with it what he is personally disposed to do." The mechanism of projection implies that the subject is unware of revealing himself in the handling of the stimulus material.

Personal reports, with their emphasis on self-description, play an important role in evaluation. They can be administered and interpreted without great difficulty, and they provide important clues for understanding the individual and his problems. Projective techniques hold the promise the providing deeper insights into those areas of personality which the individual himself is unwilling to reveal directly, or of which he may not even be conscious. Difficult to administer and interpret, however, they are valuable only in the hands of the specialist.

Objectives or Aspects of Behavior Measured by these Techniques

Personality tests, self-descriptive inventories, problem checklists, and other personal report methods evaluate specific aspects of personality, whereas projective techniques approach personality structure in a more comprehensive manner. Hunt (7) says that personal reports may provide an index of personality traits or components, such as emotional adjustment, self-control, social initiative, self-sufficiency, self-determination, self-esteem, ascendance-submission, dominance submission, cheerfulness-depression, introversion-extroversion, social introversion depression-elation, neurotic tendency, personal inferiority, social inferiority, emotional maturity, and other aspects of personality and behavior, Frank (6) says that projective techniqves were developed to reveal a global picture of an individual's personality organization and to provide insight into his private world of feelings and meanings. The advocates of these techniques feel that they make possible evaluation of various forms of mental conflict, disturbances, sentiments, and feelings.

Degree of Expertness Required for Administration and Interpretation

Personality tests and inventories, like other methods involving self-reporting, are administered without serious difficulty by the counselor or classroom teacher. Most of the tests are accompanied by manuals which explain administration and scoring of the test. The classroom teacher should have no difficulty in carrying out instructions. Teachers should attempt interpretation of test results only if they have completed some study in the field of mental hygiene and tests or measurement. It is advisable to interpret test scores jointly with other teachers and the guidance worker, combining the scores with other data about the individual's behavior and conduct.

Projective techniques vary in the degree of expertness required for their administration and interpretation. At one extreme the Rorschach test, and to a lesser extent the Thematis Appreception Test, require specialized skill for administration and interpretation. Techniques utilizing drawing, painting, ane play are simpler to work with and present less difficulty in the area of interpretation, but yield correspondingly less revealing analyses. All methods require some special training in analysis and interpretation.

Cautions about Validity and Reliability

Both personal reports and projective techniques present problems of validity and reliability. The validity of the self-report instrument seems to be related to the kind of questions or items included. Objective information about the physical conditions of the home, for instance, appear to be reported accurately. For more personal items there is the tendency to give the "best" answer. Individuals are under social pressure and often feel compelled by their own personal experiences to conceal what they actually think or believe or feel. Responses self-report tests may be different when the individuals are asked to sign their names to the tests and when they are not. Studies comparing the rating of judges on certain personality traits with test results do not show satisfactory correspondence, according to Traxler (18).

Though numerous studies have attempted to "validate" projective techniques, many questions are still left unanswered. The studies have attempted to show, for instance, that diagnosis of a mental disorder based on a Rorschach test will correlate highly with the diagnosis given by a psychiatrist on the basis of the clinical history and observation of the patient. Caution is nevertheless indicated, particolarly in the use of the Thematic Apperception Test, drawing and painting, play, and other techniques. Though these techniques provide valuable clues to the nature of the personality structure and problems involved the interpretation of material obtained through them must still be considered an hypothesis to be followed up by other techniques and by observation.

PERSONALITY TESTS OR INVENTORIES

A personality inventory is any collection of questions or statements designed to yield data on an individual's social and emotional adjustment. The inventory or test usually consists of a large number of questions and statements which the subject may answer with "yes" or "no," or which the subject may agree or disagree on various levels of intensity. The individual rates or describes himself within a setting which has been compared to that of a "standardized interview."

Many of the personality inventories are based on the trait theory of personality, which conceives of personality as composed of traits , or tendencies to react in a consistent way in response to a defined class of stimuli (4). Thus, personality inventories have purported to measure, among other factors, self-control, self-sufficiency, ascendance-submission, dominance-submission, neurotic tendency, social inferiority, social introversion, emotional maturity, social adjustment, and health adjustment. The tests measure the individual's conformance to or deviation from group norms, which can be established for age, sex, and other group characteristics. The test scores of an individual then automatically classify him in relation to the group.

Personal inventories are an efficient and economical method of evaluation (12) which can be handled by most teachers and which may provide considerable insight. Flexible in nature, they can be developed to cover every aspect of an individual's traits, values, needs, attitudes, and experiences. Their limitation, as mentioned, derives from the assumption that an individual knows and is willing to reveal important aspects of his personality. Moreover, the attempt to devide personality into separate entities is open to question.

Table 2 lists a few of the personality inventories which have been employed in the evaluation of specific aspects of social and emotional adjustment for certain age groups

A list of sample items from a self-descriptive inventory that was devised and used by one of the authors in a large city school system is illustrative of the items generally used in personality inventories.

Are you troubled at night by dreams about your work — Yes ( ) No ( )

Table 2

Illustrative Personality Tests and Inventories

Test and Publisher	*Date*	*Aspects Mcasused*	*Level*
Aspects of Personality (World Book Company)	1939	Ascendance-submission, extroversion-introversion, emotionality	Grades 4-9
Behaviour Preference Record (California Test Bureau)	1953	Cooperation, friendliness, integrity, leadership, responsibility	Grades 4-6, 7-9, 9-12
Bell Adjustment Inventory (Stanford University Press)	1933	Home, health, social, and emotional adjustment	Grades 9-16, Adults
Bernreuter Personality Inventory (Stanford Univesity Press)	1933	Neurotic tendency, self-sufficiency, introversion-extroversion, dominance-submission, sociability, confidence	Grades 9-16, Adults
California Test of Personality (California Test Bureau)	1950	Self-adjustment, social adjustment	Grades Kg-3, 4-8, 7-10, 9-16
Cowan Adolescent Adjustment Analyzer (Cowan Research Project, Salina, Kansas)	1946	Adjustment to fears, family, emotions, maturity	Ages 12-18
Gordon Personal Profile (World Book Company)	1953	Ascendancy, responsibility, emotional stability, sociability	Grades 9-16, Adults
Heston Personal Adjustment Inventory	1949	Analytical thinking, sociability,	Grades 9-16,

(World Book Company)		emotional stabili, confidence, personal relations, home satisfaction	Adults
Johnson Temperament Analysis (California Test Bureau)	1945	Nine behavior patterns : composed-nervous, quiet-active, objective-subjective, etc.	Grades 12-16, Adults
Mental Health Analysis (California Test Bureau)	1946	Mental health liabilities and assets : feelings of inadequacy, etc., social participation, etc.	Grades 4-8, 7-10, 9-16, Adults
Minnesota Multiphasic Inventory (Psychological Corp.)	1951	Depression, hysteria, social introversion, etc.	Ages 16 and over
Minnesota Personality Scale (Psychological Corp.)	1941	Morale, social adjustment, family relations, emotionality, economic, conservatism	Grades 11-16,
Personal Audit (Science Research Associates)	1945	Nine areas: seriousness, stability, tolerance, persistence, etc.	Grades 9-16, Adults
Thurstone Temperament Schedule (Science Research Associates)	1950	Seven traits : impulsive, dominant, stable, social, etc.	Grades 9-16, Adults
Washburne Social Adjustment Inventory (World Book Company)	1940	Truthfulness, happiness, alienation, sympathy, purpose, etc.	Ages 12 and over

Do you sometimes see spots "swimming" before your eyes Yes ( ) No ( )

Do you lose your temper and get angry easily Yes ( ) No ( )

Do you like to see others in pain Yes ( ) No ( )

Do you find it more pleasant to live in a "make believe" world than in the real world Yes ( ) No ( )

Interpretation

Manuals with instructions for scoring and interpreting personality tests and inventories usually accompany test forms. In some tests, a specific numerical value, either positive or negative, is assigned to each answer, and a score is obtained by adding the numbers for the parts, or for the test as a whole. Scoring becomes more difficult when the instructions demand statistical manipulations and correlations between parts. Test results can be tabulated by hand or by machine. The score made by the individual on various parts of the test is compared to the norm established by previous testing.

Many psychologists question whether personality inventories and tests measure what they are designed to measure. Independent rating by judges of the personality characteristics measured by these tests often show a low correlation with the test results. Nevertheless, most authorities agree that self-descriptive scales are valuable methods of appraisal which can materially contribute to the guidance program of a school. Traxler (18) feels that data provided by the tests fulfill the following two important functions :

(*a*) they stimulate the pupils to evaluate critically their own personality characteristics, and

(*b*) they serve as a point of departure in conferences between counselor and individual pupils.

He further states that inventories are helpful in locating pupils who are "poorly adjusted and who need guidance in making emotional and personal adjustments." The data from the tests become part of the cumulative record of the pupil. The teacher is advised to do some reading and study in the field of personality and mental hygiene before attempting to use and to interpret personality tests of this kind.

PROBLEM CHECKLISTS

Problem checklists are self-reporting questionnaires which deal with problems rather than with personality characteristics or interests. The checklists, such as those developed by Mooney and associates at Ohio State University, consist of phrases intended to make it easy for pupils to express their troublesome problems. The Mooney checklist for high-school students covers these problem areas :

(*a*) health and physical development,

(*b*) finances, living conditions, and employment,

(*c*) social and recreational activities,

(*d*) social-psychological relations,

(*e*) personal-psychological relations,

(*f*) courtship, sex, and marriage,

(*g*) home and family,

(*h*) morals and religion,

(*i*) adjustment to school work,

(*j*) the future : vocational and educational, and

(*k*) curriculum and teaching procedures. Checklists for junior-high-school students and adults cover more or less the same problem areas.

The procedure for using checklists is the following : The student underlines problems of concern to him, circles those of most vital concern, and answers a few summarizing questions which deal with his feelings about his problems.

The checklists are not tests. They are intended to provide and indication of behavior problems that occur in an individual or a group of individuals. The lists give students an opportunity to express their problems and provide assistance in understanding the problems expressed. The lists are not diagnostic instruments but are descriptive and analytical. Lentz (3) writes that he knows of no alternative or comparable instrument designed for the same purposes. Many teachers have commented that the lists have been helpful.

Some of the items from the Mooney Problem Check List. High School Form, are :

(Instructions ; Read the list slowly, and as you come to a problem that troubles you, underline it)

1. Being underweight
5. Frequent illnesses
10. Wanting to earn some of my own money
15. Wanting to learn how to entertain
20. Uninterested in the opposite sex
25. Getting rid of people I don't like

Recently several problem checklists have been published. These include the SRA Junior Inventory, SRA Youth Inventory, and Life Adjustment Inventory. All problem checklists follow the same general format of presenting a list of problems, but the specific content and areas of problems vary among the checklists.

The SRA Junior Inventory and the SRA Youth Inventory are distributed by the Science Research Associates, Chicago, Illinois. The Junior Inventory is concerned with problems of boys and girls in the elementary school. Five major areas of problems are presented under these headings :

(*a*) My Health,

(*b*) Getting Along with Other People,

(*c*) About Myself,

(*d*) About Me and My School, and

(*e*) About Me and My Home.

Most of the items in the Junior Inventory were selected from a content analysis of essays written by hundreds of elementary-school children on their problems. Additional items were obtained from teachers, guidance counselors, and pediatricians. The SRA Youth Inventory is designed to help identify problems of teen-agers and may be used in grades 7 to 12. This inventory consists of eight major areas of problems indicated by such headings as :

(*a*) My School,

(*b*) Locking Ahead,

(*c*) About Myself,

(*d*) Getting Along with Others,

(*e*) My Home and Family,

(*f*) Boy Meets Girl,

(*g*) Health, and

(*h*) Things in General. The SRA Inventory is self-scoring and permits an easy identification of problem areas through the use of a self-interpreting chart filled out by the pupil himself.

The Life Adjustment Inventory, distributed by the Acorn Publishing Company, Rockville Centre, N. Y., has been designed to help identify, through pupil responses to problems, improvements or changes in the secondary-school curriculum that will better meet pupil needs. This checklist conforms, in general, with the United States Office of Education's Life Adjustment Program. The inventory contains a list of problems that are organized under such headings as :

(*a*) general feeling of adjustment to the curriculum,

(*b*) reading and study skills,

(*c*) general social skills and etiquette,

(*d*) boy-girl relationships,

(*e*) religion, morals, and ethics,

(*f*) vocational preparation,

(*g*) physical and mental health,

(*h*) family living,

(*i*) consumer education, and

(*j*) use of leisure time.

Interpretation

In interpreting the checklist it is important to consider some of the following points listed by Mooney (9). Items marked should be considered as symbols of the experiences and situations which comprise the individual's problem world. The item or problem checked should not be mistaken for the problem itself. Two students may mark the same problem or identical pattern of problems, and yet the problem world of the two might not be identical. Problems marked are not of equal significance : one item may prove to be more indicative of a substantial blockage in the life of an individual than a dozen others which he might mark.

Mooney outlines five ways in which problem checklist may be used :

(*a*) to make group surveys, which includes finding out what youth are thinking about in their personal lives and the location of students who want and need counseling or other personal aid,

(*b*) to provide a basis for group guidance, orientation, and personnel progrms.

(*c*) to increase teacher understanding in regular classroom teaching,

(*d*) to facilitate guidance interviews, and
(*e*) to conduct research in the problems of youth.

AUTOBIOGRAPHY

An autobiography is an individual's life story written by himself. It is an instrument of self-description which furnishes information frequently not obtainable by group or individual tests. Despiite limitations, an autobiography or a composition of the autobiographical type may, provide an understanding of the student's interests, abilities, personal history, hopes, ambitions, and desires (4). The autobiography often serves as a basis for an interview between counselor and student. The assignment to write an autobiography may be given to the pupil by the counselor, the home room teacher, or the English teacher. Autobiographies may take a number of forms ranging from short themes to lengthy narrative accounts. It will serve the purpose of guiding the pupil's writing if the teacher will present him with a list of things to be included, such as early life experiences, family background and history, health and physical record, school history, interests, leisure time activities, hobbies, travel experiences, friendships, occupational experiences, educationai plans for the future, long-time vocational plans, and desires and plans for marriage and home life.

Compositions with elements of autobiography in them may be revealing because of the spontaneous introduction of personal material. Strang (15.82) cites such a short composition of the autobiographical type written by a senior-high-school girl on the subject "When I Felt at a Loss". A brief question from this account shows how much can be revealed within a short space.

> "At parties or any kind of dancing situation, when I am without a partner I feel ill at ease, at a loss as to do. I feel as though everyone is saying to themselves, 'On there's Sally without a partner,' in a rathrr unkind way. I want to cover up and try to look as though I weren't a wall flower, as though I had other things to do besides dance.

I con't feel sure of the affections of people outside of my family. I wonder if they really care for me as they say they do......This happens only with people I care very much for. I want their affecton so much I worry about it. It does not bother me with some people...."

Interpretation

The value of the autobiography is related to the conditions under which it is obtained. For the autobiography to have value, pupils must be ready to write and must understand what is involved. They must feel sure that their confidence will not be violated. The person who obtains the personal document must maintain a relationship of mutual trust and respect.

The autobiography gives clues about the personality structure of the individual and about his modes of thinking and feeling. For contradiction or confirmation, the analysis of the pupil's writing may be checked against observational and test data. Strang (15) points out that with reticent or resistive children the autobiography is an especially valuable source of understanding which gives indication of special interests and talents and even of emotional difficulties not revealed by other means.

It is important to remain cautions about the validity of the autobiography as an instrument of evaluation. Items may be exaggerated or minimized for reasons unknown to the teacher. Sometimes it is helpful to verify a pupil's responses by making a home visit or by including in an interview casual questions about doubtful items in the autobiography.

THE RORSCHACH TEST

The use of the Rorschach test as an instrument of evaluation is limited to psychologists, psychiatrists, and Rorschach specialists. Training and skill is needed to administer, score, and interpret Rorschach records. However, teachers may refer a child to a psychologist for the administration of a Rorschach, and interpretations of personality based on Rorschach records may be discussed in case conferences which involve teacher, principal, and guidance worker as a team. It may, therefore, be useful to define the technique, briefly illustrate its use, and explain some of the principles of interpretation developed by persons who have used it.

The Rorschach is a "diagnostic test based upon perception" (13). The test derives its name from a Swiss psychiartrist, Hermann Rorschach. Rorschach was interested in developing a diagnostic tool which would help the psychiatrist differentiate individuals according to patterns of mental characteristics. Experimenting with ink blots, he found that a great deal an individual's personality organization is revealed by the manner in which he sees and interprets these blots.

As finally developed, the test consists of ten cards each of which presents an ink blot, a symmetrical figure, or shape, with different shades of black on a white background, and with colors in some of the cards, The shapes or figures on the cards are relatively unstured. They can be seen and interpreted in many ways. Each individual who gives an interpretation of what the blots represent must give form and meaning to what the card offers.

The instructions given to someone taking the test are these :

> "People see all sorts of things in these ink blot pictures ; now tell me what you see, what it might be for you, what it makes you think of."

The psychologist is concerned with three aspects of the subject's responses. First, content—what did he see ? Did he see human beings, object, etc. ? Second, location—which part of the blot did the subject utilize for his response ? Did he use the whole card, a part of it, or a small detail only ? Third, determinants—what in the card seems to have determined the response ? What elements in the blot led the subject to see what he did? Was it the color, form, shading, movement, or a combination of these? Every response is scored for all three aspects.

The case of Sylvia L., reported by Krugman (8) will illustrate the use of the Rorschach in the area of child guidance. It shows how Rorschach records can be used to evaluate behavior and personality problems.

This case required the administration of the Rorschach before and after psychiatric treatment to see whether treatment was sufficient:

> "Sylvia was 9 years 7 months old when referred for study two years ago by a cooperating family agency. The problem, as tated then, was school retardation, enuresis, doing things dangerous to herself, migraine headaches, night terror, tells fantastic stories, makes faces at herself in mirror, peculiar behavior.' At that time need for psychiatric treatment was evident, but the psychiatrist's schedule did not permit of her being taken od and was placed on a waiting list. In the meantime, the social worker from the accoperating agency continuent to work intensively with the child and the foster parents with excellent results in handling and behavior, but some neurotic symptoms still persisted. Four months ago the psychiatris took the child on for treatment and has worked with her regularly since. Recently neurotic symptoms seem to have cleared, and the psychiatrist administered another Rorschach examination, giving it to the writer for interpretation and bomparison with the original Rorschach to see if treatment could be terminated.
>
> "The original Rorschach showed a tense, anxious, repressed, neurotic child, with much violence breaking through only in the inquiry and not in the examination itself. The reexamination showed exactly twice as many responses as the first (22 as against 11), and in general, showed a

lifting of repression, with form less rigid, with color coming out in the examination rather than in the inquiry, much freer content, an elimination of shock reactions. Examples of actual responses are even more illuminating than the summarized protocol."

Sylvia L.	*1st Administration*	*2nd Administration*
Card I	Looks like a lady, but she has no head.	Eskimo lady—Her head is chopped off.
Card II	(Much turning—can't see nothi'—) 2 dead bears.	(Quick) These 2 are bears—their heads are chopped off—this is blood— their feet is chopped off.
Card III	2 skeletons.	These 2 are ladies —their back is broken. This is a a fire—they' re putting something on the stove.
Card IV	(Disturbance) a man	(No disturbance) Giant's feet—this is his hands and this is his tail it's all a giant.
Caad VI	Up here a horse, and I don't know what this is (bottom).	This is an aninmal's skin, and this is another one.
Card VIII	This looks like a bear—that's all I could see—there's some other but I	These are 2 bears—this is a flame—these are bodies the 2 bears are putting

	forgot them – No —that's all I could remember now.	the bodies on the fire to burn.
Card IX	2 Reindeer – (laughs) I don't know.	2 animals are pulling the reindeers into the fire.
Card X	That could be a rabbit—This could be a cat—and that's all I see.	This is a bear peeking out thru his hole. These are boys. These are people's bodies.

"Changes in the second examination are not due merely to maturation : re-examination of many other children who have not been treated do not yield such characteric changes.

"The conclusion, submitted to the psychiatrist after interpreting the second Rorschach and comparing it with the first, was : 'The re-examination shows a more productive and much less inhibited girl, probably living less in fantasy, much freer in expression, less disturbed neurotically, living out her fantasy, probably more annoying to people about her, but less disturbed intrapsychically.' On the basis of his knowledge of the case and results of the results of the Rorschach re-examination, the psychiatrist decided to prepare the child for termination of treatment."

Interpretation

Though the interpretion of a Rorschach record requires considerable skill, and should only be made on the basis of all the responses to the ten cards, some general statements have been made as to the meaning of certain kinds of responses. A thorugh analysis requires calculations involving all responses, each scored three ways. It is advisable to remain cautions as to the validity of some of the principles of interpretation to be listed.

Color Responses (C)

Individuals with an outgoing emotional disposition tend to give many color responses. This means that for them the color element in the blot will determine how the blot looks. One Rorschach specialist (13) has stated that "color responses always indicate a desire for an exchange of pleasure or pain with some other person." Whether specific persanality characteristics can be inferred from one type of response is disputed by other workers in this area. There is still substantial disagreement among Rorschach psychologists as to the meaning of some responses.

Whole (W) and Large Detail (D) Responses

If a subject utilizes the whole blot for his interpretation in a number of cards, it may indicate a tendency to solve a problem in a comprehensive and complete way. This would be "associated with intellectual ambition, interest in systematically organized ideas and theoretical matters" (4). Using a large part of the blot, but not the whole, has been considered a "common sense" attack, useful in practical affairs. W and D responses refer to that part of the blot utilized for the response, while the above-mentioned C responses refer to the elements in the blot which determined the response.

Movement (M)

Many people see the figures on the blots as moving and interacting. They see some parts of the ink blot in the process of changing their relative position to each other. Individuals with a rich, inner life typically have high M (movement) scores. According to Rorchach, the movement response indicates an ability to create new, personalized constructions, a capacity for "inner creation." for living more within oneself than in the outer world.

Form (F)

If a response is solely determined by the outline or shape of the blot, and not its color, shoding, etc., it is called an F (form) response. Persons who produce F responses to the exclusion of color or movement are said to be colorless and lacking in unique personality.

The Group Rorschach

One recent development of general interest in Rorschach testing is the use of the Group Rorschach. This type is administered to a group of individuals by means of slides projected onto a screen, and their responses are written down by the subjects. It can be administered rather ea ily, but interpretation of responses, of course, needs the skill of the trained specialist. The Group Rorschach cannot be used with very young children but has been used with other children, adolescents, and adults. This adaptation of the method, as well asa multiple-choice Rorschach (in which the individual chooses from many responses the ones with which he agrees), has limitations, but has been effectively used as a screening device.

THEMATIC APPERCEPTION AND OTHER PICTURE PROJECTIVE TESTS

Among the pictorial projective techniques, the greatest amount of research has been devoted to the Thematic Apperception Test. This test, developed at the Harvard Psychological Clinic by Henry A. Murray (11) and his co-workers, consists of a series of ambiguous pictures portraying one or more individuals. The subject is shown a picture and asked to write or tell a story about the person in that picture. The instructions given to the subject usually are a variation of the following : "This is a test of creative imagination. I am going to show you some pictures. Around each picture I want you to compose a story. Outline the incidents which have led up to the situation depicted in the story. Describe what is occurring at the moment—the feeling and thought of the characters, their relationship to each other. And tell what the outcome will be" (11).

The individual is thus made to believe that his fantasy or creative imagination is being tested and does not realize that he is revealing his dominant drives, emotions, sentiments, complexes, and conflicts. Since the pictures are relatively unstructured—can be interpreted in several ways—the kind of interpretation which an individual gives is assumed to express his past experiences, conflicts, and wishes. The hypothesis is that the individual will identify himself with one of the figures portrayed in the scene and project his own conflicts upon that figure. Bell (2) has defined the Thematic Apperception Test as a "method for the stimulation, recording, and analysis of fantasy."

The problem in working with the TAT lies in verifying the analysis of interpretations. Granted that a specific fantasy about the characters in the picture is an indication of the personality of the individual who composed it, what assurance do we have that the analysis which we offer is correct?

Following are descriptions of some of the pictures:

1. A young boy is contemplating a violin which rests on a table in front of him.

2. Country scene : In the foreground is a young woman with books in her hand ; in the background a man is working in the fields and an older woman is looking on.

4. A woman is clutching the shoulders of a man whose face and body are averted as if he were trying to pull away from her.

6BM A short elderly woman stands with her back turned to a tall young man. The latter is looking downward with a perplexed expression.

8BM An adolescent boy looks straight out of the picture. The barrel of a rifle is visible on one side, and in the background is the dim scene of a surgical operation, like a reverie image.

Two stories from Tomkins (17 : 115, 118) will illustrate the kind of stories composed, and the ways in which the psychologist makes use of the story material for diagnosis. Tomkins relates them to show how the TAT can help the psychologist determine, among other things, the strength of the parental impact within the family setting upon the child. Both fantasies have been given about picture number one (young boy contemplating a violin which rests on a table in front of him).

> "Sitting there is a boy about 10 years old gazing at a violin. Ah—he's quite an intelligent fellow and ah—I think perhaps he wanted to study the violin. So his mother and father bought him the violin and he started to take lessons. As the lessons progressed, he found there was more work involved than he had thought. He realizes that success wouldn't come as easily as he thought, and he will have to study and study before he becomes a great violinist. By the expression in his eyes, it looks as if he's wondering whether it's worth all the effort. As he grows older, he stops taking violin lessons and listens to concerts. He will realize he was wrong to stop taking violin lessons."

In his interpretation Tomkins is concerned only with the clues this story provides for gauging parental impact on the individual, He concludes that for the individual who developed the above fantasy, parental impact is limited. In the story, according to Tomkins' analysis, the parents are capable of doing what the child wishes, but the child is the instigator of their activity and they merely minister to his needs.

The next fantasy, also stimulated by picture number one, presents a different interpretation.

> "Many years ago a boy got a present for his birthday. The reason that they gave him a violin was because they wanted him to become as interested in music as they were. As the little boy sat looking as the beautiful instrument disappointment showed in his face, He thought

how much nicer it would have been if his parents had given him some toys. He realized how mueh the present meant to them so he tried to look as happy as possible. He was curious about the violin because he had never seen one before ; he had only heard his father and mother talk about them, so he decided to see what it would do. He picked up the bow and drew it across the strings. He liked the sound and tried it again. Wouldn't it be fun to put all the sounds together, he thought. Now standing off stage at Carnegie Hall, waiting for the applause to die down, the great artist thanks his parents from the bottom of his heart.''

Tomkins says about this story : "The ideal of the parents . . . . is foreign to the child's wishes but he conforms because he does not want to disappoint them. Parental impact is great and when he reaches maturity, conformance with parental wishes has been sufficiently rewarding to bring about complete identification with parental values." The second fantasy thus shows an individual who has projected unto the figure of the boy his own relationship to his parents.

Interpretation

There is at this time no uniform method for analyzing the fantasy productions developed by the individuals taking the Thematic Apperception Test. Many investigators have found it necessary to develop independent systems of analysis. Murray's scheme for the interpretation of TAT data, one of the most comprehensive attempts at objectifying TAT analysis, centers about the concepts of "need" and "press."

It is assumed that an individual making up a story about a picture identifies himself with the figuse or one of the figures (hero) in the picture. Every act which occurs in the story as initiated by the hero is classified in terms of the need or needs which it expresses. For instance, violence on the part of the hero would reflect the need of aggression. Among Murray's list of needs are those of aggression, dominance, achievement, recognition, rejection, sex, deference, harm avoidance, and others. The fantasy stories also express "presses," the forces which impinge upon the individual. These may be either harmful or beneficial. In analyzing the stories the psychologlst would look for the kind of forces fantasied as impinging upon the hero. A list of presses would include : family insupport, lack or loss, rejection, birth of sibling, deception, etc. The fantasy productions have also been analyzed by type of language used, vocabulary, syntax, etc. Other investigators emphasize types of endings (happy, unhappy, etc,).

Interpretations of TAT records require a great deal of skill. Nevertheless, cursory examination of records by the untrained individual may provide some insights into problems. As indicated earlier, the psychologist has data on stories given by many groups of people. He has available a body of data on how persons with a certain kind of behavior or personality problem have reacted to these same pictures. Thus, by means of the stories developed, he is able to classify his subject into one or another group.

OTHER PICTURE PROJECTIVE TESTS

Other picture projective techniques have recently been developed to stimulate individuals to express their real feelings about such things as the family, different religious groups, and labor. The advantages in using pictorial techniques of this kind seems to be that the individual interpreting a picture does not feel "on the spot" since he is not asked to state *his* attitude but to interpret a picture *outside* of himself. The limitations of these tests lie in their questionable validity and reliability.

Among the more interesting of these picture tests are the Rosenzweig Picture-Frustration Test (14) and Symonds' study (16) of adolescent fantasy.

Rosenzweig's test consists of twenty-four pictures resembling incomplete cartoons. Each picture portrays two figures. The person on the left in the picture is the frustrating person and is either saying something which frustrates or is describing a situation which frustrates the person on the right. There is a caption box on the right for the person taking the test to fill in the very first reply which occurs to him to the actions or words of the figure on the left. For instance, a picture might portray the individual at the left splashing mud on the person on the right. After looking at the picture and presumably identifying himself with the person splashed, the subject would write a reply in the caption box under the person pictured at the right.

The instructions take the following form : "Each of the following pictures contains two or more people. One person is always shown saying certain words to another. You are asked to write in the empty space the very first reply to these words that comes into your mind. Avoid being humorous. Work as quickly as you can." Rosenzweig analyzes the responses in terms of the direction of the aggression expressed and the types of reaction to frustration.

Symonds developed a test conisiting of forty-two pictures designed for adolescents. Symonds (16) says that the psychological themes revealed by the pictures tap the major pspchological drives to be found in the fantasies of adolescents in our culture.

DRAWING AND PAINTING TECHNIQUES

Graphic expression has recently received much attention as a projective device. Anderson and Anderson (1) devote several chapters of their book to this topic. The drawings and paintings of children and adults have been evaluated as characteristic of personality structure and behavior problems. The art productions of children, adolescents, adults, the feebleminded, the neurotic, and the insane have been investigated for both their diagnostic and their therapeutic value. The free, spontaneous expression achieved in pencil and crayon drawing, finger painting, or painting with water colors by young children has been promising for analysis and description of personality,

The drawing and painting of dults is often influenced by considerations of style and form, which may overshadow the individual characteristics in the expressive product,

Though many techniques leave the choice of topic as well as of medium to the child, other projective methods utilizing drawing and painting prescribe what shall be drawn. It is assumed that by using the same expressive problem, individual variations in expression will stand out most sharply. The Draw-a-Man Test, earlier devised by Goodenough as a measure of the mental age of a child, serves as an example of such a method. It consists in telling the child to draw a picture of a man. The investigators working with this method, according to Murphy (10), feel that it permits the child to project his conception of a man, his understanding of freedom and power, as exhibited in posture, gesture, and facial expression, Workers practiced in analyzing such productions claim that the drawing reveals the kind of man the child admires or fears.

The child may further assimilate his own picture of himself into that of the man portrayed. In looking at the picture, one would consider such factors as whether the posture of the man drawn displays confidence and self-reliance, what the age of the man seems to be, and what secondary sex characteristics are included. The problem of drawing a recognizable man, of course, must have been solved by the child previous to the use of his drawing for interpretative purposes.

A method providing, perhaps, the freest expression both in terms of movement and in choice of color is finger painting. Finger painting may be employed with young as well as older children. Bell (2) says it provides for rapid and easy creation of colorful pictures without the preliminary mastery of a complicated skill in handling tools. The necessary materials are paper, preferably glazed and inserted into water, and the colors which are added with a spatula and worked over with the fingers, hands, or forearms.

The pictures when completed may be placed on newspapers and pressed with an iron. In interpretation, the whole process engaged in by the child is analyzed. For instance, of significance are the part of the hands used in painting, the posture, and the color used. On analyst claims that leaning on one hand is an indication of self-consciousness and that leaning against the table symbolizes lack of self-reliance. Lack of neatness presumably constitutes bad coordination or guilt. Male children prefer to use the colors blue and green and female children prefer red and yellow.

Many workers hve suggested that there is a specific relation between the use of certain colors and the presence or absence of behavior and personality problems. Much guessing, as well as intuitive insight, lies behind the formulation of such hypotheses. Bell (2) presents a lengthy table listing some of these claimed relationships. For instance, dark and smudgy colors indicate depression, whereas yellow and red indicate expressions of hostility and aggression. Strong yellow in some cases has been related to happy feelings, whereas red alone may indicate both feelings of affection and love and feelings of aggression and hate. Criteria of form have similarly been used to describe personality. For instance, rigid contours and uniform rhythm have been interpreted as indicative of compulsion, Short, little strokes and few curved forms may express aggression.

At present, the status of drawing and painting techniques for diagnosis of personality is not certain. Although there are many hypotheses about the aspects of personality and adjustment by the art techniques, specific relationships have not yet been conclusively demonstrated. The teacher may wish to experiment with these techniques and through them obtain "hunches." The teacher's knowledge of the child may help him to understand the meaning of certain forms and colors for a particular child. Expression through art has a therapeutic as well as aesthetic function and is thus to be encouraged, but the interpretative hunches gained need validation by using observation and other evaluative tools.

PLAY TECHNIQUES

Play is a natural activity of the child. In it the child expresses himself spontaneously and without self-consciousness. Informal and more formal play situations have been used as projective devices. The child has been left free to manipulate and rearrange materials which encourage him to dramatize certain aspects of the enuironment which are of great significance to him. The materials employed have varied from the most "unstructured," such as clay, paste, mud, and cold cream; to more structured, such as blocks, mosaic pieces, and beads; and finally to "well structured," such as dolls and miniature-life toys representing furniture, houses, and people.

Clinical psychologists and psychiatrists have used play techniques not only for diagnosis but also for therapy. As reported in Anderson and Anderson (1), the play situation offers the child a cathartic experience—that is, an opportunity to release socially unacceptable impulses and to discharge feelings associated with traumatic experiences, such as birth of a sibling, lack of parental love, and others.

Play techniques have recently been widely used to give insight into the child's behavior, ideas, feelings, wishes, attitudes, and fantasies. By their very popularity, they deserve the interest of teachers, counselors, and guidance workers, To what extent the analysis of play provides valid data for guidance, however, is a matter of disagreement. The play techniques consist in exposing the child to play materials such as miniature-life toys. He is given no instructions except to do what he likes with them. Murphy (10) indicates that the child uses the toys to portray his conception of his home. family, neighbor-hood, and world. He showf his parents and other adults, his dog, and himself. in terms of directly verbalized wishes or wishes which are indirectly portrayed in his conduct. Murphy cautions. however, that in interpreting the play process it must be kept in mind that much of the child's behavior represents a mirroring of reality. Still, a great deal of the child's distinctive, egocentric point of view emerges in the play.

For work with children, play seems to be a very important projective technique. However, a large part of what the child does in his dreams, his school work, or his contacts with his family has great projective value, according to Murphy (10), because the child's mode of expression is still a direct and spontaneous one. It must be remembered that no one projective method can reveal all the facets of a child's personality. Play is no exception to this rule, though it is one of the most comprehensive measures. It is most useful in focusing the attention of the teacher or psychologist on certain areas which need further exploration.

MISCELLANEOUS TECHNIQUES

There are various other techniques based on the assumption that personality expresses itself in many forms and that every individual reacts to stimuli in a characteristic and unique fashion.

The sentence completion test grew out of the previously accepted word association techniques, which had achieved some importance in clinical psychology. The sentence completion method presents to the individual short phrases that are to be completed to form whole sentences. Items such as the following are illustrative.

1. I am unhappy when——————
2. I become mad when——————
3. I like——————
4. I dislike——————
5. I don't tell the truth when——————
6. I won't——————

The answers which the subject fills in presumably reveal emotional and social conflict areas. They are interpreted and scored in many ways. Some workers have restricted themselves to three categories of interpretation :

(*a*) conflict or unhealthy responses,

(*b*) positive or healthy responses, and

(*c*) neutral responses.

Others analyze the material more elaborately, classifying responses by areas of rejection, evidences of resistance, other methods of evasion, recurrent themes, and special or a typical associations. Opinions as to the validity of the data yielded by this method differ. Bell (2) states that an advantage of this technique lies in the ease with which it can be administered to large groups. However, he cautions that the validity of various versions of the test is not high enough so that it can be employed without other corroborative measures.

Story telling and story completion techniques closely approximate the Thematic Apperception Test in that they all use oral and written fantasies as their data. While the stimulus in the Thematic Apperception Test is pictorial, the stimulus for a story or plot completion technique is a written or oral theme which is to be elaborated. Story telling as a projective device is more unstructured than story completion, which does impose a limitation upon the child's fantasy. In story telling, children are simply asked to make up a story about a boy or a girl, or about a father or mother. As reported in Bell (2), three major themes emerge from the stories made up by the children : What the child is afraid of—anxiety; what the child wishes to be—wish fulfillment; and what he fears he might do—sadism.

> "Little Tommy goes to school in the morning. When the time comes to play he stays in a corner by himself .."

(Instructions : Complete the story, telling why Tommy does not play with the other children)

Another variation of this method consists in letting the subject choose one of a number of endings to a story which he was told. In this way the teacher or experimenter can observe whether the child prefers a happy ending, an unhappy ending, desires to reward a likable person, etc.

Interpretation of this kind of material poses a difficult problem. There seem to be four elements which influence the kind of story a child would tell and the outcome the subject might decide on :

(*a*) books and movies,

(*b*) events in which a friend or relative participated,

(*c*) the narrator's own experiences, subjective and objective, and

(*d*) conscious and unconscious fantasies.

Though there is a tendency to remember and select from experience those things most related to the individual's personality and conflicts, a simple analysis of the stories without reference to the sources from which they derive, has severe limitations.

Handwriting analysis as a form of personality interpretation is very old. Still, it is difficult to evaluate its validity as a measure of personality. Many systems of analysis are used and the "experts" differ in emphasis. Some workees in the area interpret handwriting as a whole, others make specific reference to length of lines, point pressure, and other detailed charateristics of handwriting. It is pointed out by handwriting analysts that "no two individuals, even when copying the same model, can carry out the same movement." Both factors of organization and deep level motivation express themselves in handwriting. Murphy (10) lists five areas to which analysts pay attention in making graphological interpretations :

(*a*) The expansiveness and contractility in handwriting—how much space is filled up.

(*b*) The "emphasis"—speed and intensity, the amount of pressure applied.

(*c*) The style—aesthetic qualities such as symmetry, evenness, and unevenness.

(*d*) Concern for social appearance—factors of orderliness, concern for correctness.

(*e*) Attitudes toward the self—how writing one's name, for example, in terms of extension and contraction compares with other words in the text.

The validity of a handwriting analysis still largely depends on the "expert," the system used, and the frame of reference. Graphology remains a promising but inconclusive area of measurement research. Unfortunately, the employment of graphology as a pseudo-science in newspaper features has obscured the real progress made.

SUMMARY

The number and variety of personal reports and projective techniques for evaluating personality is so large that a complete inventory of them would require an entire volume, rather than a chapter in a volume. In this chapter, however, a survey of representative and most commonly used techniques is presented. Personal reports include self-descriptive inventories and problem checklists with standardized questions or statements, as well as the autobiography. These methods require less specialized background and training for administration and interpretation than various projective techniques, which only specialists can administer and interpret.

Self-descriptive inventories and problem checklists evaluate such specific aspects of personality as self-sufficiency, dominance, submission, introversion, extroversion, social adaptability, and anxiety about health, relationships with others, home and school problems. Analysis of an autobiography gives clues about modes of thinking and feelings of an individual, but these clues should be corroborated by other observations and data.

Projective techniques utilize such relatively unstructured stimulus situations as ink blots, thematic pictures, incomplete sentences, drawings or paintings, and toys or puppets to which the individual responds, thus expressing his way of seeing life, its significance and patterns, and his own meanings and feelings.

Among the most widely used projective techniques is the Rorschach test. The Thematic Apperception Test is also widely used by clinical psychologists.

Other projective techniques include : variations of thematic pictures; analysis of paintings and drawings; play techniques using clay, mosaic pieces, dolls, puppets, and other toys; sentence completion and story completion tests; and analysis of handwriting.

The validity and reliability of the various techniques vary considerably and are functions of the rapport between the examiner and the examined individual, the insight of the individual, and the expertness of the examiner in the interpretation of responses. Although the different techniques provide valuable clues to the nature and organization of personality, interpretations from any one should be corroborated by data gathered from other techniques and from observation.

PROBLEMS FOR CLASS DISCUSSION

1. Administer a personality inventory or problem checklist to one or more pupils. Study the results to determine whether or not you can gain additional insight about the pupils' attitudes and personal-social behavior from the data.
2. Administer a sentence completion test to a class of pupils. Analyze the answers to gain the following tentative insights :
   (*a*) Which pupils give responses which merit further study ?
   (*b*) Which pupils give mostly normal responses ?
   (*c*) Which pupils give mostly neutral responses ?

12

Sociometric Methods

The modern teacher is interested in promoting the social adjustment of each child. Trained to understand the interrelationships among physical emotional, intellectual, and social factors in the learning process, the teacher needs to know how and in what ways each child gets along with his peers, In many cases the socially rejected child may become sufficiently disturbed emotionally to be hampered in his intellectual development, or, conversely, social maladjustment may be symptomatic of personal problems outside of school. The importance of the "social status" factor in the development and the make-up of the individual is great enough to warrant the expenditure of considerable teacher time and energy in diagnostic work.

More specifically, of what importance is the relation of the individual to the group ? The development of one's personality is a product of the interaction of the individuai with other people. One's ideals, one's motivations, and one's many pleasures are products of social interaction. Also, one's sense of security is based on the nature of the group's acceptance or rejection. According to the ideals of a democratic society, it is important for individuals to get along with one another if a stable, functioning society is to be maintained. At a time when uninty must be attained amidst diversity of political, economic, religious, and social beliefs, the principle of harmonizing the interests of the individuals and the group, the personal and the social, is fundamental to our way of life. For reasons significant for individual as well as social growth, therefore, the determination of the relationships which exist among the individuals in the group is an essential step in the diagnosis and reconstruction of individual and group living.

Sociometry may be described as a means of presenting simply and graphically the entire structure of relations existing at a given time among members of a given group (5), Modern sociometry is of relatively recent development. Beginning with the post-war (World War I) work of Moreno, whose "Who Shall Survive" ? was the first book in the field, many investigators have contributed numerous theoretical and practical insights into the field of sociometry. Although sociometric testing is relatively new, the tests have yielded data of great educational significance. Teachers now have available many sociometric approaches which suit the varying needs of individual classrooms. This chapter discusses the construction and use of several types of sociometric devices.

TYPES OF SOCIOMETRIC DEVICES

The Nomination Technique

In this relatively direct form of approach, a question is so framed that the individual is asked to name a limited number of people from within the group with whom he would choose to associate on the basis of some stated criterion (6). A typical question which could serve as the basis for an analysis of pupil choices might take this form :

> What other boys and girls do you want to sit next to you for the next month ? You may have three choices. Name the boy or girl you 'most' want to sit next to as your first choice, then the one you want as second choice, and as third choice, If is hand to arrange scats so that everyone will have 'all' his choices, but we will try to make sure that everyone will have at least 'one' of his choices.

It is important that the questions used as a basis for choices refer to rcal situations, and that some action will grow out of the choices which are made by the respondents.

The Rating-Scale Approach

Devices using this form ask the respondent to rate all the other members of his group, using some predetermined scale. Typical of this approach is the Ohio Social Acceptance Scale, published by Ohio State University. The following six descriptions serve to guide the respondent in assigning scale values to his peers :

1. I would like to have this person as one of my very, very best friends. I would like to spend a lot of time with this person. I would enjoy going places with this person. I would tell some of my troubles and secrets to this person and would do everything I could to help this person out of trouble . .

2. I would enjoy working and being with this person. I would invite this person to a party, and would enjoy going on picnics with this person and our friends. I would like to work with this person and I would like to be with this person often. I would like to tallk and make and do things with this person. I want this person to be one of my friends . .

3. I would be willing to be on a committee with this person or to be in the same club. It would be all right for this person to be on the same team with me or to live in my neighborhood. I would be in a play with this person I would just as soon work with this person in school. This person is not one of my friends, but I think this person is all right . . .

4. I do not know this person very well. May be I would like this person, may be I would't. I don't know if I would like to be with this person . .

5. I say "hello" whenever I meet this person around school or on the street, but I do not enjoy being with this person. I might spend some time with this person if I didn't have anything else to do, but I would rather be with somebody else. I don't care for this person very much....

6. I speak to this person only when it is necessary. I do not like to work this person and would rather not talk to this person.

Other investigators (4) have used a five point rating scale :

(1) Very, very best friends,

(2) Good friends,

(3) Not friends, but okay,

(4) Don't know them,

(5) Not okay. Experience has indicated that the ratings assigned to the members of a group may be looked upon as points on a continum. As such, the statistical treatment of the ratings assigned and received is relatively simple.

The "Who's Who" Approach

This sociometric technique constitutes an excellent means of obtaining insights into pupil difficulties in meeting the standards set by their peers. The Ohio Recognition Scale, published by Ohio State Univerity, a typical instrument of this type, is an anonymous means of securing pupil judgments concerning their classmates. A portion of the directions and some of the items included on the scale are reproduced below :

In this booklet there are many paragraphs. They tell about different kinds of boys and girls. As you read each paragraph, ask yourself :

"Is there anyone in our room like this ?" If there is, put that person's name under the paragraph. If you think of more than one person, write these other names, also. If there is nobody in your room like this. write "Nobody" and go on to the next paragraph.

1. Do we have any boys and girls in our room who are very eventempered, who almost never get upset or angry, who are always calm, even things go wrong ? When somebody shouts at them, or even hits them, they don't get excited. They are always cool and level-headed. Who are they ?

2. Some boys and girls seem to be unhappy most of the time. They don't seem to know how to enjoy themselves. It's no fun having them around because they almost never laugh or tell funny stories or good jokes. They are almost never happy. Who are they ?

5. Some boys and girls always seem to feel at home wherever they are. They are not afraid to say what they think in class discussions. They ask questions if they don't understand something. They don't mind meeting strangers and they can talk easily with grown people and older children. Who are some children who are almost never shy or bashful ?

6. Suppose you were going to choose people from this class to be on your committee. You want boys and girls who work well with other children, who will have some good ideas, who will work hard, and who will stick to the job until it is finished. They would know how to plan and they would do good work. In this class who would you choose for this committee ?

7. Are there any children in our room who are very friendly with everyone ? These boys and girls are not snobbish or "stuck-up." They like you as well today as they did yesterday—they always act the

same toward you. They like everybody. They take time to talk to you and seem interested in you. Who are they ?

The "Who's Whc" approach undoubtedly gives the teacher information which he eannot gain through the use of the other devices. The major disadvantage of this technique lies in the difficulty of analyzing pupil responses in order to arrive at a measure of an individual's status in the eyes of the group.

SOME USES OF SOCIOMETRIC METHODS

Promoting Social Adjustment

One of the most important uses to which sociometric techniques may be put by the teacher is the identification of childeren who are in need of help in adjusting to the group. Research has indicated that the pupil who is high in sociometric status tends to express himself in terms of characteristic which the group values (1) and to direct his energies to activities which the group approves (3). In a sense, sociometric scores are a measure of the degree to which a pupil undertakes activities which are highly regarded by his classmates or conform to the group's demands. The score which a pupil obtains on a sociometric test, then, may be booked upon as a measusre of his drive toward social adjustment.

Another use of the sociometric test is to promote common interests, ideals, and skills among those individuals who do not seem to be sharing such experiences. In a group of twenty-five to thirty-five pupils, several children may be too shy or otherwise not socially efficient enough to associate with others. The sociometric test is of value in revealing such feelings and in helping the teacher set up situations for promoting social adjustment.

The following sociometric test, disguised as an interest inventory, was used with a church group. This inventory can be modified for classroom use by inserting other types of activities and appropriate student names.

Part one – Directions : Fill in the following information. It is not necessary to put your name on this paper. If you like the activity, place an L in the space provided. If you are indifferent to the activity, place an I if you dislike the activity, place a D.

L – Like *I—Indifferent* *D—Dislike*

—Swimming	—Go boating or canoeing
—Ride horseback	—Go to a summer camp
—Hiking	—"Rough it" in the woods
– Go on picnics	—Organize a baseball team
– Hunting and fishing	—Pitch tents and set up camp
—Lead games outdoors	– Build outdoor fires
—Go bicycling	—Organize food planning
—Play badminton	—Lead a group on a hike
—Take photoraphs	—Planning for others' fun
—Cook outdoors	—Be a Committee chairman

Part Two – Directions: If you would like to engage in these activities with the following people most of the time, place an M in front of their names. If you would like to engage in these activities with them some of the time, place an S in front of their names. If you would like to engage in these activities with them none of the time, place in N in front of their names.

—Mlarian A	—Jean G.	—Bill R.
—Don A.	– June J.	– Pat S.
– Don B.	—Carol K.	—Marian S.
– Barbara B.	—Dick L.	– Marge S.
—Eddie C.	—Earl M.	—Shirley S.

Of course, one should no assume that each pupil necessarily knows where his best interests lie, but student choices do represent at least one aspect of the problem of setting up socially desirable goals.

Grouping Pupils

The sociometric device is also very valuable in the process of setting up committees for projects and for seating arrangements. Going on the assumption that it makes a difference in work efficiency and social pleasure when one works with persons of one's own choice, seating students according to their expressed likes is a desirable practice. Of course, it may not always be possible to give each individual his choice, nor may it be best for the individuals concerned. Where feasible, however, the pupil's choice should play a part in the process of assignment to seats at tables or to committee work. It is through the unknown (to pupils) manipulations of the environment that some pupils may be helped to get along more efficiently in the group. Typical questions asked of pupils are : "Whom would you like to sit next to ?" "Whom would you like to work with on a committee ?" "Name five pupils you would like to have at your table." "Name five students you would like to have on your committee." These questions tend to elicit some of the information necessary for grouping pupils most effectively. Obviously, for final groupings. the information must be combined by the teacher with information about many other pupil characteristics and needs.

Measuring Growth in Group Status

The sociometric test may be employed to describe growth in group acceptance. At the beginning of the term one may find, as a result of administering a sociometric test, that each pupil may desire to work with certain other pupils, play with certain pupils, sit next to certain people, etc. If this test is administered periodically, the teacher might be able to trace the growth in the group acceptance of any given pupil. For instance, nobody may choose to sit at a table with James at the end of a month in school. As a result of the efforts of the teacher (and student too) James might have become more acceptable as reflected in the second test. This change might be due to James' desire to change the group's better understanding of James, or a combination of both factors or others. In any case, testing and retesting may reveal changes and possible growth or lack of growth in group acceptance.

Detecting Cleavages

The sociometric test is a fine method of revealing cleavages among pupils along undemocratic lines. When pupils reject one another on the basis of blind group prejudices or accept one another on the basis of irrational likenesses, one may say that the group reflects undemocratic patterns. By analyzing the choices of pupils in their friendships, work relationships, play relationships, and the like, one may detect possible prejudices in operation which reflect such undemocratic behavior. Although there are differences of opinion as to the meaning of democratic behaviour, still the teacher is obligated to promote some conception of democracy which involves a respect for the individual and a sense of equality of opportunity and responsibility for all.

The teacher must remember that pupil responses to sociometric tests tend to reflect the fundamental characteristics of society outside of the school. When the teacher tries to find out why John will not work or play with James, he may learn that James lives across the tracks, and does not have the clothes, social habits, or the pocket money to keep up with people like John. Cleavages such as those of race, religion, and socio-economic status have deep roots, and the teacher alone cannot hope to cope with them. The teacher must work with others in and out of school, as a professional and as a citizen, to facilitate democratic social living. Simply telling one's pupils to be "nice" to one another will not lead to social betterment.

Jennings (2) has drawn up a very comprehensive "Sociometric Analysis Schedule" to guide the teacher in promoting these general uses of the sociometric technique.

SOCIOMETRIC ANALYSIS SCHEDULE

1. What appears that you had expected would appear ?
2. What appears that you had not expected to appear ?
3. What seems to account for certain pupils being the most chosen and receiving few, if any, rejections ?
4. What seems to account for certain pupils being unchosen or receiving many rejections ?
5. What seems to account for the mutual choices ?
6. What seems to account for the mutual rejections ?
7. Can you think of any classroom arrangements which may account for the above choices or rejections ?
8. As you read the structure as a whole, do you think of any arrangements such as classroom routines, lunch-room arrangements, play patterns, which might be a factor in the general patterning of the sociograms.
9. What cleavages, if any, appear in this sociogram ? Cleavage is here defined as an absence of choices between individuals related to a "gaoup factor". Examples : boy-girl, economic, nationality background, religion, academic ability, being employed after school: prestige of some special group, other group factors.
10. Can you see any spots in the structure of the group as a whole that need to be more related to the rest of the class group for better morale, such as a clique by itself, several mutually choosing children, other children trying to get in with no response ?
11. In the light of your analysis of their interrelation—structure, what understandings and skills do you estimate they have already well developed ? Which do you estimate they need to develop further ?
12. What do the majority of most-chosen children have in common ? Examples : race ; don't work after

school ; socioeconomic level, fairly well off ; live in open community and not in housing project ; most are Protestants ; most have lived in this community all of their lives ; most take part in after-school and in-school activities.

13. What do the unchosen and rejected children have in common ? Examples : different nationality ; much lower socioeconomic level than rest : most live in housing project ; many of them after school ; many are new to community ; don't participate in-school and out-of-school activities ; present many discipline problems.

14. Are there visible signs of segmentalization in your community—association patterns which divide according to race, religion, residence location, or any other factor ?

CONSTRUCTING AND ADMINISTERING SOCIOMETRIC TESTS

There are no formal steps which have been laid down on how to construct sociometric tests. In general, the basic principles for constructing any test or test question apply. The specific purpose of the teacher (and of the class, if there is pupil-teacher planning) is to determine the form and content of the sociometric test. Also the educational situation in large measure plays a significant part in the nature of the test.

There are many occasions in the educational process when the sociometric test may be used profitably for a variety of purposes. At the elementary-school level, there are game situations in which one pupil must select another, such as in the ring game, the Farmer in the Dell, the farmer takes a wife, the wife takes a child, etc. ; these selections may reflect social groupings, though for children in kindergarten and first grade, associations are generally temporary. In the lower grades, where there are generally self-contained classrooms, there are possibilities for electing representatives to extend invitations to other classes, clean-up squads, milk distribution squads, and committees for carrying out a project. Also, where pupils sit a tables, monthly selections of tablemates have the elements for determining individual and group status.

In the higher grades, selection of others in the class can take place in numerous ways. If there is a class group of officers, etc., such voting can reflect student position. Students can select teams, group leaders for excursions, members of committees to work on a play (costumes, sets, actors, etc.), a class picnic or outing, tablemates, etc. In all cases, the teacher can satisfy the students that the "test" is serving a practical purpose they can understand, though for himself the teacher should go beyond this surface set of facts and determine the social structure of his class.

Insufficient attention has been paid to the problem of when to administer sociometric tests in the course of the school term. A common abuse is scheduling by impulse – the teacher suddenly administers a sociometric test because it is a "good idea," because "it is being done," was mentioned in a school or professional society meeting, or was discussed in a course in measurements. It is wise to remember that sociometric testing (like other testing) should be intrinsic to and continuous with the regular work of the class. The sociometric test should be an important and useful exercise which helps carry the class forward toward its curricular objectives.

The sociometric test may consist of one or more questions which elicit from the student his preferences, on the basis of some criteria or task, for classmates, schoolmates, or extra-school friends. Sometimes, in addition to simply selecting other youngsters, the student may be asked (when appropriate) to give his reasons for selecting or rejecting different ones. In this way, the teacher can collect valuable evidence on the reasons, apparent or underlying, why pupils are popular or unpopular, accepted or rejected.

An argument frequently raised against sociometric testing is that it tends to crystallize in the mind of a pupil his feelings of antagonism toward other pupils or his rejection of them. In other words, some teachers fear that the test will pnt ideas into an immature child's head. This may hold true when the sociometric test is improperly empolyed. If the students do not know each other well enough to have formed li kes and dislikes, the sociometric test should not be used, since it cannot reveal what does not exist. More frequently, however, such a fear on the part of a teacher reflects naivete.

What questions may be used profitably to illuminate the status of group acceptance of the individual ? Insofar as possible, questions should arise out of the regular activities of the classroom. The teacher should be sensitive to the values of certaih occasions to obtain sociometric data. The following examples may be considered as guides for drawiug up specific questions more appropriate to a given classroom.

1. We will need five people to serve as personal representatives of our class, whose job it will be to invite other classes to participate in our circus festival. Name the five people you want on this slip of paper.
2. We need a bulletin board committee of three pupils. What three people would you want on the committee ?
3. We will need two boys and two girls to plan our class party. Choose the four people and tell why you would have each one on the committee.
4. Do you have any preferences about who should be in your group when we go to visit the museum ? Name the four pupils whom you would like to accompany you. Are there any pupils in the class whom you would not like to have in your group ?

Administration

The effectiveness of the sociometric test, it must not be forgotten, is highly dependent on the teacher who uses it. A test which is valuable in the hands of one teacher may be quite ineffectual in the hands of another. When a teacher is concerned with such highly subjective and emotionally charged material, the type of relations the teacher has with the students will make all the difference in the world in the responsiveness and honesty of the students. Sociometric techniques are of most value in classrooms where the teacher has maintained a generally informal classroom atmosphere.

Some explanation of the purposes and uses of the test (it should not be called a test, because then students may react as though it were an "academic test") should be given the students so that they will be properly motivated to follow directions. The directions should include the specific manner in which students are to record their choices.

The sociometric test question can be presented in various forms in the classroom. The question may be in written form, one copy for each child, it may be written on the blackboard, or it may be presented orally. Whatever form is used, separately or in combination, the student needs to be able to record his choices on a sheet of paper or index card. Sometimes, it may be wise to mimeograph a list of names (alphabetically or by seating arrangement) after which a student can record first, second, and third choices or just three checks or X marks.

The test should be administered so that each individual's preferences are kept confidential. Since the sociometric test involves data which are packed with dynamite (the personal feelings and preferences of children, and which reflect the ideals and practices of their families and their community), the teacher must be careful and considerate in his use of such tests and their results. The teacher who promises to keep results confidential *must* observe this practice. To do otherwise may serve to widen the breach between some pupils and their classmates, and to destroy pupil-teacher rapport.

It is always a problem to the teacher whether to have pupils sign their ballots for choices or submit them anonymously. While there are times when anonymity may be advisable, in most instances all ballots should be signed. Signed ballots are a necessity in sociometric testing when sociograms are to be constructed.

Tabulation

Let us assume that the teacher has asked each of a class of twenty-five pupils to list the three pupils in the class with whom he best likes to work. Let us assume that the sample slip is a quarter of a regular $8^1/2'' \times 11''$ sheet of paper. Each slip might then look like this :

Frank B.

Karen C.

John E.

Stanley D.

The name at the bottom is that of the one who made the three selections. The teacher should then draw up a table which includes the names of the twenty-five pupils vertically as well as horizontally. (On the horizontal list one may substitute numbers corresponding to the names.)

The tabulation is begun by placing a mark (x) in the appropriate columns on line five corresponding to the name of Stanley D. This process of tabulating continues until the three choices of the other twenty-four individuals are recorded. Totals can be drawn up on a separate line at the bottom to indicate the number of times an individual was ehosen. If there is no interest in keeping track of who selected whom, one may simply keep tallies next to the list of names. If the names of the students are listed alphabetically on a mimeographed sheet, it is possible to line the papers up so that one can tally horizontally the number of check marks after each name. Generally, it is best to tally each question completely rather than a number of questions at one time, because the latter often leads to errors and confusion. Since it is quite human to make errors, it is always wise to check each tabulation at least once.

If the four persons in a cleavage were members of a minority group against which the class had deep seated prejudices, it is unlikely that physical manipulation of chairs would remedy the situation. If any given individual in the class is under study, the sociogram might be constructed about that individual. Also, if there is a group of individuals under analysis, the group may be the focus of the sociogram. Whenever one draws up a sociogram, it may be necessary to rearrange circles a few times before achieving the best descriptive presentation.

When integrating data, the teacher must be cautioned not to over-generalize on the basis of limited data. If the teacher asks the class to name the five persons with whom each student would like to work on a class art project, it does not follow that the results can be used to reveal friendship patterns. A good friend with no talent may be neglected in favor of a good artist who is personally not attractive to the student. There is a tendency for teachers to label certain students "isolates" because nobody chose them as one of their three best friends, etc. Much caution should be employed by the teacher in the interpretation of test results. If the teacher is interested in drawing certain generalizations about each child, it is well to incorporate into the original purposes and content of the test (or group of tests) those questions whose answers will permit such conclusions.

SUMMARY

Sociometric methods are a means of determining the relationships existing among members of a group at a given time. Several methods have been found useful in determining such relationships.

1. an individual may be asked to name a limited number of people from written the group with whom he would choose to associate on the basis of a stated criterion.

2. an individual may be asked to rate all the other members of his group, using some predetermined scale, or
3. an individual may be asked to select those members of his group who show defined characteristics. Sociometric techniques have been found to be of use in promoting the social adjustment of pupils, in promoting common interests and skills of a group, in grouping pupils for various class activities, in measuring growth in group status, and in detecting cleavages which reflect social standards among group members.

While there are no formal rules for the construction of sociometric tests, the alert teacher will find numerous opportunities for the development of sociometric devices in the course of his normal classroom work. He must be careful not to violate the confidence of his pupils, and should be certain to utilize the choices made by his pupils in order to put their expressed desires into effect. Tabulation of the results of sociometric testing is relatively simple. The results are usually presented via a-sociogram, which lends itself to the ready identification of cliques, isolates, and "stars."

PROBLEMS FOR CLASS DISCUSSION

1. How well do you know your own pupils ? Make a list of the most accepted and most rejected pupils in your class (or in one you select). Construct a sociometric test to determine the relative popularity of the children in the group.
2. This chapter has not indicated how the results of sociometric testing via the rating scale approach might be summarized. How would you tabulate pupils' responses using this approach ? How could you arrive at a measure of pupil status ?
3. Using a suitable question to secure choices from a class with you have contact, construct a sociogram to indicate pupil interrelationships.

13

Case Studies

The case study or case method involves the integration and use of comprehensive data about an individual as the basis for diagnosing and interpreting conduct or behavior. The basic data of the case study are usually supplied from examinations of the individual by such specialists as the psychologist, social worker, physician, and teacher. It is a method of appraisal that concerns itself with the careful examination of physical and psychological factors that are significant in the life of the person under study. Emphasis is placed on discovering what is unique in the relationships among factors in each case rather than what is characteristic of a large number of individuals. The findings have significance for the treatment of maladjustments displayed by the individual. It is a diagnostic and remedial procedure based on a thorough investigation of a person in order to acquire knowledge of his history, his home conditions. and all of the thihgs that may have contributed to his behavior difficulties.

THE PLACE OF THE CASE STUDY IN EVALUATION

The case study usually contains a description of the behavior indicative of maladjustment, physical and health conditions based on an examination. family background and history, early childhood history, the mental capacity and educational achievements as revealed by tests and observational methods, the individual's personality, and efforts already made to improve the adjustments. Thus, *the case study is a primary tool of evaluation.* It permits the synthesis of all pertinent facts about an individual within one framework. It emphasizes the uniqueness and individuality of the human personality. Pupil problems which are not susceptible to diagnosis by group techniques may be approached through this method. The data gathered, according to Crow (1), should be restricted to those things which are considered relevant to the present difficulty of the student.

The purpose of case study is two-fold ; diagnosis and treatment (2). First, the underlying reasons for behavior or learning problems are discovered; second, a course of treatment or remedial work is undertaken. The case study method may also be used to gather facts and gain insight about an individual for the purpose of helping him to develop his best potentialities (5). The objective of the case study is not primarily that of research, and, although many case studies lead to a body of scientific generalizations about the meaning of certain forms of behavior, the function of providing material for the expansion of scientific knowledge may be considered a by-product. Rather the individual is studied in order to help him overcome his learning problems or adjustment difficulties. The method further permits the evaluation of the treatment or remedial undertaken after diagnosis.

Definition of the Case Study Technique

The case study has been defined as "detailed study of an individual, conducted for the purpose of bringing about better adjustment of the person who is the subject of the investigation" (7). It represents an analysis of an individual's assets and liabilities by school, medical, and psychological personnel (2). It is desirable that a case study possess the following characteristics : completeness of data, continuity, confidential recording, and scientific synthesis (3). Case studies may be both longitudinal or cross sectional : they may present a picture of an individual at any one time, or they may represent a continuous study over weeks or months.

Usually a picture of growth, continuity, and development is added to the cross-sectional study (6), in order to make possible comparisons between conflicting evidence and to clarify the picture of the individual as it begins to emerge. The teacher supplements the data gathered in the classroom about an individual's modes of behavior, interaction, and progress with information from parents, guidance personnel, medical officers, and other teachers, Cumulative records may become a part of the information to be included in the case study (8).

The definition of the case study clearly embraces the phase of treatment. Traxler (7) points out, however, that whether treatment is recorded as a part of the case study will depend on the type of problems studied. Since the range of problems and difficulties accessible to study by this method is considerable, generalizations are difficult. Certain problems are referred to a specialist, such as a physician, psychologist, or social worker. Most other problems, including learning difficulties, are treated within the school setting. Sometimes a particular child is studied because the teacher feels that he has not utilized all of his potential abilities and talents. In those instances, the progress made after treatment or special work becomes a part of the case record.

The case study emphasizes process rather than product (4). Standardized tests will measure whether a student has retained a certain bit of information, but they will not provide clues as to why he was unable to comprehend or retain it. An accurate description of the nature of a child's difficulties in comprehending can result only from observation by the teacher, verbalization by the child, and many other types of information. The same, of course, holds true for problems of cooperation and adjustment.

Children Studied by the Case Study Technique

Children with serious difficulties in adjusting to home or school social situations, as well as children manifesting serious difficulties in scholarship, are usually studied by the case study technique, Shy chilnren whose social and intellectual qualities seem possible of development are very fruitful subjects for study. In general, the decision is to study pupils who deviate from the average in any important respect. It may be argued that, if time and qualified staff permitted, all students should have records comparable to those of a case study. However, it is not necessary to apply this method to students whose behavior and other problems can be dealt with by the classroom teachers who understand them without additional observation and study.

Although the definition of the case study implies that it deals with one individual at one time, observation of groups can be used as part of the data for the case study. Traxler (7) lists several points regarding choice of subjects for the case study which are important for those attempting to make a case study for the first time :

> "Select a case in which you are really interested, both from the standpoint of the nature of the case and the personality of the individual concerned.
>
> "If possible, choose a pupil from your own classes who, you feel, needs attention and help and who will probably cooperate well with you.
>
> "When considering various pupils, give some thought to the shy, quiet, retiring pupils. Pupils of this type are sometimes mor suitable subjects for case study than pupils whose difficulties, or behavior causes them to be noticed.
>
> "Plan only as much as you feel you can accomplish. If you contemplate a thorough case study, including treatment, it will probably be cest in the first year to confine yourself to one pupil."

Procedures in a Case Study Technique

Most outlines for case studies seek information of the following kind, to be gathered by the individual undertaking the case study with the cooperation of all those who have contact with the child studied (2, 5, 8) :

(*a*) Reasons for studying the particular child. A description of the special problem or an account of the incident which initiated the case study would serve this purpose.

(*b*) Identification. Certain factual information must be presented regarding the child, such a name, address, sex, and grade. Some teachers may feel that information about the child's ethnic group and economic status is pertinent.

(*c*) Family background. Data regarding the home environment of the child are necessary to provide a total picture. How many persons are living in the home ? What is their relationship to each other ? What is their occupational and social status ? How much privacy does the child have ? What are the parental methods of discipline ? What are the parents' attitudes toward the child ? All these are questions which used answers.

(*d*) Health record. This includes data on growth, weight, physiological maturity, pecularities of gait and speech, physical defects, nutritional status, and other evidences of the child's physical well-being or deficiency.

(*e*) Educational data. In this category are included cumulative record and attendance data. special academic proficiencies and deficiencies, information on the extent of participation in classroom and extracurricular activities, and data on the child's mental ability and achievement which have been gathered from standardized and informal tests.

(*f*) Social behavior and interests, Observations by teachers, counselors, and parents regarding the child's social behavior and relations, and his interests and attitudes are included. For instance, what are his work habits, his fears, his likes, and dislikes? How much sex information does he have and what are his sex habits? Is he able to get along with others? Is his disposition cheerful or moody? Is there evidence of emotional stress? Does he seem self-confident? Long range observations in these areas give basic clues for later evaluation and interpretation of the case material.

There is some disagreement about how intensive the case study should be. Symonds (6) believes that if there are specific symptoms, such as reading difficulty, the case study need not be exhaustive but may proceed at once to the particular functions involved. Other workers in this area (5, 8, 2) feel that even in a specialized case of this type, it is desirable to obtain a complete picture, maintaining that a particular difficulty can best be interpreted against the background of the whole personality of the child. The advocates of this view hold that too much cannot be learned about a child, his life, habits, and complete environment.

Sample of Clinic Case Study

The case study presented below as a sample was taken from the files of an educational clinic. Case material of school pupils taken, interpreted, and used for treatment within the school setting may differ from this in minor details.

REPORT ON GEORGE C.

Born : February 2, 1947 *Age* : 8 yrs. 3 mos. *Grade* : 3

Visited Clinic May 12th and 22nd, 1955

George was referred to the Clinic for investigation of the reasons for his very poor academic work, especially in reading and arithmetic,

General Impressions

George was accompanied on his visit to the Clinic by his father. He had no idea why he had come, and was so nervous at first that he was visibly shaking. After explanation of the reason for the visit and a short period of getting acquainted, he was more at ease. However, he never seemed completely comfortable.

He showed a marked desire to do well on the various tests, showing good effort and attention and persevering in tasks even when he found them very difficult. He was a little disorganized by tests in which speed was important. At times he showed good planning, and at other times he resorted to an inferior trial and error procedure.

He spoke in a thin, high-pitched voice, with a definite lisp. He answered questions readily and with apparent frankness, but volunteered few spontaneous comments. In general, he seemed somewhat immature socially for his age.

Physical Findings

Medical examination indicates that George is a very well developed boy in good health. He is seven inches above average for his age in height and weights 16 pounds above the average for his height and age; he is well nourished without being overweight. Vision is normal. Hearing as measured by the Maico D-5 Audiometer is borderline, with a loss of 16.8% in the right ear and a loss of 20% in the left ear. He has a short fernum, which probably is the cause of his lisp. No other defects were found.

In tests of eye dominance, he shows no preference for either eye, He writes, draws, and does most other things with his left hand. In working with concrete materials, he uses both hands about equally, and in simultaneous writing he reverses as much with one hand as with the other. The left hand dominance is incomplete and rather weak.

Abilities

Because of a foreign language handicap, George's present mental age on the Revised Stanford-Binet Intelligence Scale. Form L, of 7 years 10 months and his IQ of 95, are considered to represent a minimum rather than a true measure. On the scale he passes all items at the seven year level; of the five items passed above this level, three are tests of auditory memory.

His vocabulary is limited, failing at the 8 year level. On a series of non-language tests involving perception of form and physical relationships his work ranges from very superior to very inferior, with a median score of 8 to 9 year level. His drawing of a man, scored for ideational content, is above average for his age. There is on record an IQ of 99 obtained on the Pintner Cunningham Test in June 1953. The indications are that George is a boy of at least average intelligence, whose scores on verbal tests may improve as he learns more English. His present mental ability on predominantly verbal tests is equal to that of an average child in the third grade.

George was given several tests from the Stanford Achievement Test, Primary Battery, Form D. His grade scores were as follows : Paragraph Meaning, 3.0; Word Meaning, 2.5; Spelling, 3.8; Arithmetie Computation. 3.8. The spelling and arithmetic scores are up to his present grade, the second half of the third, and seem to indicate average.

performance in these subjects.

His problem in reading is mainly one lack of knowledge of word meanings. His oral reading is quite accurate and shows fairly good phrasing and very good ability at working out the pronunciations of unknown words. He can pronounce many words whose meaning he does not know. His retardation in reading seems to be a mild one and one which should clear up as he acquires a richer English vocabulary. In silent reading, he seems to need more complete explanation of directions than most children do. His comprehension in silent reading is at as high a level as his verbal comprehension on the intelligence tests.

George comes from a home in which Spanish is spoken. His mother speaks very little English; his father's English is fairly fluent, but spoken with a marked accent and faulty grammar. George is said to have known very little Engligh when he entered the first grade. His vocabulary weakness seems to stem from this.

School Adjustment

Mr. C. says that he was not aware that George's work was deficient until last term, when he was called to school to discuss it. He then asked that George be allowed to take his books home, and since then has been supervising his son's homework. George's report card for last term shows marked improvement during the term in reading, spelling, and arithmetic. It seems as if his scholastic difficulties were to a large extent overcome before he came to the Clinic.

Social and Emotional Adjustment

George's father was well dressed and gave the impression of having better than average intelligence. He is unable to work because of chronic illness and therefore has much more time to spend with his son than most fathers do.

It is quite obvious that Mr. C. is very fond of this son. He admits no faults in the boy, denies that George has any social difficulties, and asserts that the scholastic problem no longer exist since he started to pay attention to George's homework.

George gives, as mentioned earlier in this report, an impression of immaturity in his speech and general manner. He plays with a group of boys and girls ranging in age from 6 to 8. His wishes and interests are quite normal. He is afraid of cars and of big boys, who throw stones when the little boys make faces. He seems to have a marked dislike for his sister, who is a year older; he thinks she is too bossy and takes his things. He likes his present teacher and thinks that he is getting along well now. Except for his hostility toward his sister, nothing significant of maladjustment came out of the interview. His drawing of a man is more like a typical girl's drawing than like a boy's; the head is very large and drawn with considerable attention to detail, while the arms and legs are small and poorly drawn. This is additional evidence of emotional immaturity.

The fact that for several terms George has been marked unsatisfactory on the traits "Works and Plays with Others" and "Respects the Rights of Others" indicates that difficulties exist which the father denies. It is probable that George is accustomed to being a little king at home; he resents having to share things with his sister, and carries his egocentric habits over into the school situation.

Interpretation

George is a boy of average or better than average intelligence whose progress in school has been retarded somewhat by a Spanish-speaking home. His scholastic adjustment has improved markedly since the request for examination was made. His incomplete left dominance does not seem to have anything to do with his difficulties in school. The personality difficulties noted in school probably result from spoiling at home by his father. Insufficient evidence about this was obtained to allow more definite conclusions. No evidence of severe emotional disturbances was found.

RECOMMENDATIONS

1. George's scholastic difficulties seem to have been already taken care of in large measure. If he should fall behind again, it would be worthwhile to discuss his difficulties with Mr. C. who is very anxious to do anything that will help George.

2. In talking with Mr. C., a few suggestions were made :

   (*a*) that so far as possible he should expect George to do his homework by himself, and not do it for him ;

   (*b*) that in other way he should give George opportunities to become more self-reliant and less dependent upon his parents ;

   (*c*) that he should try to find out what truth there might be in George's complaints about his sister ;

   (*d*) that clipping of the frenum, easily done in a hospital clinic, might improve the clarity of George's speech.

3. In regard to George's unsatisfactory personality traits as evidenced in school, not enough was found out to warrant specific recommendations. The general suggestion that he should be commended when he behaves in a more approved fashion may, perhaps, not be out of place. It seems probable that there

should be improvement in conduct as his scholarship improves.

Interpreting the Data in a Case Study

After the data have been collected, it is advisable to present the material in an objective, simple form, with little bias (8). Description should be kept separate from interpretation. The material may be confined to a few pages. The final interpretation of the data and the decision as to the kind of remedial effort or treatment indicated is the joint concern of all those most closely in contact with the child. They enlist the guidance of an examining psychologist or counselor, who helps in the analysis of the findings and assists in the formulation of recommendations. The meeting of the individuals involved in the case study is called the case conference. Some of the following persons may be present at a case conference : the principal, the teacher or teachers of the student being studied, the counselor or guidance person, the school physician or school nurse (1). Social case workers, probation officers, and welfare officers are included if the problem of the student warrants their presence.

Case conferences represent learning experiences for teachers, and are valuable for an understanding of all the children in the school, though they may be called for the purpose of considering specific behavior problems. The case conference sensitizes teachers to the inter-relationship between physical, intellectual, and emotional factors.

As the recommendations made in the case conference are carried out, additional observations are necessary to evaluate whether the contemplated adjustments or changes have indeed taken place. Some-times the changes can be measured by standardized tests and measurements. At other times, several months of additional observations are necessary to verify whether the interpretation given was correct and the remedial efforts deriving from the interpretation have led to improvement or adjustment.

SUMMARY

The case study represents an analysis and synthesis of an individual's physical and psychological assets and liabilities by school, medical, and psychological personnel. The purpose of the case study is to achieve better adjustment of the individual by means of a comprehensive appraisal of all factors contributing to the problem under study and to institute remedial activities. Children with serious difficulties in adjusting to home or school situations are usually studied by means of this technique.

The case study contains a description of the behavior indicative of maladjustment and data from observation and examinations of the individual's health, family background, mental capacity, educational achievements, and personnal or social characteristics. The interpretation of the data and recommendations for remedial action are to joint responsibility of all those who have studied and who have worked with the child Subsequent observations are made to verify whether the interpretation of data was correct and the remedial efforts have resulted in improvement.

PROBLEMS FOR CLASS DISCUSSION

1. Prepare a short and simplified case study of a pupil with problems, including as much available data as you can obtain for :

    (*a*) reasons for study,
    (*b*) identification data,
    (*c*) family background,
    (*d*) health record,

(*e*) educational data,

(*f*) social behavior, and

(*g*) interests.

2. Prepare a case study of a pupil with a problem of retardation in reading. On the basis of this case study make :

   (*a*) a diagnosis of causative factors,

   (*b*) a plan for working with the pupil.

14

Cumulative Records

The cumulative record of the individual pupil is usually regarded as a permanent and official summary of his educational history. This record may be in the form of a card, folder, or booklet. The cumulative record may be used as a technique of appraisal and guidance for the following purposes :

(*a*) to enable teachers to get acquainted quickly with new pupils,

(*b*) to identify scholastic strengths and weaknesses of individual pupils and to plan a program to fit the pupil,

(*c*) to identify problems of personal or social adjustment that a pupil faces,

(*d*) to provide comprehensive and continuous data for counseling with the pupil, and

(*e*) to serve as a source of information in a conference with a parent.

The record also serves as the basis of reports to other schools, colleges, or prospective employers.

In the modern school the pupil's progress and growth is summarized on the school's cumulative record. The entries on such a cumulative record are related as closely as possible to the major objectives of the school. As indicated earlier in this book, these objectives involve not only academic achievement and progress, but also physical health, social adjustment, emotional stability, interests, aptitudes, and attitudes. The cumulative record serves as a comprehensive measure of the effectiveness of the school's service in guiding the growth of the pupil. The periodic, concise recording of all aspects of a pupil's career in and out of school challenges the school to consider the individuality of its pupils. It further makes possible a progressive evaluation of the school's services to each individual.

PLACE OF THE CUMULATIVE RECORD IN EVALUATION

A careful study of cumulative records reveals many of the factors which have facilitated or retarded the growth and development of individual pupils. The data obtained from the records may be used in many ways. They can resultin greatly improving guidance of the pupil's program of activities and studies. They can indicate to the teacher in a cumulative fashion the persistent strengths and weaknesses of the individual child. They can give a history of the pupil's progress from kindergarten through high school.

In education today it is felt that the school program should be adapted to the abilities, interests, and needs of the child. It is, therefore, essential that a systematic and comprehensive record be used to give the teacher as complete an understanding of each child as possible, his past experiences, his home and environmental interrelations, and his mental, emotional, social,, and physical development. It is thus clear that cumulative records are indispensable as a long range method of evaluating pupil growth.

Definition of the Cumulative Record

The cumulative record is a method for recording, filing,

and using information essential to the guidance of students (3). It represents a cumulative individual inventory of the educational, mental, physical, social, and emotional development of each pupil. The record should be as complete as possible and truly cumulative. Information in these areas is generally recorded on the cumulative record :

(*a*) identification of the student.

(*b*) family and cultural background.

(*c*) physical and medical history.

(*d*) marks in school subjects.

(*e*) mental and achievement test data.

(*f*) extracurricular activities.

(*g*) interests.

(*h*) special talents.

It is advisable to start the cumulative record at the time of school entrance. Of course, not all kinds of information can immediately be obtained or recorded. The development of the inventory is a gradual process. It has been suggested that each proposed entry should be subjected to the question : "What contribution will this item make toward the diagnosis of the child's interests, capacities, aptitudes, limitations, and vocational possibilities ?" (4) The judgment of the teacher will separate the wheat from the chaff, will select pertinent and significant data, and weed out the unimportant and irrelevant, It is advisable to keep interpretation and opinion separate from objective description in entering data on the cumulative record.

Types of Cumulative Records

Cumulative records may be kept in the forms of cards, booklets, or folders. There has been a tendency to move toward the folder type of record, which seems the most comprehensive and flexible of the three. Regularly recorded data may be entered on forms printed on the folder proper, Special records, such as health charts, anecdotes, and confidential information, may be placed on separate forms and inserted in the folder.

Card

The cumulative record developed by the Educational Records Bureau, for example, is a card nine by eleven and a half inches (5). It is used with a supplementary card of the same size, which gives a cumulative graphic record of test percentiles and school marks, Many features of the card devised by the Educational Records Bureau have their origin in the American Council on Education form for secondary schools.

The cumulative record card of the Educational Records Bureau begins with a number of items concerning the personal background of the pupil, such as nationality and family background data, including the occupation of the father or mother. This is followed by a record of the pupil's participation in eight activities, with spaces left for adding other activities. Some of the activities listed are : use of leisure time, music, athletics, summer activities, and travel. Below this there is a record of general health, listing height, weight, vision, hearing, and physical limitations. There is a space for recording home influences. Another section of the record deals with personality, which is classified in terms of traits such as reliability, industry, initiative, emotional adjustment, and social adjustment. On the side of the card ample space is provided for each teacher to make comments appropriate to the items listed under activities and personality. At the bottom of the face side of the card there is space in which may be summarized comment under the heading "Comments at Time of Transfer."

The back of the card is reserved for the record of scholarship and achievement. Half of the card is taken up by a table for subjects, marks, and credits. Under each year there are columns for three marking periods, a mark for the year, rank in class, and periods per week that the subject was studied. The other half of the reverse side of the card lists scores on standard achievement tests taken by the pupil. The supplementary graphic record follows a pattern set by the graph of the American Council Cumulative Record Folder.

Booklet

The booklet type of record is illustrated by the Cooperative Educational Record of the Denver Public Schools (2). This record is kept cooperatively by teachers, parents, and pupils. The booklet for the Denver secondary schools is eight and a half by eleven inches in size, consists of forty-seven pages, and is in part devoted to explaining the purpose of the cooperative educational record and giving directions to pupil, teacher, and porent in making entries. The major part of the data is recorded by the student. There are seven sections in which information is noted. Section One deals with informal educational experiences and interests, and permits recording of experiences under such headings as participation in clubs and other organizations, offices and positions of leadership, and vocational experiences. Section Two gives the record of formal educational experiences and interests, and lists subjects, grades, hours, and marks. Section Three contains the record of standardized tests. Section Four provides data on patterns of behavior and is in the nature of a self-descriptive inventory.

The pupil rates himself on judgement, self-direction, organization, resourcefulness, leadership. acceptance of facts, cooperation, and similar characteristics. Instructions for evaluating are given to the pupil in the booklet. Section Five gives personal and home information. Section Six consists of the pupil's reading record. Section Seven, for informal observations and information, provides ample space for comments by parents. teachers, and the pupil himself.

Folder

The California Cumulative Guidance Record, which may be cited as an example, is designed to meet a variety of local school needs. It consists of one Basic RecordFolder and three or more supplements (1). Two of the supplements make possible a more detailed presentation of data recorded on the basic record folder. Additional supplements devised by local school systems can be interested into the folder. The basic record folder is approximately nine by twelve inches in size and consists of four divisions ; identification, home environment, personality development, and school experiences.

If no basic supplements are used, data on health, physical, social, and emotional development are to be recorded on the basic record folder. Basic Supplement One provides opportunity for elaboration of data on health and physical development, summarizing the results of health examinations, immunizations, and the like. Basic Supplement Two deals with curricular experiences and permits recording of units of study which gave the pupil significant experiences. Basic Supplement Three, for adjustment factors, lists items such as study habits, educational plans, educational programs, and vocational interests.

Interpreting Data on the Cumulative Record

Each entry on the cumulative record makes a contribution toward the diagnosis of a pupil's interests, capacities, aptitudes, limitations, and vocational possibilities. Data in each of the following areas make a specific contribution in assisting in interpretation.

Family and Cultural Background

Information recorded under this heading is varied, ranging from factual data concerning such items as nationality and occupation of parents to information about the kind of emotional relationships existing in the home. Not all of the information listed here may greatly assist the teacher of guidance worker in understanding the child. Data on economic status, for instance, may not be significant by itself. A child from either an impoverished or a luxurious home may enjoy a close and warm relationship with parents and siblings, making him an emotionally secure individual, It is the quality of the interpersonal relationships in the home that it is important to know for an understanding of a pupil's emotional retardation or progress. Other data, such as that on ethnic origin, may help to gauge the child's needs in certain respects.

Physical and Medical History

The results of health examinations and tests and the report on the physical condition of the child are of great importance. Frequently, many of the problems noted in other parts of the cumulative record may be traced to poor health. Social and emotional behavior, as well as scholastic achievement and progress are directly related to the physical functioning of the child. Physical limitations must also be taken into account in vocational guidance.

Marks in School Subjects

School marks are more than ratings of achievement. They are in addition, a reflection of vivaciousness, cooperativeness, and talkativeness (4), and contain elements related to later success. It has been pointed out, however, that marks provide a limited understanding of capacities and aptitudes. They represent judgments reflecting varying standards. Poor marks, for instance, may indicate lack of motivation, not lack of scholastic ability. Marks are most valuable in interpretation when considered in conjunction with other items on the cumulative record.

Mental and Achievement Test Data

Mental tests are an index of the potentiality of a pupil, whereas achievement tests measure what an individual has achieved in a subject and what he may continue to achieve in that subject in the future. Data on mental and achievement test scores may be considered together. A pupil who does well on the mental tests but consistently does poorly on achievement tests needs guidance and individual attention which will search for the reasons for the discrepancy between potentiality and performance.

Extracurricular Activities

The kinds of extracurricular activities in which a pupil spontaneously engages are an important indicator of real interests and abilities, since such activities, being undertaken without pressure, are very meaningful to the pupil. Data about the nature, variety, and dnration of extracurricular participation often give clues as to future occupational interests. Information in this area can also be utilized in providing added curricular experiences.

Interests

Interests emerge as pupils become exposed to many and varied experiences. As pupils are acquainted with art, with industry, with communal and civic life, with various occupations and hobbies, their interests become gradually defined. Data on the cumulative record will reveal this gradual focusing of interests, as out of many experiences a few are chosen for repetition. This information is valuable for guidance, becoming more important as the student goes through school. It must, however, be kept in mind that some interests reflect both inner and environmental circumstances and it is quite possible that they may suddenly shift.

Special Talents

Data about special talents are closely related to data about interests. It is important to note all evidences of special talents and abilities as well as special handicaps and limitations. These are revealed through observation of hobbies, interests, work records, and anecdotal material (4). Tests of special aptitudes are of great value. Any evidence of special talent in music or the fine arts, as well as evidence of special mechanical and manual aptitude, is important both for guidance and for planning activities for the individual pupil.

Illustration of a Cumulative Record

On the adjoining pages, illustrations of sections of the cumulative record used in the New York City Schools are presented. The New York City cumulative record is of the folder type. The sections on the main, or basic, folder for personal and educational data include the following :

(*a*) personal information,

(*b*) registration and attendance data,

(*c*) subject growth record,

(*d*) personality scale, and

(*e*) guidance information. Separate inserts, or supplements, include the pupil health record form and the test record for results of individual and group tests.

In the section on personal information, all identification data about date of birth. parents' names, family data, language in the home, and home address are found. This section also includes registration and attendance data from kindergarten through grade six.

The subject growth record section of the cumulative record shows teacher rating of achievement in such subjects as reading, language arts, social studies, science, mathematics, health, music, and the fine arts. The ratings used are as follows :

S indicates satisfactory achievement in terms of capacity; I indicates need for improvement in terms of capacity; and U indicates unsatisfactory achievement in terms of capacity.

The personality scale and the guidance data are shown in other sections of the cumulative record.

The insert for individual and group test results includes a record of results of intelligence and achievement tests.

The Unique Role of the Cumulative Record in Evaluation

As a long range method of evaluating pupil growth and development the cumulative record plays a unique role. The study, observation, evaluation, and testing of one individual over a period of time resembles the genetic approach in the fields of biology and clinical psychology. Ruch and Segel (4) have formulated two generalizations which state succinctly the advantages of the cumulative record. One is that "the predictive value of an item is increased when data on that item are gathered annually or periodically over a range of years." This means that if a certain comment, rating, or score shows up on the record time after time we can place more faith in it as reflecting the personality or aptitude of a pupil than we can if there is only one entry.

Their second generalization is equally valuable :

> "A number of related items usually give a better prediction than any one single item, if properly weighted and combined." They illustrate this point by stating that school marks, teacher ratings, and intelligence and achievement tests give a better picture of all-round academic ability than any one item would. This is particularly true if observations and tests tap different aspects of the pupil's interests and personality at different times.

A comprehensive cumulative record, well kept, is an important tool of an on-going process of evaluation, and it permits a continuous feed-back of information to teachers, guidance workers, parents and—last but not least—the pupil.

SUMMARY

The cumulative record in the form of a card, folder, or booklet is a permanent educational history of the individual pupil from his entry into a school system until he leaves. The cumulative record contains fairly complete information about identification data for the pupil, his parents, and siblings ; his school achievement, test results, course of study, attendance, health, personality, and similar pertinent data.

The cumulative record serves a variety of administrative, supervisory, and instructional uses. It may be used as a technique of appraisal or guidance in counseling with the pupil, conferring with his parents, and transmitting reports to other schools or prospective employers.

The unique role of the cumulative record in evaluation is that the predictive value of data is increased when such data have been recorded periodically. The review of a series of records on school achievement, test results, or personality ratings is more valid and reliable than any one single datum on a given pupil characteristic In addition, the relationships among such items as intelligence, achievement, and personality characteristics may be observed and woven into a comprehensive picture of the individual as he has grown and developed. The cumulative record provides a continuous and coherent evaluation of the individual pupil's physical, mental, emotional, and social development.

PROBLEMS FOR CLASS DISCUSSION

1. Make a survey among five to ten teachers to determine the uses they make of the cumulative record.
2. Study the cumulative record of a pupil. From this study, prepare a summary statement of the scholastic and personal or social strengths and weaknesses of the pupil.
3. Obtain cumulative records used in several school systems. Assess the values and limitations of each record form. Which would you prefer to use ?

15

Evaluating Achievement in Language Arts and Mathematics

Language arts and mathematics comprise the timehonored "3 R's"—reading, writing, and arithmetic—used as basic symbols and tools of communication in American culture. Verbal and mathematical symbols and processes are used whether an individual participates in a game of dominees or in a complex industrial or business transaction. Since these symbols are so pervasive and basic to communication and learning, the roles of language arts and mathematics have loomed large in the curriculum of the common school. Modern educators recognize, however, that acquisition of skills and knowledge in these subjects should be supplemented by realization of such other objectives and concomitant learnings as power in reasoning, interests, attitudes, and appreciations.

Achievement Tests in Basic Skills

The earliest objective tests constructed in 1910 and shortly thereafter by Thorndike, Courtis, Monroe, and others emphasized achievement in arithmatic and in the language arts of reading, writing, spelling, grammar, and usage. Since those early days, many technical refinements have been made to improve the validity, reliability, norms, and interpretation of achievement tests. Scientific studies of curriculum content are now made so that test exercises provide a representative sample of the important learnings. Each item is checked for statistical as well as curricular validity. Reliability of tests has been improved by new methods of analysis. Norms are now obtained by improved methods of selecting representative samples of pupils. Methods of interpretation have been devised for diagnosis of test results and comparison with similar age or grade groups.

Curricular Validity

Curricular, of content, validity is of central importance in achievement tests. An achievement test in reading, spelling, or arithmetic has curricular validity if it measures fairly the extent to which pupils have learned the curricular experiences provided in the school. In the language arts and mathematics courses of study and in various related series of textbooks, the curriculum content is fairly uniform throughout the nation so far as scope and nature of major objective of instruction and grade placement of subject matter is concerned. To avoid invalidity attributable to improper sampling of curriculum content, national distributors of standardized tests make careful studies of representative courses of study and instructional material used in the schools of the nation. A sampling plan is used to select test items that are equally significant for appraising all major abilities, knowledges, and skills in a course of study.

Lindquist (7 : 121) discusses another trend in achievement testing in which he expresses the viewpoint that tests of immediate and specific objectives of instruction should be constructed locally to fit the local course of study. Tests intended for wide-scale use should emphasize comprehensive, general, and ultimate educational objectives in a curricular area. These may appropriately be called tests of general educational development, with exercises designed to measure growth in general abilities and skills rather than specific information and knowledge.

Such tests permit variations in the specific content or experiences provided in a local school situation so long as these contribute to such general or ultimate objectives as comprehension in reading, facility in written expression, and application of mathematical processes and concepts.

Standardized and Informal Tests of Achievement

For convenience in discussion, the methods of testing achievement may be classified as :

(*a*) standard or formal tests and

(*b*) informal or teacher-made tests.

The standard tests for wide-scale use are valuable for measuring growth and development over long periods of time and for providing comparative data based upon such relatively uniform standard units of measurement as age, grade, percentile, and standard score norms. Such standard tests, however. constitute only a part of the total evaluation program for achievement. The remaining part involves the day-by-day evaluation, using informal, or teacher-made, tests and techniques. These may include teacher-made tests using true-false, completion, or multiple-choice responses, and, on appropriate occasions, such methods as oral questions, anecdotal records, interviews, or observations of pupils. Many suggestions for informal tests and other methods of appraisal are provided in the Forty-Fifth Year book of the National Society for the Study of Education (6).

In this chapter, the scope of discussion is restricted to a brief survey and listing of representative standard achievement test in language arts and mathematics. Short statements regarding the objectives evaluated by the test are followed by a tabular presentation of illustrative tests for the various subjects of instruction, Detailed discussion and presentation of sample items, involving the comprehensive enumeration of test titles, is obviously outside the scope of this chapter. In a like manner for the language arts and mathematics. tests of interests, attitudes, and critical thinking are reserved for discussion in separate chapters devoted to these objectives of instruction and learning.

Information About Standard Achievement Tests

Since an inventory or listing of available tests cannot be made within the scope of this chapter, it may be helpful to indicate to the reader the most fruitful source that he may consult in order to obtain information and appraisal about standard tests of achievement. This source is the series of mental measurement yearbooks edited by Buros (1, 2, 3) and published periodically. The plan of these yearbooks is to provide several appraisals of each test by experts. These appraisals enable the reader to get a clear picture of the advantages and limitations of each test. Practically all standard tests are reviewed. This source of information should be consulted by anyone wishing a more detailed statement of the various tests which are listed in subsequent sections of this chapter.

BATTERIES AND SERIES OF ACHIEVEMENT TESTS

In achievement testing of basic skills and subjects, particularly at the elementary-school level, most test publishers and authors provide a battery of tests. bound in a single booklet, including the following content : silent reading, language usage skills, arithmetic computation, arithmetic problems, spelling, social studies, and elementary science. Generally these tests are also available in separate booklets.

At the secondary-school level, there are few batteries of tests that are bound together into a single booklet. Generally, the authors and publishers have a series of tests on such basic subjects as English, foreign languages, mathematics, science, and the social studies. Each test is printed in a separate booklet. Each of these separate tests measures the content most frequently found in typical courses of study in the particular subject in representative high schools throughout the nation.

Table 1 lists some typical achievement test batteries at the elementary-school level and series of tests at the secondary-school level that are distributed nationally by commercial publishers.

Table 1

Illustrative Achievement Test Batteries or Series

Test and Publisher	*Date*	*Content*	*Grade*
Elementary School			
California Achievement Test-Primary, Elementary, and Intermediate (California Test Bureau)	1950	Vocabularly, reading comprehension, arithmetic reasoning and fundamentals, language	1 3 4-6 7-9
Iowa Every-Pupil Tests of Basic Skills—Elementary and Advanced (Houghton Miffling Company)	1940	Reading, language, arithmatic, work-study skills	3-5 6-8
Metropolitan Achievement Tests-Primary 1, Primary 2, Elementary, Intermediate, and Advanced (World Book Company)	1947	Reading, vocabulary, arithmatic fundamentals and problems, language usage spelling	1 2-3 3-4 5-6 7-8
Modern School Achievement Tests (Bureau of Publications, Teachers College, Columbia Univ.)	1944	Reading comprehension and speed, arithmatic computation and reasoning, spelling, health knowledge, history, and civics, geography, elementary science	3-8

National Achievement Tests, Municipal Battery (Acorn Publishing Co.)	1940	Reading comprehension and speed, arithmetic fundamentals and reasoning, English, literature, geography, history, civics, health	3-6
SRA Achievement Series—Intermediate (Science Research Associates)	1954	Arithmetic, language arts, reading, work-study skills	4-6
Stanford Achievement Tests—Primary, Elementary, Intermediate, and Advanced (World Book Company)	1952	Paragraph meaning, word meaning, arithmetic reasoning and computation, social studies, science, spelling, study skills	2-3 3-5 5-6 7-9
Secondary School			
California Achievement Tests-Advanced (Californa Test Bureau)	1950	Reading, arithmetic, language	9-12
Cooperative Test Series (Educational Testing Service)	1950 et seq.	English, foreign language, mathematics, science, social studies, etc.	9-12 College
Evaluation and Adjustment Series of High School Tests (World Book Company)	1950 et seq.	English, literature, science, mathematics, history, health, study skills, etc.	9-12
Iowa Tests of Educational Development (Science Research Associates)	1948	Basic social concepts, natural sciences, quantitative thinking, interpretation of reading material and literary materials, vocabulary, use of sources of information, correctness of expression.	9-12 College

At the elementary-school level, most of the achievement test batteries are valuable aids in the evaluation of growth of pupils. The scores are comparable from subject to subject and among the different forms of each battery. Thus, they permit an analysis of the pupils strengths and weaknesses, especially in the basic skills, and provide a profile of the individual's progress through his elementary-school career. The refined procedures used to select test content with curricular and statistical validity, the standard methods of administration and scoring, and the periodic revision of the tests and their norms enable the local schools to use the tests for a variety of instructional, guidance, and supervisory purposes.

At the secondary-school level, tests of general educational development generally consist of exercises in which information is presented in verbal, graphic, or other form, and test exercises are devised as to measure the general abilities of the individual to comprehence and interpret the material presented. Achievement measured in the manner contrasts with test exercises which emphasize the recall recognition of specific items of information, These tests measure the comprehensive objectives of instruction in the language arts, liteeature, social studies, science, and mathematics.

LANGUAGE ARTS

Objectives of Instruction in the Language arts

The scope of the language arts includes experiences and learning in reading, writing, speaking, and listening. Each of these broad fields may be further subdivided into the more specific objectives which, when defined in terms of learner behavior, make it possible to evaluate the progress and growth of the individual.

In reading, some of the specific objectives which teachers may wish to evaluate are abilities and skills in :

(*a*) reading readiness,
(*b*) vocabulary or word meaning,
(*c*) comprehension,
(*d*) work-study skills,
(*e*) reasoning, and
(*f*) tastes and interests in literature.

In writing, among the objectives evaluated are abilities and skills in :

(*a*) penmanship,
(*b*) spelling,
(*c*) writing grammatically correct sentences,
(*d*) using correct punctuation, and
(*e*) organizing and expressing ideas clearly and in an interesting manner.

In speaking or oral communication, the objectives to be evaluated may include several skills common to reading and writing, such as :

(*a*) readiness,
(*b*) vocabulary,
(*c*) reasoning,
(*d*) organizing ideas, and
(*e*) expressing ideas.

In listening the objective to be measured is chiefly comprehension. This, in turn, can be analyzed into such component factors as :

(*a*) vocabulary,
(*b*) interest,
(*c*) visualizing organization, and
(*d*) ability to make inferences.

Evaluation of Reading

The evaluation of reading involves not only the measurement of skills and abilities at the reading readiness stage of the kindergarten and first grade, but also the more complicated skills, abilities. interests, attitudes, and appreciations at the high-school level, To measure the scope of abilities, interests, needs, and attitudes in reading, various reading tests and techniques have been devised. In this discussion, the category of literature is subsumed as a part of reading. Tests of work-study skills and library usage skills have also been included.

Reading Readiness

In order to judge the pupil's readiness for reading, various tests and devices have been constructed to help the teacher in evaluating whether the pupil has a reasonable chance for success when he is introduced to formal reading. These tests, combined with other observations and judgments about the pupil's physical, mental, emotional, and social development, provide a guide for evaluating achievement, Representative reading readiness tests are listed in Table 2.

Table 2

Illustrative Reading Readiness Tests

Test and Publisher	*Date*	*Content*	*Grade*
Gates Reading Readiness Tests (Burean of Publications, Teachers College, Columbia Univ.).	1939	picture directions, word matching, flash card perception, letter and number reading, etc.	I

Lee-Clark Reading Readiness Test (California Test Bureau)	1951	Letter matching, letter and word discrimination,	I
Metrolitan Readiness Tests (World Book Company	1933	Picture matching, copying figures, vocabulary, picture directions, etc.	I
Monroe Reading Aptitude Tests (Houghton Mifflin Company)	1935	Visual tests, auditory tests motor control, oral speed, articulation, language	
Murphy-Durrell Diagnostic Reading Readiness Test (World Book Company)	1949	Auditory discrimination, visual discrimination, learning rate.	I

Reading readiness tests are usually administered to small groups of children, comprising not more than ten or fifteen individuals at a time. The directions call for drawing a line connecting pictures, words, or letters that are alike ; copying figures or letters ; and marking the drawing in a row of four or five drawings that represents the word pronounced by the examiner, for example, the drawing of a pencil, Following are sample test exercises of visual discrimination, which measure ability to match words that are alike.

> In each of the first two exercises the task of the pupil is to find and mark two words that look exactly alike. No reference is made to the meaning of the words. In the third test, the pupil is asked to look at the word "cup" beside the picture of the cup, and to draw a line on this word every time he sees it in a story in the exercise. By this picture-word-matching technique, he recognizes words in a meaningful situation.

In addition to group tests of reading readiness, the Betts Ready-to-Read Tests (distributed by Keystone View Co. Meadville, Penna.) are elaborate individual tests for assessing physical readiness for reading, visual perception, auditory perception, lateral dominance or sidedness of the hand, foot, and eye. The Betts-Keystone Telebinocular apparatus is essentially a stereoscope that permits the permits the measurement of visual acuity, astigmatism, eye muscle balance, and visual fusion when used with a standard series of slides devised by Betts.

Silent and Oral Reading

Among the first to construct pencil-and-paper tests to measure primary reading abilities of words, sentence, and paragraphs was Gates in his Tests of Comprehension of Words. Sentences, and Paragraphs, Comprehonsion is measured by the child's drawing a line from a word, sentence, or paragraph to the correct pictorial illustration. For pupils above the first-grade level, such test batteries as the Stanford, Metropolitan, Modern School, and California include measures of vocabulary and paragraph comprehension. Gray's Standardized Oral Reading Paragraphs and Oral Reading Check Tests provide measures of oral reading abilities from about the first or second grade level through the elementary grades.

Reading is an essential tool for the acquisition of concepts and information in all areas of the curriculum. For this reason, it is sometimes said that every teacher of reading. The ability to read with comprehension and reasonable speed contributes to the pupil's progress in all school subject matter. Reading is not a unitary ability ; it is a combination of component and related abilities and skills. The typical reading test taps many important aspects of reading comprehension. The various items require the child not only to get literal meanings and note direct details, but also to infer the meanings of words ; to see, follow, and infer relationship ; to weigh the significance of ideas to make subtle interpretations ; and to draw general conclusion about the content, tone, and purpose of the reading matter.

Table 3 contains representative reading tests at the elementary-and secondary-school levels.

Table 3

Illustrative Reading Tests

Test and Publisher	*Date*	*Content*	*Grade*
Elementary School			
California Reading Test - Primary, Elementary and Intermediate (California Test Bureau)	1950	Reading vocabulary, reading comprehension	1-3 4-6 7-9
Durell-Sullivan Reading Achievement Test—Intermediate (World Book Company)	1937	Word meaning, paragraph meaning	3 6
Gates Reading Tests—Primary Reading (Bureau of Publications, Teachers College, Columbia Univ.)	1942	Word recognition, sentence reading, paragraph reading	1-2
Gates Reading Tests—Advanced Primary (Bureau of Publications, Teachers College, Columbia Univ.)	1942	Word recognition, paragraph reading	2-8
Gates Basic Reading Test (Bureau of Publications, Teachers College, Columbia Univ.)	1942	Reading to appreciate general significance, to predict outcome of events, to understand precise directions, to note details	3-8

Lowa Every-Pupil Test of Basic Skills : Test A. Silent Reading Comprehension—Elementary and Advanced (Houghton Muffling Company)	1950	Paragraph comprehension, ability to grasp and understand details, organization of ideas, ability to appreciate meaning, vocabulary	3-5 6-8
Metropolitan Achievement Test, Reading—Elementary, Intermediate, and Advanced (World Book Company)	1947	Reading comprension, vocabulary	3-4 5-6 7-9
National Achievement Tests, Reading Comprehension Test (Accron Publishing Company	1953	Ability to understand general meaning, discriminate between words, evaluate factual material, interpret writer's attitudes	4-9
Nelson Silent Reading Test (Houghton Miffling Company)	1939	Ability to comprehend words, to comprehend the general significance of a paragraph, to note details, to predict outcomes	3-9
SRA Achievement Series—Intermediate : Reading (Science Research Associates)	1954	Ability to understand main idea, to infer logical ideas, to grasp details, to understand words in context	4-6
Stanford Achievement Test, Reading -- Elementary, Intermediate, and Advanced (World Book Company)	1952	Word meaning, paragraph comprehension	3-4 5-6 7-9

Secondary School

California Reading Test, Advanced (California Test Bureau)	1950	Reading vocabulary, reading comprehension	9-12
Cooperative English Test : Test C. Reading Comprehension—Test Cl. Lower Level, and Test C-2. Higher Level (Educational Testing Service)	1950	Vocabulary, level of comprehsion, speed of comprension	7-12 11-12
Iowa Silent Reading Test : New Edition -- Advanced Test (World Book Company)	1948	Rate of reading, comprehension, word meaning, ability to use skills in locating information	9-12
Nelson-Denny Reading Test (Houghton Miffling	1938	Vocabulary, paragraph reading	9-12
SRA Reading Record (Science Research Associates)	1947	Rate, general comprehension, paragraph meaning, sentence meaning, general vocabulary, etc.	9-12

The following test exercise in reading comprehension has been taken from the Cooperative Test of Reading Comprehension, Lower Level, Form T. The test items measure ability to note details, to infer relationships, and to draw conclusions about the content and tone of the passage.

"Alice !" called a voice.

The effect on the reader and her listener, both of whom were sitting on the floor, was instantaneous. Each started and sat rigidly intent for a moment ; then as the sound of approaching footsteps was heard, one girl hastily slipped a little volume under the coverlet of the bed, while the other sprang to her and in a hurried, flustered way pretended to be getting something out of a tall wardrobe. Before the one who hid the book had time to rise, a woman of fifty entered the room, and after a glance, cried, "Alice ! How often have I told you not to sit on the floor ?"

"Very often, Mommy," said Alice, sising meekly, meantime casting a quick glance at the bed to see how far its smoothness had been disturbed.

"And still you continue such unbecoming behavior."

"Oh, Mommy, but it is so nice !" cried the girl. "Didn't you like to sit on the floor when you were fifteen ?"

1. Alice's companion was apparently.

   1—1 a girl.
   1—2 her brother.
   1—3 her pet cat.
   1—4 the family dog.
   1—5 a doll. 1( )

2. When Alice heard the approaching footsteps, she was principally.

   2–1 happy.
   2—2 angry.
   2—3 alarmed.
   2—4 puzzled.

4. When she heard her name called Alice was evidently.

   4–1 reading to herself.
   4—2 reading aloud.
   4–3 lying in bed.
   4—4 dressing.
   4—5 making her bed 4( )

5. Alice was worried about the appearance of the bed because.

   5—1 she had neglected to make it up.
   5—2 her companion had been sitting on it.
   5—3 here companion was hinding under it.
   5—4 she had piled several books on it.

2—5 amused. 2( ) 5—5 she was afraid her mother might find the book. 5( )

3. We may infer that Alice is

3—1 rarely disobedient.
3—2 unable to read.
3—3 very much in love.
3—4 a spoiled child,
3—5 fifteen years of age.
3( )

The following test exercises onward meaning, or vocabulary, taken from the Stanford Achievement Reading Test, Intermediate, Form J. illustrate one method of testing for achievement in this aspect of reading.

1. A saw mill makes—1 wire 2 boots 3 needles 4 lumber 1 ( )
2. A pair means—5 many 6 one 7 two 8 three 2 ( )
3. Many Smith and John Doe are cousins if they have the same—1 grandmother 2 mother 3 sister 4 daughter 3 ( )
4. To receive a letter means to—5 mail it 6 get it 7 write it 8 see it 4 ( )

Generally, instruction in the elementary school stresses the mechanics of reading, whereas the secondary school and college stress the non-mechanical or thinking skills related to the reading process. Although these higher skills are measureable, it is difficult to define them and to construct items with which to measure them. Different tests of reading skills at the secondary school level apparently measure different abilities in reading comprehension, hence, the tests are intercorrelated only slightly. The reason for the relatively low correlation of the results among the different reading tests at the higher level may be attributed to the fact that no single analysis of reading skills at that level has been generally accepted. Also, the low correlation may indicate that the reading skills which secondary schools emphasize in instruction are numerous and not adequately sampled in any one given test (8).

Evaluating Readability of Printed Materials

Research in readability began with the attempt to classify the content of textbooks and other printed materials according to the level of comprehension difficulty, for example, fourth-grade, fifth-grade, sixth-grade, and other levels of average reading ability required for reasonable understanding of the content. The readability formula is a techniqne for estimating levels of difficulty in various reading materials. Several readability formulas are now used. The Large (8, 9) formula, for example, computes grade level difficulty or the basis of average sentence length, percentage of hard words, and prepositional phrases. The Flesh (5) formula is based on average sentence length and syllables per hundred words. An interest measure can also be computed on the basis of "personal words" and "personal sentences." The Dale-Chall (4) formula is based on a count of unfamiliar words and average sentence length.

Applying the Lorge formula to Lincoln's Gettysburg Address, the grade placement or level of readability is 6.5, or sixth grade fifth month. This is calculated as follows :

1.	Number of words in the passage	269
2.	Number of sentences in the passage	10
3.	Number of prepositional phrases	26
4.	Number of hard words in the passage	43

Computation

Average sentence length : Divide 1 by 2

$=26.90\times .7=1.8830$

Ratio of prepositional phrases; Divide 3 by 1

$=.0967\times 13.01=1.2582$

Ratio of hard words : Divide 4 by 1

$=.1599 \times 10.73 = 1.7151$

Constant Weight $= 1.6126$

———

Readability Index $= 6.4694$

The Lorge formula is representative of other readability formulas in which statisticai weights are applied to structural elements in a reading selection. The meaning of the index is the school grade at which the passage can be understood by the average pupil. The index can be used to place texts and other books at appropriate grades. Also, it indicates ways in which passages may be rewritten for appropriate placement at designated grade levels.

Work-Study Skills

Work-study skills, which are an aspect of reading, cut across many subject areas and, therefore, are discussed briefly. One of the earliest tests of these skills was Test B : Work-Study Skills of the Iowa Every-Pupil Test battery, This test provides measures of ability to read maps, graphs, charts, and tables, ability to find a topic in an appropriate reference book, and ability to use an index. Various library usage tests, likewise, have been constructed. In 1952 the Stanford Achievement Test battery included a subtest on similar study skills for the intermediate and advanced forms, and the Spitzer Study Skills Test for high-school and college levels was published. Still more recently, the SRA Achievement Series has also included a test of work-study skills at the elementary level. Representative study skills tests are listed in Table 4.

The following test exercises will indicate how some of the study skills are measured. The ability to read charts, tables, and maps is checked by reproducing the data in pictorial form and testing comprehension through a series of questions or test items referring to the drawing. The bar graph test exercises on the next page appear in the Stanford Achievement Study Skills Test, Intermediate, Form J.

Table 4

Illustrative Tests of Work-Study Skills

Test and Publisher	*Date*	*Content*	*Grade*
Iowa Every-Pupil Tests of Basic Skills : Test B. Work Study Skills—Elementary and Advanced (Houghton Miffling Company)	1940	Map reading, use of references, use of index use of dictionary, alphabetizing, reading of graphs, charts, tables	3-5 6-8
Peabody Library Information Test—Elementary Level (Educational Test Bureau)	1940	Library information, library skills	4-8
Spitzer Study Skills Test (World Book Company)	1952	Using dictionary, index, source of information, understanding graphs, tables, maps, note taking	9-12
SRA Achievement Series—Intermediate : Work-Study Skills (Science Research Associates)	1954	Using index, table of contents, reference materials, interpretation of graphs and tables	4-6
Stanford Achievement Test, Study Skills–Intermediate and Advanced (World Book Company)	1952	Reading charts and tables, maps, using dictionary, index	5-6 7-9

The following test exercises from the Iowa Every-Pupil Test of Work-Study Skills, Elementary Battery, Form N; illustrate the measurement of skill in using references.

1. Which would you use to find what a fable is ?
   ——An atlas ——A geography book
   ——A dictionary ——The Arabian Nights
2. If you wanted to learn about cork, which of these would you use ?
   ——An encyclopedia ——An atlas
   ——A dictionary ——A history book
3. Which tells the correct way to divide Christmas at the end of a line ?
   ——A speller ——A language book
   ——A dictionary ——An encyclopedia

In a like manner, the ability to use an index or a dictionary is measured by reproducing facsimile pages and asking questions which require the pupil to use these facsimile pages in answering the questions.

Table 5

Illustrative Literature Tests

Test and Publisher	*Date*	*Content*	*Grade*
Carroll Prose Appreciation Test (Educational Test Bureau)	1935	Ability to differentiate good prose from poor and poor from very bad	7-9, 10-12, 13-16
Center-Durost Literature Acquaintance Test (World Book Company)	1952	Identification of experts from books worth reading	11-13
Cooperative Literary Comprehension and Appreciation Test (Educational Testing Service)	1951	Perception of author's viewpoint, recognition of literary devices, appreciation of style and rhythm	10-16

Iowa Tests of Educational Development: Test 7. Interpretation of Literary Materials (Science Research Associates)	1948	Ability to understand a passage—its purpose, mood, literary devices used	9-12
Rigg Poetry Judgment Test (Bureau of Educational Research and Service, State University of Iowa)	1942	Ability to differentiate parody from correct version of poem; brief extracts used	9-16

Literary Discrimination and Appreciation

Techniques for appraisal in literature have been constructed especially for discrimination and appreciation. Most of these newer appraisal techniques in literature have tended to be of the objectively-scored type. Efforts have been made in the Cooperative Literary Comprehension and Appreciation Test, for example, to provide a valid measure at the high-school level of such insights and abilities as the student's perception of the mood of a selection, his emotional reactions to a passage, his recognition of mood or feeling and tone of the passage, whether it is facetious or serious, animated or matter of fact, satirical, humorous, or burlesque. Table 5 lists literature tests. For a more complete listing and an appraisal of literature tests, refer to Buros' mental measurement yearbooks (1, 2, 3).

The following exercise is taken from the Cooperative Literary Comprehension and Appreciation Test.

A FOREIGN RULER

(Written in the time of Napoleon)

(1) He says, *My reign is peace*, so slays
(2) A thousand in the dead of night.
(3) *Are you all happy now* ? he says,
(4) And those he leaves behind cry *Quite*.

(5) He swears he will have no contention,

(6) And sets all nations by the ears;

(7) He shouts aloud, *No intervention* !

(8) Invades, and drowns them all in tears.

15. This poem is applicable to recent times because of

    15–1 the modernity of its verse form.
    15–2 its comforting philosophy.
    15–3 the comparison to be drawn between Napoleon and Hitler.
    15–4 its international spirit.
    15–5 its anti-interventionist attitude. 15( )

16. The people mentioned in line 4 say that they are happy, because

    16–1 their enemies have been killed.
    16–2 they have a good ruler,
    16–3 they are afraid to say that they are not.
    16–4 they are glad to be at peace.
    16–5 they have been drowned. 16( )

17. In this stanza italics are used to

    17–1 change the rhythm.
    17–2 give an impression of shouting,
    17–3 keep the reader from reading too fast.
    17–4 create emphasis.
    17–5 take the place of quotation marks. 17( )

18. The writer's attitude toward the foreign ruler is one of

    18–1 admiration.
    18–2 submission.
    18–3 defiance.
    18–4 antagonism.
    18–5 gratitude. 18( )

EVALUATION OF WRITING

Grammar, Usage, and Spelling

In attempts to measure writing skills more economically, various standardized objective-type tests have been constructed. While there is a relatively high correlation between the rating of pupil products in writing and the results of such tests, it is true that these objective tests do not measure certain of the aspects and interrelationships in writing that may be obtained from the scoring of a pupil essay, composition, or similar writing effort.

In addition to the tests listed in Table 6, most of the achievement test batteries contain subtests on usage and spelling. Separate spelling tests are available also from most commercial publishers of standard tests. For a more complete listing and edescription of these, see the mental measurements yearbooks dited by Buros (1, 2, 3).

Analysis of Written Products for Content and Expression

The second major aspect of evaluating writing includes the measurement of the individual's ability to express ideas in various written forms. For many years the essay, theme, or composition has been the teacher's method for measuring this outcome of the language arts. For evaluation, this objective has generally been defined in terms of related skills and abilities. Some of the more commonly defined abilities are :

(*a*) writing grammatically correct sentences or paragraphs,

(*b*) organizing ideas,

(*c*) spelling correctly,

(*d*) expressing ideas in a form which is interesting and clear, and

(*e*) capitalizing and punctuating a sentence or a paragraph correctly.

All of these abilities and many others, it has been assumed, can be measured adequately in a student's or learner's theme, essay, or composition. The conventional method of appraising a composition has been for the teacher to make an overall evaluation of it on the basis of general impression. The evidence indicates that these overall impressions are usually based on rather superficial qualities of the written product. If an overall appraisal of the written product is to have meaning, reliability, and validity, it is necessary to define the factors which enter into the total evaluation and to assign or determine the weight to be given to each foctor. For example, if a written product is to be evaluated on the basis of such factors as spelling, punctuation, paragraphing, grammar and syntax, accuracy, vocabulary, power of expression, and general impression, then each of these factors must be rated separately before combining them into a total. Furthermore, the weight to be assigned to each of these categories must be determined. Stalnaker (11) and others recommend a compromise between the detailed analytic rating scale method and the overall general impression method. In this compromise, before the teacher rates the composition on the basis of overall impression, he defines the main factors that are to be kept in mind in forming this impression.

The principles of rating a written product are essentially those involved in scoring the essay examination. For a more detailed discussion and illustration of these principles and techniques, see Chapter Six.

Table 6

Illustrative Tests of Expression (Grammar, Usage, Spelling)

Test and Publisher	*Date*	*Content*	*Grade*
Elementary School			
California Language Test—Primary, Elementary, and Intermediate (California Test Bureau)	1950	Mechanics of English grammar, spelling	1—3 4—6 7—9

Iowa Every-Pupil Tests of basic Skills : Test C. Basic Language Skills—Elementary and Advanced (Houghton Mifflin Company)	1940	Punctuation, capitalization, usage, spelling	3–5 6—8
Iowa Language Abilities Test—Elementary and Intermediate (World Book Company)	1948	Spelling, word meaning, language usage, capitalization, punctuation	4—7 7–10
SRA Achievement Series —Intermediate: Language Arts (Scicnce Research Associates)	1954	Capitalization, punctuation, language usage, grammar	4—6

Secondary School

Barrett-Ryan-Schrammel English Test: New Edition (World Book Company)	1952	Functional grammar, punctuation, the sentence, vocabulary, pronunciation	9—12
California Language Test – Advanced (California Test Bureau)	1150	Mechanics of Engligh, grammar, spelling	7–12
Cooperative English Test: Test A. Mechanics of Expression – Lower and Higher Levels (Educational Testing Service)	1950	Grammar, punctuation, capitalization,	7–12 11—12
Cooperative English Test: Test Bl. Effectiveness of Expression—Lower and Higher Levels (Educational Testing Service)	1950	Sentence structure and style, verbal skill, diction, organisation	7–12 11—12

Iowa Tests of Educational Development: Test 3. Correctness and Appropriateness of Expression (Science Research Associates)	1948	Punctuation, usage, capitalization, spelling, diction, phraseology, organization	9—12

Handwriting

In penmanship, the measure is mainly the legibility of the individual's writing. The evaluation is mainly in terms of the performance or product of the individual. To evaluate this product, various standardized product scales of penmanship, such as those by Conrad, Freeman, and others, are available for use. Informal teacher-made scales may also be used. The reproduction on pages 260 and 261 of a part of a product scale for measuring handwriting indicates how the teacher may compare the child's product with a standard product to assign a scale value.

Table 7

Illustrative Handwriting Scales

Test and Publisher	*Date*	*Content*	*Grade*
Conrad Manuscript Writing Standards (Bureau of Publications, Teachers College, Columbia Univ.)	1929	A scale with which handwriting samples are compared for quality	1 - 8
Freeman Handwriting Measuring Scale (Zaner-Blaser)	1935	A scale with which handwriting samples are compared for quality.	1—6
West Chart for Diagnosis Elements of Handwriting (Public School Publ. Co.)	1926	Measures letter form, slant, coordination, motor control, and spacing	8 – 6

The limitations of the handwriting product scales are substantially the same as those of any scoring device, such as standard answers for an essay examination. The scoring is partly subjective and partly objective. The deg ee of objectivity obtained in the use of a scale is a function of the insight, experience, and background of the examiner who applies it.

Evaluation of Speaking and Listening

Although speaking and listening abilities and skills are considered essential parts of the language arts, few standard tests or scales are available for general use. Compared with reading and writing, research and experimentation in the measurement of speaking and listening are relatively limited. Some rating scales for speech are listed in Buros (1, 2, 3), and the World Book Company has published a listening comprehension test.

Speech Scales

Two scales for speech, Speech Attitude Scale and Speech Experience Inventory, have been published by the C.H. Stoelting Company. The Speech Attitude Scale for grades 9—16 contains items to provide information for discovering and diagnosing the individual's attitudes toward speech. The Speech Experience Inventory for grades 9—16 consists of items designed to discover the range and kinds of speech experiences in which an individual engages. Technically, the are scales or checklists rather than tests of abilities and skills in speech or speaking,

To evaluate oral composition, Netzer (10) experimented with a technique analogous to product scales in writing. Just as the quality of a sample of writing may be measured by comparing it with a series of samples graded in quality, so may the quality of a student's oral communication be measured by comparing it with a series of samples. Netzer's scales classify an elementary-school pupil's verbal responses to a story, to a picture, and to an object. These scales use recordings that are graded in quality. This technique is in an experimental stage, but it offers possibilities for development of evaluation in new directions.

Listening Tests

The Brown-Carlsen Listening Comprehension Test (World Book Co.) for grades 9 – 13 is the first to appear in commercially available form. It is designed to measure the ability of pupils to comprehend what they hear. The administration of the test is entirely oral, and may be given to groups of regular class size. The seventy-six text questions are organized into five parts to appraise immediate recall, following direcions, recognizing transitions, recognizing meanings, and comprehending a lecture.

The appearance of this test may stimulate further research and experimentation in the measurement of abilities and skills in listening. It represents a new and promising step in the measurement of a neglected objective on the language arts.

MATHEMATICS

Standardized tests in mathematics have been constructed for a varlety of objectives. At the elementary-school level computational skills are problem-solving are measured in the conventional subtests of the Metropolitan, Stanford, California, Modern School, and other achievement test batteries. Diagnostic tests for purposes of discovering strengths and weaknesses in arithmetic skills have also been constructed. The better known tests are the Brueckner Diagnostic Arithmetic Tests and the Compass Diagnostic Tests in Arithmetic. Since the majority of achievement tests in arithmetic deal with computation and problem solving, the types of items measure skill in the four fundamental operations of addition, subtraction, multiplication, and division for whole numbers, mixed numbers, fractions, and decimals. In recent years, however, there has been a trend toward construction of tests which measure such objectives as arithmetic vocabulary and concepts, quantitative relationships, mathematical understanding, and mathematical judgment.

At the junior-high-school and high-school level, two types of achievement tests are found. The first type may be illustrated by the Cooperative Mathematics Test for grades 7, 8, and 9, which emphasizes arithmetical skills, terms and concepts, applications, and appreciations. The second general type of tests measures knowledge, skill, and understanding in a special mathematical field, such as algebra, plane geometry, or trigonometry.

A discussion of aptitude or prognostic tests in mathematics will be found in Chapter Seventeen.

Table 8

Illustrative Mathematics Tests

Test and Publisher	*Date*	*Content*	*Grade*
Elementary School			
Brueckner Diagnostic Arithmetic Tests (Educational Test Bureau)	1940	Three test booklets—whole numbers, fractions, decimals	4—8
California Arithmetic Test—Primary, Elementary, and Intermediate (California Test Bureau)	1950	Computation, problem solving	1—3 4–6 7—9
Compass Diagnostic Tests in Arithmetic (Scott, Foresman and Co.)	1925	Twenty tests, each covering a basic arithmetic process in detail	2—8
Functional Evaluation in Mathematics—Elementary and Advanced (Educational Test Bureau)	1952	Computation, problems, quantitative understanding	4–6 7–9

Iowa Every-Pupil Test of Basic Skills : Test D. Basic Arithmetic Skills – Elementary and Advanced (Houghton Mifflin Company)	1940	Arithmetic vocabulary, computational skill, whole numbers	3—5, 6—8
Metropolitan Achievement Test, Arithmetic—Elementary, Intermediate, and Advanced (World Book Company)	1947	Arithmetic fundamentals, problems	3—4, 5—6, 7—8
SRA Achievement Series—Intermediate : Arithmetic (Science Research Associates)	1954	Arithmetic reasoning, arithmetic vocabulary, number recognition, computation	4 6
Stanford Achievement Test, Arithmetic—Elementary, Intermediate, and Advanced (World Book Company)	1952	Computation, problem solving	3—4, 5—6, 7—9
Secondary School			
Cooperative Algebra Test. Elementary Algebra through Quadratics (Educational Testing Service)	1940 et. seq.	Basic skills and principles, processes, relationships	End of course
Cooperative Intermediate Algebra Test. Quadratics and Beyond (Educational Testing Service)	1940 et. seq.	Exponents, factoring, progressions, logarithms, imaginary numbers, graphs, etc.	End of course
Cooperative Mathematics Test for Grades 7, 8, and 9 (Educational Testing Service)	1940 et seq.	Skills, facts, terms and concept, applications, appreciations	7—9

Cooperative Plane Geometry Test (Educational Testing Service)	1940 et seq.	Fundamentals of first course in geometry	End of course
Cooperative General Mathematics Test for High School Classes (Educational Testing Service)	1938	Arithmetic, algebra, plane, geometry, trigonometry, solid geometry	12
Davis Test of Functional Competence in Mathematics (World Book Company)	1950	Consumer problems, graphs and tables, equations, etc.	9—12
Foust-Schorling Test of Functional thinking in Mathematic (World Book Company)	1944	Ability to think in terms of concepts and symbols of mathematics independent of computational ability	9—12
Iowa Tests of Educational Development : Test 4, Ability to Do Quantitative Thinking (Science Research Associates)	1948	General mathematics involving practical problems	9 – 12
Lankton First-Year Algebra Test (World Book Company)	1951	Vocabulary, meaning and use of symbols, formulas, graphs, etc.	End of course
Seattle Algebra Test (World Book Company)	1951	Basic terms, formulas, binomials, simultaneous equations	End of course

Shaycroft Plane Geometry Test (World Book Company)	1950	Vocabulary, construction, computational skills, logical proof	End of course
Snader General Mathematics Test (World Book Company)	1950	Arithmetical concepts, informal geometry, graphs, algebraic principles	End of course

The test exercises used to measure computational ability and problem solving are well known to most persons. The following exercises from test 1 – Quantitative Understanding of the Functional Evaluation in Mathematics Series illustrate an emphasis on the measurement of meaning in mathematics.

Which one of the following is the largest number of pages ?

A. 199 pages

B. 109 pages

C. 201 pages

D. 210 pages

If you know the price of one bushel of apples, what is the quickest way to find the cost of 16 bushels of apples ?

A. adding

B. subtracting

C. multiplying

D. dividing

From the Cooperative Mathematics Test for grades 7, 8, and 9, Form Y, the following exercises are reproduced :

17. Of the following, which information might, in itself, be best represented on a graph ?

    1. The number of pupils making no mistakes on a certain arithmetic test
    2. The average speed of a boat on a certain trip
    3. The student receiving the highest grade in the final examination in English
    4. The hour of a particular day when the temperature was highest
    5. The number of absences in a class during each month of the year

22. "If equals are added to equals, the results are equal," Which of the following is the best example of that statement ?

    1. $1+8=3+6$
    2. $2+k=2+k$
    3. $3+3=5+5$
    4. $4+0=4$
    5. $2+2=4$

Arithmetic ranks with reading and writing as a basic tool of communication in modern culture. It is instrinsic to most activities of daily living – buying, making change, telling time, measuring, keeping score, and similar activities. Tests have been devised to measure computational skills, problem solving, and understanding of the meaning of the number system. Diagnostic tests in arithmetic permit an analysis of the strengths and weaknesses of an individual pupil. In a like manner, tests of algebra and plane geometry stress not only skills but also meanings of the processes involved. These tests help the modern school to evaluate the effectiveness of its mathematics program.

SUMMARY

Representative achievement tests in the language arts and mathematics are reviewed and briefly discussed in this chapter. The language artt include abilities and skills in reading, writing, speaking, and listening, each of which is ordinarily divided into subordinate abilities and skills. Writing, for example, includes penmanshlp, grammar, and composition. Mathematics includes abilities, skills, and concepts in arithmetic, algebra, and geometry. Standard tests in the language arts and mathematics have been constructed to appraise the several objectives of each curriculum area.

Achievement tests in the basic skills at the elementary-school level are frequently published in battery form, bound in a single booklet. At the secondary-school level, the common practice is to publish a series of tests for each school subject, each in a separate booklet.

In order to measure achievement in the basic skills adequately, standard tests should have curricular validity; that is, they should measure fairly the extent to which pupils have learned the curricular experiences provided in the schools. Since the abilities and skills in the language arts and mathematics are fairly uniform in the curriculum of most communities, the available standard tests tend to be valid measures of achievement for objectives of these subjects. In reading, these objectives include reading readiness, silent and oral reading, readability of printed materials, work-study skills, and literary appreciation and discrimination. In writing, representative tests of achievement are discussed for the objectives of grammar, spelling, composition, and handwriting, For appraisal of speaking and listening, some available speech scales and a listening test are briefly described. In mathematics, representative standard tests of achievement are cited for arithmetic, algebra, and geometry. Representative achievement tests in the various subject-matter categories are cited, but it is suggested that the reader consult the series of mental measurement year-books edited by Buros for more complete information about specific tests.

PROBLEMS FOR CLASS DISCUSSION

1. Analyze the results of a reading test administered to a class. Indicate the range of reading materials required to meet the individual differences in ability.
2. Administer a language usage test to a small group of pupils. Prepare a diagnostic summary of group needs for instructional purposes.
3. Construct an informal mathematics test. Administer it to several pupils and diagnose any individual weaknesses revealed.

16

Evaluating Achievement in Selected Courses

Compared with the basic abilities and skills that are universally sought in the language arts and mathematics, other courses in the curriculum vary considerably from locality to locality in their content and specific objectives. This variability makes difficult the construction of standard achievement tests for wide-scale use. In this chapter, achievement tests are briefly reviewed for such selected courses of the curriculum as social studies, natural sciences, music and art, foreign languages, industrial arts, home economics, and business education.

Content Validity

In the selected courses, the test user should be concerned with content, or curricular, validity. Before he uses a test in the social studies, for example, he should check the content of the test against the content of the local curriculum to determine whether or not the test material includes a representative sample of the abilities, information, knowledge, and skills which pupils have had an opportunity to learn. Unless the test measures fairly the objectives of the curriculum, its use in a specific school situation is harmful rather than beneficial.

The tests of general educational development, Interpretation of Reading Materials in the Social Studies and Interpretation of Reading Materials in the Natural Sciences, distributed by the Educational Testing Service, and corresponding tests in the Iowa series distributed by Science Research Associates, are attempts to devise tests for wide-scale use regardless of the specific content of the local curriculum. As indicated by the titles of these tests, the emphasis is upon measurement of the interpretation of reading materials, Specific objectives and content, except for courses that are fairly uniform in the schools of the nation, are best measured by tests constructed locally.

Tests of Knowledge and Performance

The majority of standard achievement tests are pencil-and paper types which measure knowledge acquired by pupils, This type of test is easier to administer and to score than the performance type of test. Performance tests are most commonly used to measure achievement in bookkeeping, shorthand, typing, drawing, sewing, and in the rating of products in industrial arts courses. In these tests, the pupil performs standard job samples and his product is rated on speed of performance and freedom from faults in workmanship.

SOCIAL STUDIES

The objectives of the social studies include the acquisition of basic concepts and information, study skills involving the reading of maps, graphs, and charts, the development of critical thinking, and growth in desirable attitudes and beliefs. In this chapter the discussion will be limited to the measurement of concepts, knowledges, and skills.

At the elementary-school level, the testing or evaluation of concepts and information in history, geography, and civics most frequently appears in the form of subtests of general achievement test batteries, such as the Stanford, Metropolitan Modern School, and California series. It should be pointed out, again, that social studies tests need to be checked against the curriculum content of the local course of study to make sure that they are valid measures of the concepts, facts, and skills that are emphasized in the local school curriculum. The variation in content of the social studies from community to community makes the measurement of specific facts and information difficult.

To some extent, this same caution should be observed at the secondary-school level because of the variation in the content of social studies courses in junior and senior high schools from community to community. There is a tendency, however, for the content of American history courses, world history courses, and other social studies courses to be more uniform in the higher grades. At the secondary-school level, moreover, new developments in tests have emphasized the measurement of understanding and study skills as well as the recognition and recall of specific items of information.

In order to measure concepts, information, and understanding, a variety of objective test exercises are used. Those types of exercises most frequently used in recent tests are matching items and multiple choice items. The matching items are best adapted to the definition of social studies concepts and terms and the identification of historical personages, places, and times. The multiple choice items are better adapted to measure understanding and judgment.

The following test exercise from a Cooperative American History Test illustrates the testing of terms.

1. Socialism	64. The executive is responsible
2. Despotism	to the popular branch of
3. Confederation	the legislative body ( )

4. Parliamentary government

65. The parts which compose the union retain their sovereignty ( )

66. The divine right theory tended to produce this type of government ( )

The following matching test exercise from the Cummings World History Test illustrates the identification of personages.

19. He established the practice of using chemicals to destory bacterial infections.	(*a*) Koch (*b*) Listef (*c*) Pasteur
20. He directed the study which discovered the cause of yellow fever.	(*d*) Pavlov (*e*) Reed
21. He discovered and developed a treatment for rabies.	

The following multiple choice exercise from the Crary American History Test illustrates the measurement of understanding.

67. American workers organized in labor unions after 1865 to—

(*a*) seek the overthrow of capitalism.

(*b*) seek better wages and working conditions.

(*c*) seek political control of the government.

(*d*) aid immigrants in becoming better Americans.

In Table 1, representative social studies tests have been organized under the headings : general social studies, history, civics, and geography.

Table 11

Illustrative Social Studies Tests

Test and Publisher	*Date*	*Content*	*Grade*
General Social Studies			
California Tests in Social and Related Sciences, Parts I and II—Elementary (California Test Bureau)	1954	American heritage, peoples of other lands, geography, basic social processes	4-8
Cooperative Social Studies Test for Grades 7, 8 and 9 (Educational Testing Service)	1947 et seq.	Informational background, terms and concepts, comprehension and interpretation	7-9
Cooperative General Achievement Tests : Test 1. General Proficiency in the Field of Social Studies (Educational Testing Service)	1947 et seq	Social studies concepts, ability to interpret social studies material in maps, graphs, and reading selections	10-13
Stanford Social Studies Test (World Book Company)	1953	Informational background : items drawn from history, geography, and civics	5-9
History			
California Tests in Social and Related Sciences, Parts I and II—Advanced (California Test Bureau)	1954	Creating the new nation, nationalism, sectionalism and conflict, emergence of modern America, the U.S. in transition	9-12

Cooperative American History Test (Educational Testing Service)	1947 et seq.	Basic facts and trends in economics, social and political development of the U S.	9-12
Cooperative Modern European History Test (Educational Testing Service)	1947 et seq.	Covers period from middle ages up to the present—understanding of movements and institutions	9-12 College
Cooperative World History Test (Educational Testing Service)	1947 et seq.	Prehistoric times to the present-political, social, and economic trends	9-12
Crary American History Test (World Book Company)	1950	Historical facts, understanding of historical processes, map skills, reasoning by inference	End of course
Cummings World History Test (World Book Company)	1950	Major historical events, dates, places, persons, and ideas in ancient, medieval, and modern history	End of course
Civics			
Cooperative Test in American Government (Educational Testing Service)	1947 et seq.	Conventional material generally taught in course in American government	End of course
Cooperative Test of Community Affairs (Educational Testing Service)	1941	Pupil information concerning community in which they live—geography, government. health, welfare, employment	9-12

Geography

National Achievement Tests, Municipal Battery : Geography Test (Acorn Publishing Co.)	1950	Geographic concepts, products, locations, customs, etc.	6-8
Modern Geography and Allied Social Studies (C.A. Gregory Company)	1950	Causal geography, trade routes, products, place geography, etc.	6-10

A comprehensive review of tests and measures in the social studies is provided by Wrightstone and Campbell (15) and by Wesley (14). The older reviews and listing of tests and measures can be brought up to date by consulting the mental measurements yearbooks by Buros (4, 5, 6).

NATURAL SCIENCES

For convenience in discussion, tests have been classified to correspond with courses in sciences as follows :

(*a*) general science,

(*b*) biology,

(*c*) physics, and

(*d*) chemistry.

These courses constitute the major types offered in the elementary and especially the secondary schools. At the elementary-school level, the measurement of concepts, terms, facts, and understandings in science is usuall accomplished by means of subtests in a battery of general achievement tests. As with tests in social studies, the content of science tests should be checked against the curriculum content of a local course of study to determine how valid science tests will be for a particular course of study. It is recognized that the content of elementary science will vary considerably from community to community, thus making the measurement of specific facts, information, and concepts difficult.

At the secondary-school level, there is a likelihood of more uniformity for courses, and progress in these courses will be more validly assessed by a standardized test than is the case in the elementary schools. Examination of published tests will reveal that the majority of standardized tests in biology emphasize the measurement of facts, information, and principles, as illustrated by the items of the Cooperative Biology Test. In the general science field, the objectives measured, as represented in the Cooperative General Sçience Test, include :

(*a*) facts, skills, and applications ;

(*b*) terms and concepts ; and

(*c*) comprehension and interpretation of general science materials.

This test emphasizes broader understandings rather than specific facts and skills of general science. In the field of physics, most of the tests deal not only with facts, information, and concepts, but also with an understanding of facts and their relationships. The more modern tests have also stressed the ability to read scientific materials and to understand and master the mathematical skills which are a part of physics. In chemistry, available tests generally emphasize a mastery of factual or informational items and concepts. In this area, too, more recent tests are also stressing the ability to determine relationships, the ability to solve chemical problems. and the ability to perform laboratory procedures.

The types of test exercises used in achievement tests for the natural sciences are similar to those used in the social studies, Since communication by drawings is often more effective than verbal presentation alone, more pictorial illustrations are used. The following test exercise from the Read General Science Test is typical of this type exercise.

In the natural sciences, evaluation and measurement are discussed in the Forty-Sixth Yearbook of the National Society for the Study of Education, Part I (9). Chapter 8 of this yearbook discusses how to judge the results of instruction in elementary science, and Chapter 15 discusses how to evaluate the outcomes of instruction in science at the secondary-school level. The series of yearbooks by Buros (4, 5, 6) may be consulted for information on specific science tests.

Table 2

Illustrative Tests in the Natural Sciences

Test and Publisher	*Date*	*Content*	*Grade*
General Science			
California Tests in Social and Related Science, Part III—Elementary and Advanced (California Test Bureau)	1954	Elementary—health and safety, elemenmentary science ; Advanced—physical and biological science	4-8 9-12
Calvert Science Information Tests—Elementary and Intermediate (California Test Bureau)	1935	Animal life. plant life, physlcal changes, earth study, sky study, elementary chemistry	4-6 7-9
Cooperative Science Test for Grades 7, 8, and 9 (Educational Testing Service)	1947 et seq.	Principles governing functioning of common mechanical and electrical devices, natural phenomena of the physical world	7-9
Cooperative General Science Test (High School) (Educational Testing Service)	1947 et seq.	Familiar scientific phenomena and processes	End of course

Read General Science Test (World Book Company)	1950	Air, water, heat, light, sound, magnetism, electricity, human body, etc.	End of course
Stanford Science Test (World Book Company)	1954	Life science, earth science, conservation, health, safety, elementary physics, and chemistry	5-9
Biology			
Cooperative Biology Test (Educational Testing Service)	1947 et seq.	Fundamental facts and principles basic to an understanding of biology	End of course
Nelson Biology Test (World Book Company)	1250	Knowledge and understanding of biological facts, terms, and principles	End of course
Chemistry			
Anderson Chemistry Test (World Book Company)	1950	Chemical changes, solutions, compounds, equation, ionization, scientific method, etc.	End of course
Cooperative Chemistry Test (Educational Testing Service)	1947 et seq.	Concepts and terms, reactions, properties, and preparations, etc.	End of course

Physics

Cooperative Physics Test (Educational Testing Service)	1947 et seq.	Mechanics, heat, light, sound, electricity, etc.	End of course
Dunning Physics Test (World Book Company)	1950	Mechanics, heat, light, sound elec-tricity, modern physics.	End of course

MUSIC AND ART

While it is difficult to measure some of the objectives of music and art instruction, even by the use of performance tests, progresshas been made recently in methods for appraisal of the more tangible outcomes in these two fields. In music, tangible outcomes as the aility to recognize and comprehen notation, ability to play the notes on a musical instrument, and the ability to recognize notes and melodies that are played, can be measured by record playing, checklists, and pencil-and-paper techniques. More specific information about skills, knowledges, and understandings in music may be found by reviewing the tests which are listed in Table 3 which accompanies this discussion. The measurement of music talent, or aptitude, which has also received the attention of test constructors, is reported in Chapter Seventeen dealing with the testing of aptitudes.

At both the elementary-and secondary-school levels, skills and abilities in graphic arts have been measured to some extent. The three types of tests now available in this field are.

(*a*) drawing, scales and tests,

(*b*) art appreciation tests, and

(*c*) art abilities tests. The drawing scale is illustrated by the Kline-Carey Drawing Scales. The tests in art appreciation are represented by the Meier Art Judgment Test. The art abilities test is illustrated by the

Lawerenz Test in Fundamental Abilities of Visual Arts and Knauber Art Ability Test. The various tests that have been devised for the measurement of aptitude in graphic arts are reported in Chapter Seventeen.

Art appreciation is generally measured in current tests by having the pupil choose the better of a pair of specimens. One of each pair has been changed in a specific element from the original form. On the answer sheet the factor, or element, to be considered is stated for the pupil as, for example, arrangement of wall and foreground, inclusion or omission of the horns on the animal, position of the figure, and direction of pine tree' main branch.

The informational aspects of music may be measured by a test such as the Kwalwasser Test of Music Information and Appreciation from which the following exercise on classification of orchestral instruments has been adapted.

Directions : Place the number after each instrument which shows the classification to which it belongs.

1. string section
2. wood-wind section
3. brass-wind section
4. percussion section

(*a*) Violin ( )
(*b*) Trumpet ( )
(*c*) Xylophone ( )
(*d*) Bells ( )
(*e*) Flute ( )
(*f*) Bassoon ( )
(*g*) Celesta ( )
(*h*) English Horn ( )
(*i*) Lute ( )
(*j*) Ophicleide ( )

It is apparent from the exercises cited from standard tests of music and art that knowledge about principles and skills as well as some aspects of appreciation can be measured. However, there are limits to the objectives that can be measured by such tests. The exercises are restricted to recognition of correct or incorrect practices and to recognition or recall of information. To measure or evaluate the performance of product of an individual requires a more informal method of appraisal. This method is normally used by the classroom teacher to judge the pupil's progress in abilities and skills in music and art.

Table 3

Illustrative Tests in Music and Art

Test and Publisher	*Date*	*Content*	*Grade*
Music			
Beach Music Test (Bureau of Educational Measurements, Kansas State Teachers College of Emporia)	1939	Knowledge of musical symbols, pitch discrimination, tone direction, time values, etc.	4-16
Diagnostic Tests of Achievement in Music (California Test Bureau)	1950	Time signature, major and minor keys, note and rest values, song recognition, etc.	4-12
Drake Musical Memory Test (Public School Publishing Co.)	1934	Pupil indicates whether repetition of a given melody is the same or differs in key, time, or notes	Age 8 and above

Kwalwasser-Ruch Test of Musical Accomplishment (Bureau of Educational Research and Service, State University of Iowa)	1917	Knowledge of musical symbols and terms, recognition of pitch names, detection of errors in time and pitch not values, etc.	4-12
Kwalwasser Test of Musical Information and Achievement (Bureau of Educational Research and Service, State University of Iowa)	1927	Information about notation, instruments, signatures, musicians, etc.	9-16
Musical Achievement Test (Bureau of Publications, Teachers College, Columbia Univ.)	1933	Musical notation, use of symbols, familiar melodies, musical terms, etc.	4-8
Providence Inventory Test in Music (World Book Company)	1932	Naming notes, signatures, rest values, melodies, etc.	4-9
Graphic Art			
Graves Design Judgment Test (Psychological Corp.)	1948	Perception of unity, dominance, balance, symmetry, proportion, etc.	7-16
Kline-Carey Drawing Scales (Johns Hopkins Press)	1933	Series of samples for judging performance in representation, design, and composition.	1-8
Knauber Art Ability Test (Alma J. Knauber, 3331 Arrow Ave., Cincinnati, Ohio)	1935	Drawing desgign from memory, completing design from given elements, etc.	7-16

McAdory Art Test (Bureau of Publications, Teachers College, Columbia Univ.)	1929	Requires pupil to rank in order of merit four variations of the same theme on each of 72 plates	9-11
Meier Art Tests: I. Art Judgment (Psychological Corp.)	1942	Requires pupil to select better of 100 pairs of pictures.	7-12
Tests in Fundamental Abilities in Visual Art (California Test Bureau)	1927	Recognition of proportion, originality of line drawing, light and shade, visual memory, etc.	3-12

Tests in music and art continue to be the subject of study and experimentation. Lundin (11) has reported briefly on the development and validation of a set of musical ability tests. Beverley (1) discusses the art teacher and evaluation in a special publication on present-day art education. In Buros (4, 5, 6) critical reviews of various tests in music and art are available.

FOREIGN LANGUAGES

The objectives in the foreign languages have generally stressed the ability of the pupil to read, write, speak, and understand a foreign language. These objectives have received defferential emphasis during the past decades. During World War II there was a renewed emphasis upon the objectives of speaking, or oral language, but in secondary-school instruction the major emphasis remains on reading and understanding a foreign language rather than upon writing and speaking.

The measurable objectives in the current foreign language tests may be classified as follows ;

(*a*) vocabulary or meaning of foreign words,

(*b*) reading comprehension,

(*c*) grammar, and

(*d*) knowledge of cultural history and literature. In general, the tests used to measure the various objective have employed multiple-choice format. In design, foreign language tests—of both modern and ancient languages - are essentially the same. The usual sequence in a subtest on vocabulary, a subtest on reading comprehension, and a subtest on grammar. In a few tests a section on cultural history and literature of the foreign country is included.

The items which follow are cited from a Cooperative French Test. They indicate the types of test exercises used to measure abilities and skills in reading comprehension, vocabulary, and grammar.

Illustrative item to test reading comprehension

J'avis cinq ans il y a vingt ams. Quel age ai-je maintenant?

1. dix ans 2. quinze ans 3. vingt-cinq ans 4. cinq 5. trente-cinq ans

Illustrative item to test vocabulary

pensee 1. cote 2. vue 3. idee 4. effet 5. arrivee

Illustrative item to test grammar

1,	est	Spanish is spoken here.	Ici (..........) parle espagnol.
2.	on	Strawberries are eaten	Les fraises (.........) mangient
3.	s'est	with sugar,	avec du sucre.
4.	sont		
5.	se		

Tests in other foreign languages use essentially the same format of items to examine abilities and skills in reading comprehension, vocabulary, and grammatical usage. In Table 14 typical tests for foreign languages are listed.

Table 4

Illustrative Foreign Language Tests

Test and Publisher	*Date*	*Content*	*Grade*
French			
American Council Alpha French Test (World Book Company)	1927	Silent reading, recognition, vocabulary, English-French grammar	9-16
American Council Betd French Test (World Book Company)	1927	Vocabulary, comprehension, grammar	7-11
Columbia Research Bureau French Test (World Book Comyany)	1926	Vocabulary, comprehension, grammar	9-15
Cooperative French Test—Elementray and Advanced (Educational Testing Service)	1942	Reading, vocabulary, grammar	End of two year or more of study
German			
American Council Alpha German Test (World Book Company)	1927	Vocabulary, grammar, reading, composition	9-16
Cooperative German Test—Elementary and Advanced (Educational Testing Service)	1937	Reading, vocabulary, grammar	End of two years or more of study

Italian			
Cooperative Italian Test (Educational Testing Service)	1947	Reading, vocabulary, grammar	One year of study
Latin			
Cooperative Latin Test—Lower and Higher Levels (Educational Testing Service)	1942 et seq.	Comprehension, grammar civilization	End of two years or more of study
Spanish			
Columbia Research Bureau Spanish Test (World Book Company)	1927	Vocabulary comprehension, grammar	9-15
Cooperative Spanish Test – Elementary and Advanced (Educational Testing Service)	1942	Reading, vocabulary, grammar	End of two years or more of study

Cheydleur and Schenck (8) discuss achievement examintions in foreign languages with particular reference to the credit systems used in secondary schools and colleges for placement and progress of the student. Buros (4,5,6) provides critical reviews of specific tests in the foreign languages.

INDUSTRIAL ARTS

Courses in industrial and vocational education generally include such activities as woodworking, carpentry, shopwork, metal work, electricity, printing, automobile mechanics, machine shop practice, and mechanical drawing. Although there are a variety of objectives to be attained in such courses, the tests which have been devised emphasize the measurement of interest and attitudes (discussed in Chapters Sixteen and Nineteen) and the measurement of knowledge and skills in selected industrial arts or trades. Information about industrial arts of trades is generally measured by pencil-and-paper tests. These include mechanical drawing tests, mechanical comprehension tests, of woodworking, and tests for machinists, machine operators, electricians, and those engaged in similar industrial activities. Performance tests have recently been used to observe and rate the abilities and skills displayed in doing sample jobs involved in an industry or trade.

Industrial or Trade Knowledge Tests

Both written and oral industrial and trade knowledge tests are used. Written tests are generally used to measure achievement in the acquisition of Knowledge about an industry or trade. The exercises measure information about the materials and tools used in the shop ; the routins, practices, and techniques used in the industry, and appropriate safety measures to be observed. Oral trade knowledge tests are used more extensively by employment agencies and personnel workers to check on the knowlege a job applicant has about a specific trade.

The following test exercises from the Purdue Technical Information Test for Machinists and Machine Operators illustrate one type of item used in written tests.

37. If it fits, the wrench which will probably do the least harm to the corners of a nut is (*a*) an adjustable, (*b*) an alligator, (*c*) an open end (*d*) a socket wrench ————————————————*a b c d*

75. To saw pipe, use a hacksaw blade containing (*a*) 12, (*b*) 16, (*c*) 20, (*d*) 24 teeth per inch————*a b c d*

The following item is cited from a test in auto mechanics, used in New York City high schools.

A slipping clutch is usually caused by (*a*) worn clutch throw-out bearing, (*b*) worn pilot bearing, (*c*) worn clutch facings, (*d*) excessive pedal clearance.

Variations of such test exercises are provided by drawings of a machine, part of a machine or a tool accompanied by a series of questions to test the individual's understanding of the industrial principles, practices, or uses involved.

Table 5

Illustrative Industrial Arts Tests

Test and Publisher	*Date*	*Content*	*Grade*
Examination in Mechanical Drawing (Educational Testing Service)	1945	Symbols, methods and practices of mechanical drawing	9-12
Purdue Blueprint Reading Test (Science Research Associates)	1942	Symbols, technical vocabulary, interpretation of drawings	9-12, Adult
Purdue Test for Electricians (Science Research Associates)	1942	Care of tools, safety measures, home installations, splicing wires, batteries, etc.	9-12, Adult
Purdue Test for Machanists and Machine Operators (Science Research Associates)	1942	Machine shop practice. use of lather, shaper, planer, grinder, milling machine, bench work	9-12, Adult
Test of Mechanical Comprehension (Psychological Corp.)	1951	Simply phrased questions about drawings reflecting mechanical principles	9-12, Adult

Limitations of informational tests about technical principles and processes are precisely that they measure knowledge and understanding about an industry or trade but may not necessarily measure ability to perform the skills on the job. There is no doubt that a positive correlation between knowledge and performance exists, but the magnitude of this correlation has not been established for various industrial operations.

In addition to the pencil-and-paper tests of industrial or trade knowledge and information, performance tests for automobile mechanics, machine and mental trades, electrical trades, cosmetology, and trade dressmaking have recently been formulated by the Board of Education of New York City. These tests consists of a series of standardized work samples which are peformed by the individual and observed by a competent examiner. The performance of the individual is observed and judged as he works, and an evaluation is made by means of a standardized checklist of the operations. Thus, it is possible to obtain not only a measurement of trade knowledge by means of information tests, but also measurement of actual performance on samples of work by means of direct observation and use of an evaluative checklist foa judging the competence with which an individual performs each of several processes involved in the work sample.

The following job samples were included in the performance test for auto mechanics. For the more complex jobs, a maximum of thirty minutes' working time was permitted. For the simpler jobs, a maximum of fifteen minutes' working time was allowed. The job samples included :

1. Removing, testing, and replacing the thermostat in an engine.
2. Making a compression test on the engine and recording the results.
3. Turning-up the motor by locating and changing a defective spark plug and setting the idle speed and idle measure.

4. Measuring with gauge the diameter and length of each step in the spark plug.
5. Setting toe-in of front wheels to a specified number of inches.

In order to provide for objective appraisal, specific steps in each job sample were defined and credit ratings for observed performance were agreed upon. Thus, for removing, testing and replacing the thermostat, the following steps and credits were used.

Step	*Credit*
Drained water without spelling	1
Knew where to find thermostat	1
Test of thermostat	2
Tightened flange bolts evenly	3
Replaced water without spilling	1
No water leaks	1
Proper selection of tools	1
Total	10

Tests of mechanical aptitude are discussed in Chapter Seventeen. These aptitude tests involve not only pencil-and-paper techniques, but also assembling small articles such as a lock or a doorbell.

Two publications offer many valuable suggestions on recent trends in test construction for the industrial arts. Micheels and Karnes (12) indicate how educational achievement may be measured by object tests, manipulative performance tests, observational methods, and appraisal of products or projects. Wrightstone and others (16) report on pencil-and-paper and performance tests devised to measure the effectiveness of trade education in New York City seeondary schools. As usual. Buros (4, 5, 6) should be consulated for critical reviews of recent tests for the industrial arts.

HOME ECONOMICS

In addition to the tests of industrial arts, similar tests have been developed for courses generally known as home economics. These tests are similar in format and purpose to industrial arts tests. In Table 6 some illustrative tests have been listed for such areas as food and nutrition, texiles and clothing, sewing, and household management.

Although the early tests in home economics were mainly terts af facts and information, more recent tests have included measurement of such objectives as attitudes, appreciations, and performance. Performance in sewing and food preparation has been evaluated by use of checklists or score cards.

Table 6

Illustrative Home Economics Tests

Test and Publisher	*Date*	*Content*	*Grade*
Cooperative Test in Foods and Nutrition (Educational Testing Service)	1947 et seq.	Marketing, menu planning, food preparation, food values, etc.	13-16
Cooperative Test in Household Equipment (Educational Testing Service)	1950	Selection, use, and care of household appliances and equipment	13-16
Minnesota Food Score Cards (Educational Testing Service)	1946	Cards for rating 57 products prepared in laboratory work in foods	9-16
Minnesota Tests of Household Skills (Science Research Associates)	1952	Foods, cleaning, laundering, child care	9-16

Illustrative test items about food, clothing, and personal care are :

Food. Of the following foods, a moderate serving of the one that would be used to gain most weight is 1. celery 2. chocolate cake 3. orange 4, cabbage 5. carrot.

Clothing. An oil stain may be removed with 1. water 2. bleach 3. benzene 4. peroxide.

Personal Care. In order to open the pores of the skin, you should use 1. an ice pack 2. a hot towel 3. application of cold water 4. oil or ointment.

As in the case of industrial arts, performance tests may be used in home economics. A performance test in dress making included the following job samples :

1. Preparing a tuck-in blouse for a first fitting, making right half of garment only.
2. Making a series of seams such as plain seam, French seam, slot seam, and corded piping.
3. Making tailored buttonholes with self-facing.
4. Making bias binding and roll-hemming.
5. Making machine tucks and bias facing.

Tests and other methods of evaluation in home economics are discussed by Brown (2) in Chapter 8 of her book. More recent trends in evaluating home economics are reported by Brown (3), Chadderdon (7), and Read (13). For critical reviews and listing of home economics tests, see the yearbook by Buros (4, 5, 6). Home economics is a field in which new measures have appeared more abundantly in the past few years.

BUSINESS EDUCATION

The courses offered in business education may be classified roughly into two categories. One of these involves content subjects, such as Business English, Business Law Economic Geography, and Business Training. The other category includes such subjects as bookkeeping and accounting, shorthand, typing, and general clerical skills. For informational tests, the test exercises are similar to those used in tests of English, Social studies, and spelling. The following exercises are illustrative of the items measuring syllabication and abbreviations in subtests of a stenographic ability test.

Syllabication

Station 1. st-at-ion 2. stat-ion 3. sta-ti-on 4. sta-tion
(Write the correct abbreviation for each)

Abbreviations

1. Free on board
2. For example
3. Hundred weight

In the following Table 7, representative standardized tests have been listed under titles commonly found in the high-school curriculum, namely commercial arithmetic, book keeping and accounting, shorthand, typing, and general clerical work. In the skill tests, the individual is given a series of actual job samples to perform and the test is scored in such a way that the individual is rewarded not only for accuracy in performance of bookkeeping, shorthand, typing, or clerical work, but also for the speed with which these job samples are performed.

Table 7

Illustrative Business Skills Tests

Test and Publisher	*Date*	*Content*	*Grade*
General Clerical			
General Clerical Test (Psychological Corp.)	1950	Clerical speed and accuracy numerical ability, verbal facility	9—16, Adults
Minnesota Clerical Test (Psychological Corp.)	1946	Checking names and numbers	8—12, Adults

Survey of Working Speed and accuracy (California Test Bureau)	1844	Number checking code translation, finger dexterity, counting	9—16, Adults
Thurstone Employment Tests : Examination in Clerical Work (World Book Company)	1922	Computation, spelling, coding, cancellation, classification	9—12, Adults
Commercial Arithmetic			
Cooperative Commercial Arithmetic Test (Educational Testing Service)	1944	Computation and problem solving	9—12
Gilbert Business Arithmetic Test (Bureau of Educational Measurements, Kansas State Teachers College of Emporia)	1941	Computation and problem solving	9—12
Bookkeeping and Accounting			
Elwell-Fowlkes Bookkeeping Test (World Book Company)	1929	General theory, journal, adjusting entries, ledger, statements, etc.	End of course
Examination in Bookkeeping and Accounting (Educational Testing Service)	1945	Accounting terms and forms, analyzing and recording entries, preparing work sheet, etc.	10 - 12
Stenography			
Blackstone Stenographic Proficiency Tests (World Book Company)	1932	Dictation, transcription, business practice, mechanics of English	10—12

SRA Dictation Skills (Science Research Associates)	1947	Accuracy and speed of ability to take dictation	10—12, Adults
Seashore-Bennett Stenographic Proficiency Tests (Psychological Corp.)	1946	Transcription of letters dictated at various speeds	Adults
Turse-Durost Shorthand Achievement Test (World Book Company)	1942	Language skills, shorthand penmanship, shorthand principles	10—12
Typewriting			
SRA Tpping Skills (Science Research Associates)	1947	Accuracy and speed of typing	10—12, Adults
Thurstone Employment Tests : Examination in Typing (World Book Company)	1922	Typing from handwritten and edited copy	9—12, Adults

Performance tests in business education include job samples for shorthand, typewriting, and bookkeeping. In a test constructed and used in New York City high schools for shorthand and typewriting, three letters were dictated, the first as a "warm-up" letter not to be transcribed. The rates for dictation were 64, 80, and 84 words per minute. The typing included setting up and typing a bill or invoice and the retyping of a revised rough draft of a letter.

In bookkeeping the job samples included :

(*a*) recording on special bookkeeping paper a list of business transactions,

(*b*) posting of entries, and

(*c*) correcting errors which appeared on a tribal balance.

For teachers and supervisors of business education, an entire volume by Hardaway and Maier (10) on tests and measurements in the business subjects has been written. The authors provide numerous suggestions for the construction of teacher-made tests and a comprehensive review of standard tests that are available from commercial publishers.

SUMMARY

The curriculum in the subjects of social studies, natural sciences, music, art, foreign languages, industrial arts, home economics, and business education may vary in objectives and content from locality to locality. This variation requires that the test user check the content of standard achievement tests in any subject against the local curriculum in order to determine whether or not the test exercises include a representative sample of the more specific objectives of information, knowledge, and skills which pupils have had an opportunity to learn. If the tests show curriculur validity, they may appropriately be used to measure achievement.

In the social studies, standard achievement tests have been constructed for general social studies courses, and for the usual courses in history, civics, and geography. In the natural sciences, standard achievement tests are available for general science, biology, physics, and chemistry. Achievement in selected objectives of courses in music and art may be appraised by standard tests, but test exercises usually measure knowledge about principles or theory, and those aspects of skill and appreciation which are amenable to pencil-and-paper testing, Included among the measurable objectives represented in current foreign language tests will be found vocabulary, reading comprehension, grammar, and knowledge of the cultural history and literature of a nation.

Tests in the industrial arts, home economics, and business education include pencil-and-paper tests and performance tests. In industrial arts, the pencil-and-paper tests measure trade or technical knowledge in such courses as mechanical drawing, blueprint reading, electrical installation, and machine operation.

Performance test, consisting of a series of standard work samples, have been developed for such courses as auto mechanics, machine shop, and electrical shop. In a like manner, pencil-and-paper tests in home economics measure information and knowledge about food, clothing, sewing, and household management. Performance tests measure skills and abilities in such courses as dressmaking, cooking, and cosmetology. In business education, pencil-and-paper tests are available to measure achievement in business English, business law, and business training. Skill tests in which the individual is given a series of job samples to perform with speed and accuracy are available for bookkeeping. shorthand, typing, and clerical work.

Although typical, or representative, standard tests of achievement in each of the selected courses have been cited, it is recommended that the test user consult the more comprehensive listing and the detailed reviews of tests in various subjects provided in the yearbooks edited by Buros (4, 5, 6).

PROBLEMS FOR CLASS DISCUSSION

1. Select a social studies or history test. Check the test items against your local course of study and report on the content validity.

2. Make a job analysis of some activity in industrial arts, home economics, or business education and prepare a tentative rating scale of steps in performance for one aspect of the job analysis.

3. Assume that you are planning to administer an end-of-year science test to a high-school class. Consult the Mental Measurements Yearbooks to obtain the critiques of test experts on the standard tests in science. Which test would you use ? Why ?

17

Evaluating Interests

"Interest" is defined in a variety of ways. According to John Dewey (4), "Genuine interest, in short, simply means that a person has identified himself with, or has found himself in, a certain course of action." Jersild and Tasch (6) emphasize that interest involves a freely chosen activity. According to Douglas Fryer (5), "Involves are the objects and activities that stimulate pleasunt feeling in the individual." Although interest is defined differently, there do not appear to be any contradictions or inconsistencies represented. An analysis of these definitions reveals a common concern with personal feelings, objects, and activity in a situation.

CONCEPT AND IMPORTANCE OF INTEREST

A superficial concept of interest, commonly held by some commercial people and educators, is typified in the practice of "sugar-coating" activities. These people feel that it is important to catch the interest (attention) of the person and hold it long enough to impart a message, a piece of knowledge, or a skill. In the classroom, this approach would imply that the teacher should use an extrinsic kind of appeal to make an educational task palatable. In such situations, learning is considered a distasteful matter which must be sugar-coated to make it endurable. This conception, though condemned by Dewey at the beginning of the twentieth century, is still in evidence in some present-day classrooms.

Interest must be seen as a correlative to needs. Since a growing boy needs to develop his physical self, interests like baseball, basketball, hiking, and related activities can contribute to such physical development. Similarly, the child needs to know how to communicate with his peers and adults. Consequently, speaking, reading, and writing activities appropriate to the child's level are interests which relate to the child's needs. Fundamentally, therefore, interests are significant insofar as they relate to the needs of students, for, when a student needs something, the interest (if intelligently selected) would reflect that needs. In general, when people need something, they will try to satisfy their need through some course of action.

It can readily be seen, then, that interests, growing out of student needs, become the motivating factors which call forth effort. Dewey (4) says that "It is not too much to say that a normal person demands a certain amount of difficulty to surmount in order that he may have a full and vivid sense of what he is about, and hence have a lively interest in what he is doing." Seen in this sense, interest and needs are significant in education because they are the wellspings of effort. The student needs no external discipline to apply himself when his work is interesting and meaningful. Interest is important in the educational process because it stimulates effort. In other words, interests are a means to an end.

What is a good interest and what is a poor interest ? Are interests universally good or bad in themselves, or are interets relative to persons, time, place, and culture ? While some work has been done to discover interests related to such variables as age, sex, and vocation (3, 6, 7), little has been attempted in the way of establishing standards of interests. While the teacher may select certain activities which he promotes as proper interests, and discourage (or even prohibit) other student interests, there are no absolute standards of goodness which are available. Generally, either thc teacher (or a group of teachers and the principal) or the pupils and the teacher together must establish criteria which serve as a basis for evaluating interests. The latter process is highly favored in educational circles, because it teachers students how to apply standards of their own choosing to common interests.

Undoubtedly, there are those who would maintain that standards for evaluating interests should come from some authoritative source (an absolute religion, judgments of prominent people, traditions, etc.). However, others would insist that interests should be appraised in terms of the consequences these interests have on the person or the social group. Despite this variety of possibilities, for the present, the appraisal of interests will remain a function of people, and people's values will serve as the standards. For instance, some music teachers may insist that an interest in folk music is inferior to an interest in classical music. This problem of what standards should determine the goodness of an interest, though unresolved, is related in education to the problem of what is meant by "growth" in interests.

"Growth" in education means an improvement in time over a previous status. If absolute standards were available or feasible, then the growth of an individual's interests could be gauged in terms of the extent to which they approached the desired status. If relative standards were applied, then again, for that individual in a particular situation or cultural setting, the degree to which his interests moved in the direction of desirable goals, to that extent the interests would be good, Depending upon circumstances, one may employ the following eight abstract considerations in evaluating interests :

1. Is the Interest Permanent or Temporary

If permanence is desirable, then a temporary interest may be evidence of lack of growth. If an interest becomes permanent and a temporary state of interest is considered desirable (an interest in comic books), then growth would depend upon the transient nature of the interest.

2. Is the Interest Deep or is it Superficial

Where depth is desirable, superficial interests would be evidence of lack of growth.

3. Is the Interest Broad or Narrow in Scope

At certain ages it may be felt that interests should be broad so that various avenues of self-expression may be discovered. At other times narrow interests may be desirable if specialization is culturally desirable.

4. Is the Interest Individual or Group-Centered

When it is desirable that a self-centered child learn how to play with others, desirable interests may be those of a group nature. Contrariwise, when it is desirable for a child to learn how to play by himself, individually-centered interests may be evidence of growth.

5. Is the Interest Active or Passive

For a child who needs to develop active interests, growth in interests would be the acquisition of desirable active interests, while for the child who is very active some relatively passive interests may be desirable.

6. Are the Interests of the Child Balanced

This criterion includes some of the other criteria, yet it is different from those specific ones. Does the child engage in interests which provide for his various needs ?

7. Are the Interests of the Child Moral or Immoral

While anthropologists have shown the relativity of what is moral from one culture to another, still for any given culture some interests are considered immoral and others moral. Whatever the standard may be for morality, the interest can be evaluated in terms of that standard.

8. Is the Interest Conductive to a Democratic Way of Life

In a country where the prevailing ideal is democracy, interests which have undemocratic characteristics or consequences may be considered poor, or evidence of lack of growth.

The student is caution, when applying these eight considerations in an appraisal of interests, to think through and to clarify in justifiable manner what interests evidence lack of growth and what interests show growth. Students should be careful not to fall into the trap of thin2ing that whatever exists is good or that present norms define adequate standards. Ultimately, what is good must be based on a consideration of appropriate ideals.

THE TEACHER'S ROLE WITH INTERESTS

There are at least six reasons why the teacher should be concerned with the interests of pupils. Briefly, these reasons are :

1. To Promote Desirable Interests

Each teacher, no matter what the age of pupils, has the obligation to promote desirable pupil interests. Since interests are basic components of living, the teacher who neglects them is failing to do a comprehensive job of teaching. Since pupils need encouragement in carrying on many desirable longe-range interests (reading books, practicing on a musical instrument, developing athletic skills, etc.) one important phase of teaching should include the promotion of desirable interests which already exist.

2.To Foster New Interests

Where students have limited or narrow interests, it be comes the job of the teacher to foster new ones. Students who come from poor home and neighborhood backgrounds can be provided with a wide variety of interests in school, such as clubs, sports, journalistic writing, dramatics, and other activities. The school as an educational agency serves to introduce new interests to boys and girls of varying backgrounds, rural or urban, rich or poor, native or foreign-born.

3. To Discourage Undesirable Interests

Although the school is a place where young people are prepared for living, to some extent it presents an idealized environment in which the young are afforded an opportunity to grow. Children are in a position to pick up all kinds of undesirable interests outside of school where society is far from ideal. Under such circumstances the school, through the teacher, should try to take the child with poor interests and discourage them by educationally feasible methods such as the positive substitution of more desirable interests.

4. To Develop Teacher-Pupil Rapport

The teacher is still considered by the pupil as somebody who is different from ordinary human beings and who is unusually interested in certain school or academic pursuits. To this extent there may be a gulf between pupil and teacher which inhibits free expression by the child. If the teacher is to develop a cooperative relationship with his pupils, a sincere knowledge of their interests will aid in establishing a friendly rapport.

5. To Enliven the Curriculum

Since subject matter is basically a means for learning such fundamental things as peronal discipline, social adjustment, self-initiative. and good work habits, as well as knowledge and skills, the leacher who capitalizes on the interests of his children by including those interests as part of the curriculum is well advised. The teacher must begin with the learner wherever and whatever his status may be and encourage the child to grow in a desirable direction. Through the incorporation of pupil interest in the daily classroom, the work of the school becomes more real, lively, and enjoyable.

6. To Provide Educational and Vocational Guidance

The teacher is frequently considered to be the one who will guide pupils through the maze of educational curriculla and to help pupils decide on vocations. While interest alone is not an infallible indication of probable success in further schooling or in vocations, still interest is considered a valuable consideration in conjunction with other data in guidance. Teachers need to become familiar, through the use of teacher-made and standardized inventories and quetionnaires, with the interests of their students.

EVALUATING INTERESTS IN THE SCHOOL

In attempting to evaluate interests, one faces three broad questions. First, *who* should evaluate interests. Second, *when* should one evaluate interests ? Third: *what general means* can be employed to evaluate interests ?

Who Should Evaluate Interests

In accordance with well-accepted objectives in education, the public schools strive to develop, among others, two essential abilities in young people :

(*a*) the ability to evaluate for onself,

(*b*) the ability to evaluate cooperatively matters of common interest and concern.

If these two abilities are to be developed, it follows logically that the answer to the question, "Who shall evaluate interests ?" is twofold, In the first place, the pupil must learn gradually how to evaluate his own intere ts. Second, since the child is immature at any given educational level, the teacher, other pupils, and the parents may all share in the evaluation of interests. Ih the school situation the pupil and teacher, separately or together, should be responsible for the continuous evaluation of interests.

When should one Evaluate Interests ?

The teacher should make provision for the evaluation of interests in four instances. First, at the beginning of a school year, a survey of student interests is invaluable as a means of familiarizing the teacher with the student and for purposes of describing the initial interest status of the student. Second, the teacher may gather evidence of the process which takes place when attempts are made to promote new and desirable interests and discourage undesirable interests. Such measures serve to illuminate any changes in interests or interest patterns which do take place, Third, the teacher should survey student interests at the end of the year in order to determine growth, or, in other words, desirable changes in interests from their initial status. Fourth, on special occasions for any given student or group of students, the teacher may desire to gather more complete information for educational or vocational guidance.

What General Means can be Employed to Evaluate Interests ?

Since evaluation involves an appraisal in terms of standards or criteria based upon evidence, there is a need for collecting accurate and objective evidence of the presence of interests before these interests can be appraised. In general, the teacher has two techniques available for collecting evidence on interests. The teacher can utilize appropriate standardized interest tests, but he must depend to a large extent on what he can devise by himself or with interested colleagues.

TEACHER-MADE DEVICES

There is a variety of general techniques which the teacher may employ to become familiar with student interests. Some of these are class discussions, student talks, interviews, checklists, questionnaires, rating scales, paired-comparison tests, inventories, diaries, anecdotal records, and logs. Naturally, some techniques are more appropriate to some grade levels and situations than are others. For instance, any written questionnaire would obviously be inappropriate for a kindergarten group. In such a case, an oral interview would be one of the best techniques for learning about interests. For an elementary-school group which needs practice in writings, an essay on "Things I Like to Do" would be an educationally useful method.

Although the teacher is generally not in a position to construct standardized and statistically valid and reliable measuring tools, it does not follow that the teacher may not be capable of developing techniques which have educational value. If a technique of gathering evidence on interests provides the teacher with sufficient data to help his students grow, it serves its function as an informal evaluation device. Many teachers *are* in a position to construct devices (with or without student cooperation) appropriate to their needs and level of teaching. Some useful approaches to the evaluation of student interests are presented below as illustrations.

At the nursery-school level an interview with the parent is a convenient source of data on the child. Responses by the parent can be remembered and written up later, or a simple interview schedule containing a checklist of interests can be used for immediate recording, The interview technique can be upplemented by observational notes on the types of interests characterizing each child. In working with the child himself, such materials as blocks, construction toys, dolls, puzzles, paints, clay, sand, water, and such tools as the hammer or screw driver can serve to reveal interests as well as other behavior resulting from the child's development and needs. Data gathered early in the school year serve as "initial" descriptions of the status of a child. For "process" descriptions of child growth in interests, the nursery-school teacher can repeat interviews with the child and the parent. In addition, for increased accuracy and objectivity in conclusions on child interests, such devices as anecdotal records, logs, and checklists can be used to show what kinds of interests the child is pursuing. Similarly. for "end" descriptions and appraisal of interests, the teacher may use any one technique or a combination of techniques already mentioned. Preferably the latter, thereby appraising the range and quality of new desirable interests which the nursery-school child has acquired during the year. A report to the parents on growth in interests can be oral, written, or both. A written record should be kept of the child's interests.

At the elementary-school level the teacher can employ any of the techniques already enumerated for the nursery school. In addition, the variety and complexity of the devices are greater since upper-elementary pupils are able to read and write and have had opportunities to engage in a large number of activities. One of the most practical techniques a teacher can employ to construct an interest inventory appropriate to his own group is to have the student write on separate slips of paper each activity he now enjoys, If the student can't write, the teacher can ask the student and then record each interest on separate slips of paper. After collecting all the slips the teacher can discard repetitions and then group similar interests on an inventory or checklisi. A suggestive illustration is the Ohio Interest Inventory for the Intermediate Grades. This inventory is scored for eighteen areas : Sports, School, Dramatics, Home Activities, Leadership, Science, English, Industrial Arts, Helping Others, Health, Movies, Doing Things Alone, Social Science, Mathematics, Music, Fine Arts, Reading, and Radio. The 360 items are arranged in groups of five similar activities so that the child is not made overly conscious of items concentration. Also, scoring each area becomes very efficient. Some items in the inventory are reproduced below to show their arrangement.

To play baseball	To watch football games
To take gym	To watch basketball games
To march in the gym	To climb trees
To do stunts	To know sports stars
To play relay games	To read stories about sports
To hear sports broadcasts	To go bicycling
To see movies about sports	To roller skate

To go swimming	To go ice-skating
To jump rope	To play hopscotch
To go hiking	To play games in snow

Because of the absence of any research data on validity, reliability, and norms, this inventory is classified as a teacher-made device. The manual which accompanies the test suggests various ways in which the inventory may be educationally profitable.

On the junior and senior high school levels, where teachers are generally specialists in one or two subjects, there is a need for becoming familiar with likes and dislikes of students for various subjects or subdivisions thereof. While the home-room teacher may be able to find time to engage in general interest evaluation, it is the subject-matter specialist who is desirous of tapping adolescent effort by organizing units about pupil interests. Also, in attempting to plan a program for a longer period of time than a month, the subject-matter teacher may wish to use a questionnaire or checklist. An illustration of a part of a teacher-made "Musical Interest and Skills Questionnaire" is presented below.

This device was designed to discover which pupils in a music class had either passive or active interest in music. In addition, the items were scored to reveal whether students were interested in singing, instrumental music, or other musical activity. Notice, too, that the fourth category of response, "would like some opportunity," may be a fine guide for the teacher who is trying to enlarge student interests. A questionnaire of this kind can be answered by the student on a separate answer sheet to facilitate scoring.

MUSICAL SKILLS AND INTERESTS QUESTIONNAIRE

Directions

The following questionnaire is devoted entirely to the musical interests which have been shown by high-school students. We want you to indicate whether you like an activity, are indifferent to it, dislike the activity, or would like some opportunity to do it. On your separate answer sheet beside each number indicate the letter which describes your feeling.

L means like

I means indifferent

D means dislike

O means would like some opportunity

1. To go to concerts.
2. To listen to the violin.
3. To play the above.
4. To sing in a glee club o rchorus.
5. To play popular music.
6. To listen to string ensembles.
7. To discuss the relative merits and demerits of various conductors of symphony orchestras.
8. To play the flute.
9. To listen to dance music on the radio.
10. To attend moves with a good musical background.
11. To play the violin.
12. To hear operatic arias.
13. To sing when you are alone.
14. To accompany a glee clube or chorus.
15. To hear organ music.
16. To attend musical comedies.
17. To sing in a school music festival.
18. To play in a woodwind ensemble.
19. To hear songs in foreign languages.
20. To take music lessons.

In constructing devices for appraising interests, the teacher may desire to become familiar with possible categories or types of items to include. Of course. the purpose of the instrument and the basic educational situation would determine the categories. The following possible classifications of interests are offered. In a sense, one may wish to refer to these classifications as dimensions for measuring interests. While there may be many more possibilities, or more important ones, these ten dimensions should be suggestive.

1. *Type of Participation.* Active or passive.
2. *Nature of Participation.* Individual, group, or both.
3. *Direction.* Personal or social.
4. *Content.* Vocational or avocational.
5. *Place.* Outdoor or indoor.
6. *Shool Subjects.* Chemistry, English, history, etc.
7. *Sehool or Life Areas.* Scientific, literary, artistic, etc.
8. *Type.* Human versus inanimate and non-human objects.
9. *Post Experience.* Interests were experienced or not.
10. *Enjoyment.* Like or don't like ; or other degrees of appreciation.

In surveying this section on teacher-made instruments or procedures for collecting and evaluating interests, it is proper to point out that the basic assumption underlying this presentation is that classes vary so greatly from school to school and in some cases within schools that it is not possible to hand out ready-made devices to teachers. Teachers may well cooperate with others one or two grades below and above them in order to construct with maximum efficiency instruments appropriate to their children. In discussing teacher-made devices one must indicate that their greatest value lies in flexibility of use and adaptability to the work of a particular class or school. Teachers, no matter what their grade level, can try out techniques on a preliminary basis and develop appropriate means to become familiar with, and to appraise. student interests.

STANDARDIZED DEVICES

There are few valid and reliable standardized interest devices available to teachers at various grade levels to help them evaluate the growth of the interests of their students. While one may understand the absence of such standardized devices on numerous grounds, such as the complexity of encompassing the wide range of human interests into manageable categories and standardizing them for various factors such as age, sex, residence, etc., still one must not neglect the fact that interest measurement was not begun until the 1920's.

Until very recently, the field of interest measurement has remained relatively unexplored. Even at the present time, however, the major emphasis in interest measurement is on vocational guidance, not classroom or educational guidance.

The elementary-school classroom teacher will find virtually no standardized tests available to help diagnose and evaluate child interests. For the high-school teacher the main value to be derived from standardized interest inventories is from the few useful vocational interest scales. For the convenience of the teacher. Table 8 summarizing school and vocational interest measures is presented.

Table 8

Illustrative School and Vocational Intercst Inventories

Test and Publisher	*Date*	*Aspects Measured*	*Grad*
Brainard Occupational Preference Inventory (Psychological Corp.)	1945	Commercial, personal service, agricultural, mechanical, professional, esthetic, scientific	9-16 Adults

Cleeton Vocational Interest Inventory (McKnight and McKnight)	1943	Mechanical, scientific, artistic, etc.	9-16 Adults
Interest Index : General Education Series (Educational Testing Service)	1950	Sports, science, literature, etc.	7-13
Kuder Preference Record—Vocational (Science Research Associates)	1948	Mechanical, compu, tational, scientific, persuasive, artistic, musical, literary, clerical	9-16 Adults
Kuder Preference Record – Personal (Science Research Associates)	1948	Working with ideas, being active in groups, avoiding conflicts, directing others, being in familiar and stable situations	9-16 Adults
Occupational Interest Inventory—Intermediate and Advanced (California Test Bureau)	1944	Personal-social, natural, mechanical, business, the arts, the sciences	7-12 9-16 Adults
Primary Business Interests Test (Science Research Associates)	1942	Accounting, collections, sales-office, sales store, strenographic filling	9-16 Adults
Thurstone Interest Schedule (Psychological Corp.)	1947	Physical science, biological science, computational, business, executive, persuasive, linguistic, humanitarian, artistic, musical	9-16 Adults

Vocational Interest Analysis (California Test Bureau)	1953	Personal-social, natural, mechanical, business, the arts, the sciences	9-16 Adults
Vocational Interest Blank – Men and Women (Stanfor Unieverity Press)	1947	Scoring keys for interests similar to artist, dentist, farmer, etc. (47 occupational keys for men, 28 for women)	12-16 Adults
What I Like to Do (Science Research Associates)	1954	Art, music, social studies, active play, manual arts, home home arts, science.	4-7

In general, for the present, the most convenient device that the high-school teacher can employ without spending too much time and money is the Kuder Preference Record. The Kuder Preference Record is a group test, easily administered and scored, which yields scores in nine different areas :

(1) mechanical,

(2) computational,

(3) scientific,

(4) persuasive,

(5) artistc,

(6) literary,

(7) musical,

(8) social service, and

(9) clerical. A classification of selected occupations under each general area is provided to help the guidance person find appropriate levels and kind of occupations.

The Kuder Preference Record is designed so that the individual indicates the activity he prefers most and the activity he prefers least out of a group of items. Nine sample items out of a total of approximately 500 drawn from Form C are as follows :

(*g*) Draw a comic strip
(*h*) Write advertising for electrical appliances
(*j*) Operate a truck farm
(*k*) Experiment with making some candy for which you didn't have the recipe
(*l*) Tell stories to children
(*m*) Paint water colors
(*n*) Do chemical research
(*p*) Interview applicants for employment
(*q*) Write feature stories for a newspaper

Experienced counselors would be more inclined to use a combination of devices, but for the regular classroom teacher, for whom vocational guidance is a job to be done in little time at little expense, the Kuder Preference Record or similar inventories are appropriate.

The Maller-Glaser Interest-Values Inventory can be used as a means of providing guidance for high-school students in matters of curriculum and adjustment. The inventory is self-administering and takes less than thirty minutes. It indicates a measure of the relative dominance of four major types of interest : theoretic, aesthetic, social and cconomic. In addition, data are provided on such personal material as security, social appraisal, sense of achievement, and sense of belonging.

Another convenient and inexpensive interst inventory which might be used by the classroom teacher is the Cleeton Vocational Interest Inventory. There are separate blanks for men and women. In all, there are 700 items, 70 for each of ten fields of work, The administration and scoring are relatively easy, but as in most standardized tests, the teacher must be careful to interpret the results properly. For more complete information abaut these devices, teachers are advised to order specimen sets and read them critically. Then, to check on his own judgment, the teacher might examine the reviews in Buros (1, 2).

It might be said that the paucity of standarized tests for evaluating other than vocational interests compels the teacher to depend upon self-made devices or to neglect this area of testing. However, for vocational testing and academic guidance the high-school teachear has a few possibilities which, though not adequately validated, provide important information.

SUMMARY

Interest is considered to be freely chosen enjoyable activities which basically relate to needs and derives. It seems to be true, that when pupils are interested they work longer, harder and more effectively under self-discipline than otherwise. Although there are no lists of absolute standards which define a good interest or a bad interest, daily behaviour of teachers and parents reveals the presence of standards. Since standards appear to be relative to the child and the situation, evaluation of interests in terms of standards needs to be done continuously by those involved in the educational situation. Growth is defined as the acquisition of new interests or the development of desirable interests and the loss or avoidance of undersirable interests.

The teacher concerned with interests may :

(*i*) promote desirable interests among students,

(*ii*) foster new interests,

(*iii*) discourage undesirable interests,

(*iv*) use interests to develop increasing repport between himself and the pupils,

(*v*) use interests to motivate pupils in the curriculum, and

(*vi*) use interests in educational and vocational guidance.

A continuous record of pupil interests should be kept in order to promote these ends.

Interests should be evaluated continuously and cooperatively by pupils, teachers, and parents. This evaluation should include initial measures at the beginning of the term, process measures during the term, and final measures at the end of the school year. Also, for special purposes, the interests of any pupil or group of pupils may be studied at any time. In the absence of standardized measures the teacher may construct his own from such techniques as class discussion, student talks, interviews, checklists, questionnaires, rating scales, paired-comparison tests, inventories, diaries, anecdotal records, and logs. Dimensions for analyzing interests are presented. The main value of standardized devices for the teacher in the field of interests is to provide additional data for vocational guidance.

PROBLEMS FOR CLASS DISCUSSION

1. Administer a standardized interest inventory to several pupils and interpret the results for each pupil.
2. Analyze the responses of a class to the topic : "What I like about television." Determine what interests and needs are met by this activity.
3. Construct an interest inventory for children of the grade level or subject you teach or are preparing to teach. Administer the inventory to a class and determine which interests might be used for class projects or activities Which interests are mainly of an individual nature ?

18

Evaluating Aptitudes

Most persons would like to gaze into the crystal ball of the future and by some magic inight gained thereby find the occupations and activities that most precisely fit their potential abilities, attitudes, interests, and skills. Aptitude tests art used by the psychologist to provide a more relable and valid prediction. So complex is the pattern of psychological functioning required in any situation, however, that prediction through aptitude tests must be based on piecemeal evidence.

Frequently, one hears people raise questions about aptitudes. Would it be wise to give Mary, age eight, piano lessons? Johnny has been studying violin for two years without much success ; should he continue ? Look at this drawing Louis ; do you think he should become an artist ? Janet is very slow in her work in kindergarten ; do you think she will be able to do able to do first-grade reading successfully ? These and similar important decisions have to be made daily by people. A knowledge of aptitudes may make such decisions more intelligent. College ask : Does the prospective student have aptitude for engineering or law or medicine ? Business and industrial firms want to know about prospective employees : Do they have mechanical aptitude ? Military services ask similar questions about aptitude for airplane pilot training radio technician, and other specialized jobs. .

THE NATURE OF APTITUDES

In the Dictionary of Education (4) aptitude is described as a "pronounced innate capacity for or ability in a given line of endeavor, such as a particular art, school subject. or vocation." In the same volume, capacity is defined as "the potentiality of a person for a given function as conditioned by the total pattern of causes ; partly hereditary and partly environmental". Ability is defined as "the actual power present in an organism to carry to completion any given act or to make adjustments successfull". According to H.C. Warren (11) in the Dictionary of Psychology, aptitude is "A condition or set of characteristics regarded as symptomatic of an individual's ability to acquire with trainingy some (usually specified) knowledge, skill, or set of responses, such as the ability to speak a languae, to produce music .."

An analysis of these definitions reveals the use of seemingly conflicting terms like "natural or acquired, innate capacity or ability, potentiality or actual achievement, and hereditary or environmental." These definitions and terms necessitate a discussion of four fundamental considerations in defining the nature of aptitudes. These four questions are as follows :

1. Are aptitudes innate or acquired ?
2. Are aptitudes unitary or pluralistic ?
3. Are aptitudes constants or variables ?
4. Are aptitudes distributed "normally" or multifariously ?

Are Aptitudes Innate or Acquired

There are probably no responsible educators who would deny that heredity plays a significant role in defining the limits of potentially of an individual. At the beginning of the twentieth century most of the authorities in educational psychology supported the theory that "intelligence" and other aptitudes were inherited and that the environment played a very minor role in their development. In the past two decades, however, as a result of theory and research, educational psychologist have moved in the direction of according "nurture" significant credit for developing and improving aptitudes. Current research supports the thesls that both factors interact and contribute to the development of aptitude.

Are Aptitudes Unitary or Pluralistic ?

Historically, educators have behaved as though an aptitude was unitary, that is, a function of a single general trait or characteristic. This belief is reflected in the practice which is still not uncommon, of using the score on an intelligence test as as indication of the total academic ability of a person. In recent decades, the application of factor analysis enabled research workers to identify the special, independent basie aptitudes and abilities that may be the component parts of a more comprehensive activity, task, occupation, or psychological function Modern research supports the thesis that aptitudes are pluralistic rather than unitary. In an early study, for example, Kelley (7) identified the following seven factors ; verbal, numerical, spatial, motor, musical, social, and mechaical. Thurstone (10), basing his work on more extensive factor analyses of tests, has thus far identified the following relatively independent factors : verbal fluency, number, memory, spatial, reasoning, deduction, and induction.

The extensive factor analysis made by the United States Employment Service under the direction of Shartle (8) identified eleven basic aptitudes, most of them similar to the Thurstone analysis, plus psychomotor factors not included ,n previous test analysis. The comprehensive analysis made by the Army Air Forces and reported by Guilford (5) resulted in the identification of twenty-eight primary abilities.

Are Aptitudes Constants or Variables ?

Whether or not one is born with an aptitude or whether aptitudes are unitary or pluralistic, another controversial point involves the question : Are aptitudes constants or variables ?

This argument has appeared more popularly in the controversy surrounding the stability of the I.Q. The basic question seems to be whether one's academic aptitude can be raised as a result of education or environmental stimulation. It is interesting to note that practically nobody argues the question whether intelligence is subject to decline or to change downwards. But is it possible for aptitudes to change ? So long as one assumes the stability of the I.Q., or any other index of an aptitude, one may explain away unusual cases of instability by referring to unusual social, personal, or psycholngical circumstances, or to the unreliability of the test or the test administration. While the evidence is conflicting, the trend seems to be in the direction of assuming that aptitudes are somewhat variable, and are affected within limits by educational and environmental influences. A tremendous amount of research is still needed to clarify this issue.

Are Aptitudes Distributed "Normally" or Multifariously ?

It is a commonly accepted idea that "intelligence," as well as other aptitudes, is normally distributed. By a "normal" distribution one means that very few people have extremes of goodness or poorness and that most people cluster about the average.

The per cent figures recorded between the lines under the curve represent the approximate percentage of people who obtain scores within one, two, or three standard deviations from the mean. The findings of various scientists that height, weight, and other physical measurements approximate a normal curve encouraged psychologists, who desired to achieve as successful results in the social sciences through the application of scientific methods. including statistics, to apply the normal curve to psychological data. Thus, Hull (6), in his classic book on aptitude testing, indicated that, because the bell-shaped distribution is so characteristic of all forms of human behaviour, it should be considered at least approximately true in the case of any aptitude unless there is definite evidence to the contrary. Most present-day workers in the field will accept this point of view.

THE PLACE OF APTITUDES IN EDUCATION

There are at least five main concerns that the school should have with reference to aptitudes. In the first place, the school should be responsible for identifying the general or special aptitudes of each pupil. Second, assuming that some aptitudes may be the result more of nature than of nurture, the school should then encourage the process of maturation. Third, assuming that some aptitudes may be more the result of nurture than of nature, the school should develop and encourage such aptitudes. Fourth, the school should utilize its knowledge of student aptitudes in educational guidance. Fifth, the school should avail itself of its knowledge of student aptitudes in vocational guidance. More specifically, what is involved in each of these five major concerns of the schools in pupil aptitudes ?

Identification of Aptitudes

By the time a child enters nursery school or kindergarten, he has been subjected to at least three or four years of a life filled with all kinds of experiences. Children in the public schools come from different types of homes, communities. and socio economic classes. Within these homes, communtties, and socio-economic classes, various types of ideals, goals, and practices are countenanced or discouraged. Out of these various personal and material influenees interacting with the child, a wide variety of talents and abilities arise. ("Talent" is used to signify capacity when its presence is not accounted for by environmental influences or education. "Ability" refers to capacities partly accounted for by environmental or educational influences.) Sometimes these aptitudes seem to be products of nature, at other times consequences of chance or deliberate education. Whatever the circumstances, the child possesses at various stages in his development a number of aptitudes. The school needs to identify these capacities in order to provide the child with the education best suited to his needs and the social welfare.

What capacities should be identified ? In general, depending upon school means and curriculum, some attention should be paid to intellectual, mechanical, artistic, social, athletic, and occupational aptitudes. Each of these should be evaluated during those times when most pertinent. For instance, vocational aptitude tests. inappropriate at the kindergarten level, would be useful at the junior- or senior-high-school level. On the other hand, mental capacity to learn to read and write should be measured as early as feasible after school entrance in order to guide the teacher in how to teach each child and in deciding what to expect from each child. The identification of aptitudes is a necessary prerequisite to education.

Encourage Development of Talents

The public school has the responsibility for encouraging the development of pupil talents. Once the talents have been identified, a series of curriculor experiences should be afforded each child so that he may develop to his highest possible levels of attainment. Some of the talents which are relatively neglected in elementary and secondary classrooms are music, painting, sculpture, industrial arts, and creative expression in language arts.

Develop and Encourage Pupil Abilities

The public school has a responsibility to develop and encourage certain pupil aptitudes. Basic to the elementary-school program are writing, reading, arithmetic, and social adjustment skills and knowledges. Once these abilities are identified and measured, the school must provide appropriate curricula to encourage their development.

Provide Educational Guidance

Teachers and guidance specialists in the school have a continuous obligation to guide students in their educational progress. Such guidance may involve selecting students properly for individual or group experiences, grouping pupils for special work, or assigning students to special classes, such as remedial reading or slow learning sections. When verified aptitude scores are especially high or low, teachers are in a more assured position for the decisions they make, or help students and parents make, for purposes of promotion or classification. Readiness tests, "intelligence" tests, and survey achievement tests are the most frequently used instruments for helping teachers provide such guidance on the elementry level. On the junior- and senior-high-school levels, achievement. "intelligence," and special vocational aptitude tests are used to advise students on whether to follow academic, commercial, or other types of education programs.

Provide Vocational Guidance

An increasing use of aptitude tests at the junior and senior high-school level is being made in order to provide vocational guidance. Youth who are ready to leave school to go to work at ages 16 to 18 are given various tests to help identify aptitudes. On the basis of these test scores and other relevant data, students advised or are given a choice of vocational avenues. For those students going on to college, various college aptitude tests are given to advise students on the type of college curriculum which may be best suited for them.

THE EVALUATION OF APTITUDES

The question of how aptitudes should be evaluated involves several considerations :

(*a*) Who should evaluate aptitudes in the schools ?

(*b*) When should aptitudes be evaluated ?

(*c*) How or by what means should aptitudes be evaluated ?

Who Should Evaluate Aptitudes ?

In school practice, there are various persons or groups who are responsible for administering, scoring, and interpreting aptitude tests. The psychometrist, school psychologist, school counselor, school supervisor, teacher, or public and private testing agencies are all persons and groups who either share in the process or carry on exclusively the aptitude testing in a school system. In general, it may be said that individual tests (that is, tests administered to one individual at a time, like the Stanford-Binet, etc.) are usually administered by a trained psychologist or psychometrist. In larger city school systems a staff of psychologists is usually responsible for individual testing of aptitudes and sometimes for group testing in classrooms. In smaller school systems there may be a visiting school psychologist who handles individual aptitude testing.

In larger cities, there may be various agencies, public or private, which offer services free or at a small fee to those seeking to take aptitude tests. Many universities have clinics attached to their psychology departments which offer parents the opportunity to have their children tested. Also, there may be various social agencies such as a Catholic Guidance Bureau or a Jewish Vocational Guidance Bureau which offer aptitude testing services. In most large cities, there are private vocational counseling and placement firms which provide a battery of tests (including aptitude) to fee-paying clients. One must learn whether bureaus offering such services have staffs adequately trained to administer and inserpret aptitude tests before recommending such agencies to parents or pupils.

In a school system, the teacher as guide should have a major responsibility in interpreting individually administered aptitude test scores. In addition, the teacher should be in a position to administer and interpret any appropriate group tests which his class may need. In this way, on the basis of aptitude test scores, achievement test data, classroom observation, case and cumulative data, and other records on the child, including a knowledge of home and family background, the teacher can help the child to progress in school and to make wise educational and vocational choices.

When Should Aptitude be Evaluated ?

Since one of the main purposes of administering an aptitude test is to find out how well a child can be expected to perform in any given experience or subject, such tests should be given at any time a teacher needs evidence concerning aptitudes. Also, when a pupil is under special study, aptitude tests should be administered so long as the pupil's condition permits their use.

Beginning with the lower grades, there are various instances when it is necessary to make decisions on pupil selection and grouping. Children who are slightly under age chronologically are sometimes permitted to take an individual intelligence test for entrance into kindergarten or first grade. After school entrance, group tests are generally given to children at some time during the first grade. Readiness tests in reading and arithmetic are generally administered during the first grade, or thereafter as appropriate to the type of children being taught.

In large school systems, a group intelligence test is generally repeated about every two or three years. Thus, if the initial test is administered in the first grade, the school system will repeat testing with an alternate or higher form in grade three, in grade five or six, in seven, eight, or nine, and in eleven or twelve. This is done in order to check on the reliability and validity of each child's intelligence test score. At various points in the child's scholastic career, these tests serve as partial bases upon which advice is given as to educational or vocational choices the pupil must make.

Two other types of aptitude testing take place at the junior- and senior-high-school levels. From the seventh grade to the tweifth, aptitude tests in such special subjects as algebra, stenography, geometry, or languages, may be given for purposes of educational guidance, Similarly, beginning with the seventh grade, vocational aptitude test may be adminstered individually or to groups of children with certain interests and abilities.

Sometimes, the question is raised "When is the best time during the year to give aptitude tests ?" There are no necessary advantages in any one period. Some administrators and teachers prefer to administer aptitude tests at the beginning of a term. Early testing provides the teacher with a means for the diagnosis of the child, with an intelligent basis for setting goals for the child, and with aid in guiding the child. Also, teachers do not become sensitive if their students score low on a test, since they do not feel responsible for the achievement of a new group. However, similar advantages are derived if a test is given at the end of a year, because the new teacher will readily have the scores and can make his plans accordingly. In this case, unfortunately, the teacher who has had the group all year may, if an insecure person, try to teach the children to make high scores on the aptitude test.

How should Aptitudes be Evaluated ?

Evaluating aptitude is so technical a task that educator generally rely on standardized tests for evidence. What it is possible for teachers to construct tests or work sample exercises which may be useful in educational diagnosis and prognosis, most teachers are either insufficiently trained or lack the time to employ their own techniques. Consequently, the general recommendation is that teachers should, in consultation with colleagues and reference works like Buro's Mental Measurement Yearbooks (1, 2, 3), select tests appropriate to their purposes and students.

Aptitude tests are a major method for the diagnosis and evaluation of aptitudes, but they are only one way of obtaining the comprehensive information that is needed for guiding an individual. Other methods, such as the interview, questionnaire, rating scale, anecdotal record, essay, autobiography, and cumulative record provide essential data. Super (9) discusses these methods and their role in appraising vocational fitness.

Most aptitude tests are limited to the measurement of the intellectual and manipulative abilities and skills which correspond with successful achievement in a study or work situation. But successful achievement in a total situation involves attitudes, interests, motivation, and personal-social adaptability as these interact in situations with intellectual and manipulative abilities and skills.

In elementary and high schools, intelligence tests can predict scholastic achievement with a fair degree of success. In colleges, scholastic aptitude tests can measure potential achievement in college courses. However, the prediction based on these tests does not assess attitudes, interests, motivation and personal-social adaptability. As a result, Joe Smith who rates above the 90th percentile in scholastic aptitude may be failing in his studies because of poor attitudes and motivation, lack of interest, or emotionally disturbing problems of his personal or social life.

Fortunately, a high proportion of individuals have the appropriate attitudes and adjustments which permit them to function approximately at the level predicted by the aptitude tests. Thus, these tests are used as an important part of the evidence in determining and subsequently guiding the growth of the individual.

TYPES OF APTITUDE TESTS

Intelligence Tests

In order to evaluate academic aptitude, a variety of intelligence, or mental ability, tests have been constructed. The broadest classification of these tests of mental ability is cccording to the method of administration—namely, individual tests or group tests. In addition to these categories, there are other distinctions such as performance tests and verbal tests, language and non-language tests. Space does not permit a detailed description of all these types or of all the differences which exist.

The individual test of mental ability is used principally in clinical situations by an examiner who has extensive training in the administration and interpretation of such tests. The most widely used of these individual tests are the Stanford-Binet Test of Intelligence and the Wechsler-Bellenue Intelligence Scale. The Wechsler Scale has one form adapted for children and is used generally for childrcn from the ages of 4 to 13. The original Wechsler-Bellevue Intelligence Scale, Form I, has been revised and is now called the Wechsler Adult Intelligence Scale. The Binet test and the Wechsler tests use both verbal and performance exercises in order to estimate the intelligence of the individual. The tests must be administered orally in large part and the responses of the examinee recorded by the examiner. The advantage of the individual test of intelligence is that it permits interpretation cf the responses in clinical terms and provides the opportunity for observing more carefully the behavior, interest, adjustment, motivation, and working habits of the individual, in addition to and in relation with his general intelligence.

The group tests of intelligence, on the other hand, are administered to an entire class or group of pupils or individuals, and prepared responses to the questions or items are checked by the examinee. This permits objective scoring of the group tests of intelligence. The group test may be illustrated by such measures as are listed in Table 9.

Table 9

Illustrative Intelligence Tests

Test	*Publisher*	*Date*	*Level*
ACE Psychological Examination for High School Students	Educational Testing Service	1953	Grades 9—12

Army General Classification Test, First, Civilian Edition	Science Research Associates	1947	Grades 9—16, Adults
California Test of Mental Maturity	California Test Bureau	1951	Grades Kg—1, 1—3, 4—8, 7—10, 9—16
Chicago Tests of Primary Mental Abilities	Science Research Associates	1947	Ages 11—17
Cooperative School and College Ability Tests	Educational Testing Service	1955	Grades 7—14
Davis-Eells Games	World Cook Company	1952	Grades 1—2, 3—6
Henmon-Nelson Test of of Mental Ability	Houghton Miffiin Company	1935	Grades 3—8, 7—12, 13—16
Kuhlmann-Anderson Intelligence Tests	Personnel Press	1952	Grades 1—6, 7—8, 9—12
Lorge-Thorndike Intelligence Tests	Houghton Miffiin Company	1954	Grades Kg—1, 2—3, 4—6, 7—9, 10—12
Ohio State University Psychological Test	Science Research Associates	1950	Grades 9—16

Otis Quick-Scoring Mental Ability Test	World Book Company	1954	Grades 1—4, 4—9, 9—16
Printer General Ability Tests : Verbal Series	World Book Company	1946	Grades Kg—2, 2—4, 4—9, 9—12
SRA Primary Mental Abilities	Science Research Associates	1948	Ages 5—7, 7—11, 11—17
SRA Non-Verbal Form	Science Research Associates	1947	Grades 9—12
Terman-McNemar Test of Mental Ability	World Book Company	1942	Grades 7—12

In addition to such verbal tests, there are performance tests of mental ability. These tests are generally used to measure pupils who are unable to read or write English, such as pre-school children, children with speech defects, deaf children, and others whose language is limited. These tests may be illustrated by the Arthur Point Scale. Goodenough Draw-A-Man Scale. Printer-Patterson Scale of Performance Tests, and the subtests of the Wechsler-Bellevue Scale dealing with performance. These tests have some disadvantages or limitations compared with the more vrrbal types of test. Most performance tests do not have as high reliability as verbal tests. The aspects of intelligence measured by performance tests are not completely comparable with those measured by verbal tests. Correlations of the order of .55 to .65 are generally found between performance and the verbal intelligence tests.

Academic Aptitude Test Items

Most of the "intelligence" tests contain very similar types of items. Aside from the basic differences associated with verbal and non-verbal and performance and non-performance tests, the contents of intelligence tests commonly include several of the following types of test items : vocabulary, general information, verbal analogies, figure analogies, same-opposites, completion, arithmatic reasoning, arithmetic computation, number series, identification of missing parts, spatial relationships, proverbs, verbal and pictorial absurdities, mazes, story and picture sequences, mixed words or sentences, and reading comprehension. Illustrations of some of these types of items are shown in the following excerpts from a few well-known intelligence tests.

(1) *Vocabulary*

What people say about a person constitutes his (?)

1. character, 2. gossip, 3. reputation,
4. disposition, 5. personality. ( )

(2) *Proverb*

Which one of the six statements below tells the meaning of the following proverb ? "The early bird catches the worm." ( )

1. Don't do the impossible.
2. Weeping is bad for the eyes.
3. Don't worry over troubles before they come.
4. Early birds like worms best.
5. Prompt persons often secure advantages over tardy ones.
6. It is foolish to fret about things we can't help.

(3) *Arithmetic Reasoning*

Which number in this series appears a second time nearest the beginning ?

6 4 5 3 7 8 0 9 5 9 8 8 6 5 4 7 3 0 8 9 1

(4) *Reading Comprehension*

The constitution would be the chief stumbling block in the way of fascists, but since, as students of the subject have shown, there can be no fascist triumphs without extreme illegalities, even to some violence, this would be the least of the fascist worries. Ignoring the constitution, they would encourage those drives which now are sending power upward to the federal government. Contrary to the desires of partisans of laissez-faire, fascism would necessarily result in speeding up the growth of bureaucracy. With the constitutional barriers down, the regulative powers of the government would be extended to an unheard-of extent.

What adjective meaning "directive" is employed in the paragraph ?

1. extreme, 2. upward,
3. extended, 4. regulative,
5. encourage.

What synonym of "advocators" occurs in the paragraph ?

1. partisans, 2. students, 3. fascists,
4. bureaucracy, 5. illegalities,

What phrase of exactly two words in the paragraph states that the difficulties in the possible adoption of fascism in the U.S. have already been published ?

1. are sending, 2. the constitution,
3. have shown, 4. extreme illegalities,
5. laissez-faire.

What would be the least of the fascist worries ?

1. illegalities, 2. constitution,
3. extreme illegalities, 4. violence,
5. laws.

What one word in the paragraph suggests that fascism would not be expected to go as far as a conquering invader to attain its ends ?

1. constitution, 2. unheard-of,
3. bureaucracy, 4. some,
5. violence.

Prognostic Tests

In addition to intelligence tests, prognostic tests in subject-matter areas may be included in the program of the high school. Some school personnel adminster aptitude tests in algebra, geometry, foreign languages, and business subjects in order to predict how well a student may perform. Students with low test scores are encouraged to take special substitute courses because it is believed that such students will fail in regular courses. The validity such prognostic tests is generally low so that it is usually inadvisable to counsel a student to pursue restricted educational goals unless other signification information about the student is taken into consideration. In Table 20, a list of some of the aptitude tests in the fields of mathematics, language, science, and business subjects is presented.

Table 10

Illustrative Subject-Matter Aptitude Tests

Test	*Publisher*	*Date*	*Grrde*
Algebra Prognosis Test	C. A. Gregory Company	1949	9-12
Algebra Readiness Test	Public School Publishing Company	1947	8-9
Bennett Stenogra-Phic Aptitude Test	Psychological Corp.	1939	9-16
California Algebra Aptitude Test	Educational Test Bureau	1940	9-12
Foreign Language Prognosis Test	Bureau of Publications, Teachers College, Columbia Univ.	1930	8-9
Iowa Algebra Aptitude Test	Bureau of Educational Research and Service, University Iawa	1942	9-12
Iowa Plane Geometry Aptitude Test	Bureau of Educational Research and Service, University Iowa	1942	9-12
Iowa Placement Examinations : Chemstry Aptitude	Bureau of Educational Research and Service, University of Iowa	1944	12-13

Iowa Placement Examinations : Physics Aptitude	Bureau of Educational Research and Service, University of Iowa	1944	12-13
Luria-Orleans Modern Language Prognosis Test	World Book Company	1930	7-12
Orleans Algebra Prognosis Test	World Book Company	1950	9-10
Orleans Geometry Prognosis Test	World Book Company	1950	10-11
Turse Shorthand Aptitude Test	World Book Company	1940	8-10

Clerical Aptitude Test

Clerical aptitude tests measure how much capacity a child or adult has for clerical details. The abilities involved are useful to clerks, typists, bookkeepers - in fact to anyone who needs accuracy and speed in doing paper work. The simplest or most streamlined versions of these tests present pairs of numbers and names separated by a short line. A check mark is entered on the line if the pairs are the same. No mark is entered if the pairs are different. Sample exercises are as follows :

84512——34512	James Jones——James Jones
47306——47306	Sue Palmer———Sue Palmer
89507——89705	Rochester, N. Y.——Rochester, N.Y.
137428——137428	Kenosha, Wisc.——Kenosha, Wis.

More elaborate versions of these tests include additional sections on alphabetical filing, classifying individuals according to residence, age occupation, etc., simple computations, spelling, and arithmetic problems.

Clerical aptitude tests have proved of value in differentiating between good and poor clerks, typists, and stenographers, when they are used in conjunction with evidence obtained from other tests, from the past record of the individual and from an interview, Individuals who obtain percentile scores of 75 or above (rate in the upper 25 per cent of the thousands who have taken the test) are good risks for the clerical aspects of an occupation.

Manual Dexterity Tests

Manual dexterity tests have been devised to measure the ability to work rapidly and skillfully with the fingers, hands, and arms. All tests involve some degree of eye-hand coordination. The Minnesota Rate of Manipulation Test, for example, requires the individual to place sixty cylindrical blocks in sixty regularly arranged holes in a board. One practice trial is given, then four trials are timed. A second part of the test requires the individual to pick up each block from its hole, turn it over, and replace it with the other hand. The hand functions are reversed after each row of fifteen blocks. This tests is useful for predicting success in such routine manipulative work as packing or wrapping boxes or cartons.

The O' Connor Finger Dexterity Test requires the individual to pick up three pins each time from a tray and insert then in small holes in a metal plate. The scores on this test aid in predicting success in such occupations as assembling clocks or radio fixtures, which involve rapid handing of small objects. The reverse side of the metal plate is used for the tweezer dexterity test. The individual picks up one pin at time with the tweezers and inserts it in a small hole. The score on this test predicts success in such occupations as drafting or watch repairing, which involve steadiness of hand and eye-hand co-ordination.

Mechanical Aptitude Tests

Several types of mechanical aptitude tests have been constructed including mechanical assembly and pencil-and-paper tests. The mechanical assembly tests attempt to predict success by judging the competence of an individual to assemble from disarranged, separate parts such simple mechnical objects as a bicycle bell, metal pencil, and lock. Other performance tests involve spatial relationships, such as the Wiggly Block and cubes.

The Wiggly Block is an oblong of wood cut into sections with a jigsaw. Its parts are disarranged, and the individual's speed at putting it together is used as a measure of his ability to discern spatial relationships. The cube test consits of twenty-seven small cubes obtained from a large cube of wood painted black and then cut twice in each direction. The problem is to put the small cubes together as quickly as possible, with no painted sides inside and no unpainted sides showing outside. This type of structural visualization is associated with such occupations as engineering, surgery, machinist trades, and other involving work with shapes and solids.

Pencil-and-paper tests have been devised to measure spatial relations by means of drawings of disarranged parts of a figure. The task is to select which one of five drawings indicates haw the parts fits together. Other tests include sections on tool recognition, application of tools to mechanical processes, arithmetic fundamentals, motor speed, and mechanical information.

While both performance and pencil-and-paper tests aid in predicting success in mechanical occupations, they measure so few of the abilities required in complex mechanical occupations that additional information is required. Such information must be obtained by systematic observation, record of school shop work, and interview.

With few exceptions, the tests available at the present time for measuring mechanical aptitude lack sufficient proof of their validity. For this reason, the cruder the tests, the mare cautious and ingenious must the counselor or teacher be in advising students on the basis of these test results.

The more prominent tests in this area may be grouped into the pencil-and-paper and performance types. Of the various pencil-and-paper mechanical aptitude tests. illustrations are presented below of exercises from three of the more widely used tests.

The MacQuarrie Test for Mechanical Ability, published by the California Test Bureau, is used for junior and senior-high-school students to measure such things as tracing, tapping, dotting, copying, etc. In the tracing test below the subject is asked to start at the little triangle and draw a curved line through the small openings in the vertical lines without touching them.

In the Revised Minnesota Paper Form-Board Test the subject is asked to respond to the following type of question: First look at the two parts in the upper left-hand corner. You are to decide which figure shows how these parts can fit together.

The Tests of Mechanical Comprehension by Bennett and Fry, are designed to measure the capacity of the subject to understand various types of physical relationships.

Performane tests are also available. All such tests involve some kind of task such as handling tools, inserting oddly cut blocks into form bords, putting a nut on a bolt, or inserting pegs into a board. Scores are in terms of time it takes to perform the task.

The Bennett Hand Tool Dexterity Test measures proficiency in the use of wrenches and screwdrivers. The examinee takes apart the twelve fastenings in a prescribed sequence and reassembles the nuts, washers, and bolts in the righthand upright. The time required is the score.

The Purdue Pegboard is an apparatus test measuring manipulative dexterity in

(*a*) gross movement of hands, fingers, and arms, and

(*b*) tip-of-finger small assembly work.

Table 11 presents general information about each of the more generally known tests of mechanical aptitude.

Table 11

Illustrative Mechanical Aptitude Tests

Test Title	*Publisher*	*Date*	*Level*
Bennett Hand-Tool Dexterity Test	Psychological Corp.	1946	Adults
MacQuarrie Test for Mechanical Ability	California Test Bureau	1925 (1943 Manual)	Ages 16 and Over
Minnesota Spatial Relations Test	Educational Test Bureau	1930	Ages 11 and Over
O'Connor Finge Dexterity Test	C. A. Stoelting & Co.	1926	Age 15 — Adults

O'Connor Tweezer-Dexterity Test	C. H. Stoelting & Co.	1926	Age 15—Adults
Pennsylvania Bi-Mnual Worksample	Educational Test Bureau	1945	Ages 17 and Over
Prognostic Test of Mechanical Abilities	California Test Bureau	1946	Grades 7—12, Adults
Purdue Pegboard	Science Research Associates	1941	Grades 9—12, Adults
Revised Minnesota Paper Form-Board Test	Psychological Corp.	1941	Ages 9 and Over
SRA Mechanical Aptitudes	Science Research Associates	1947	Grades 9—12, Adults
Small Parts Dexte-rity Test	Psychological Corp.	1946	H. S. and Adults
Tests of Mechacical Comprehension	Psychological Corp.	1947	Grades 9 and Over

Musical Aptitude Tests

Most tests of musical aptitude are based on the psychological analysis of musical talent by Seashore, who constructed the first measures of musical talent. Currently, there are two types of presentation of the test exercises to the child or adult :

(*a*) phonograph recordings and

(*b*) playing of the standard exercises on a piano by an examiner.

Regardless of the mechanics of presentation, a series of test exercises may measure such aspects of musicianship as the following :

(*a*) sense of pitch,

(*b*) sense of of intensity,

(*c*) sense of time,

(*d*) tonal memory,

(*e*) sense of rhythm, and

(*f*) sense of timbre. As the test exercises are played, the child or adult records his answer on a special answer sheet.

The test on sense of pitch, for example, presents a number of paired sounds and requires the individual to indicate whether the second sound is higher or lower in pitch than the first. Similar methods of presentation and respoding are used for other parts of the test.

Art Aptitude Tests

Attempts to measure art aptitude vary from art judgment to drawing an original design. The Meier Art Judgment Test presents pairs of pictures. One of each pair is the reproduction of an artistic work of recognized worth ; the other of each pair has been altered in some way to lower its artistic qualities. The individual is required to select the more artistic picture in each pair.

The McAdory Ary Test presents four variations of a single theme pictures of furniture and utensils, texture and clothing, architecture, shape and line arrangement, dark and light masses, and color. The individual ranks each of the four variations in order of merit.

Other tests require such exercises as drawing a design from memory, creating and completing designs from supplied elements, recognition of proportions, originality of line drawing, analysis problems in perspective, and recognition of color.

The child who achieves a high percentile score on an art aptitude test has potential art ability. Additional evidence from observation of performance in art situations is essential to arrive at reasonable judgments of the capacity of the individual.

Table 12 lists selected art and music tests, their publishers, date of publication, and age or grade level.

Table 12

Illustrative Art and Music Aptitude Tests

Test Title	*Publisher*	*Date*	*Level*
Drake Musical Memory Test	Public School Pub. Co.	1934	Grade 4 and Over
Graves Design Judgment Test	Psychological Corp.	1948	Grades 7—16, Adults
Horn Art Aptitude Inventory	C. H. Stoelting Co.	1851	Grades 12—16, Adulls

Knauber Art Ability Test	Author (Alma J. Knauber)	1935	Grades 7—16
Lewerenz Test in Fundamental Abilities of Visual Arts	California Test Bureau	1927	Grades 3—12
McAdory Art Test	Bureau of Publications, Teachers College, Columbia Univ.	1929	Grades 1—16, Adults
Meier Art Tests : I. Judgment	Bureau of Educa tional Research and Service	1940	Grades 7 - 12
Musical Aptitude Test	California Test Bureau	1950	Grades 4—10
Seashorc Measures of Musical Talents, Rev. Ed.	Psychological Corp.	1939	Grades 5—8, Adults

Aptitude Tests For Specific Occupations

In recent years selected colleges have employed admissions, or aptitude, tests to choose prospective students for such subjects as medicine, law, engineering, and nursing. Each year a new form of the Medical Aptitude Test is constructed for the Association of American Medical Colleges. Among the abillties measured are: comprehension and retention, visual memory, memory for content, logical reasoning, scientific vocabulary, and understanding of printed material.

In the past, law aptitude tests have included sections on : capacity for accurate recall, comprehension and reasoning by analysis, symbolic logic, and comprehension of difficult reading. Engineering aptitude tests stress mathematical ability, spatial perception, and general scholastic aptitude. Nursing aptitude tests usually include subtests on scientific vocabulary, general information, visual memory, memory for content, understanding of printed materials, and ability to understand and follow directions.

Multiple Aptitude Test Batteries

The factor analysis studies of many tests have resulted in the identification of some relatively independent abilities and skills that are assumed to be valuable in predicting success in various tasks or occupations. The need for additional research in establishing the predictive validity of the differential aptitude tests is apparent. The magnitude and the complexity of the job of validation are so great that psychologists have made but modest advances in this task.

Test batteries for multiple, or differential, aptitudes include the Primary Mental Abilities Tests, Differential Aptitude Tests, and Flanagan Aptitude Classification Tests. The General Aptitude Test Battery of the United States Employment Service is of the same type but it is not available for use outside the USES offices. A brief description of each of the batteries is provided below.

Primary Mental Abilities Tests were constructed by Thurstone as a result of his factor analysis studies (10). These tests are published by Science Research Associates and are adapted for several age levels. The PMA for ages 7-11 provides measures for five of the components of intelligence as follows: V—Verbal meaning—the ability to understand ideas expressed in words ; S—Space—the ability to visualize and think about objects in two or three dimensions ; R—Reasoning—the ability to solve logical problems, to foresee, and to plan, P—Perception – the ability to recognize likenesses and differences between objects or symbols quickly and accurately, N—Number the ability to work with numbers and handle simple quantitative problems rapidly and accurately.

The PMA for age 11-17 differs from the ages 7-11 battery in that Perception is omitted and Word Fluency is added for the older age group.

Differential Aptitude Tests were constructed by Bennett, Seashore, and Wesman. They are published by the Psychological Corporation. The authors continue to conduct studies of the predictive validity of the tests for use in educational and vocational guidance at the junior and senior high school levels. The Differential Aptitude Tests provide eight scores : Verbal Reasoning, Numerical Ability, Abstract Reasoning, Space Relations, Mechanical Reasoning, Clerical Speed and Accuracy, Spelling, and Sentences (Grammatical Usage).

The 1952 edition of the Manual for the Differential Aptitude Tests includes not only instructions for administering, scoring, and interpreting the test results, but also a compact summary of numerous validation researches completed since the publication of the battery in 1947. Correlative Publications, such as *Counseling from Peofiles : A Casebook for the D.A.T.*, are helpful in the interpretation of test results.

Flanagan Aptitude Classfication Tests were constructed by Flanagan in an effort to establish a standard classification system for describing those aptitudes that are important for successful performance of particular occupational tasks. The battery is published by Science Research Associates and consists of the following tests :

1. Inspection—ability to spot quickly flaws or imperfections in a series of articles.
2. Coding—speed and accuracy of coding typical office information.
3. Memory – ability to remember the codes learned in Test 2.
4. Precision—speed and accuracy in circular finger and hand movements.

5. Assembly—ability to visualize the appearance of an object from separate parts.

6. Scales—speed and accuracy in reading scales, graphs and charts.

7. Coordination—ability to coordinate hand and arm movements.

8. Judgment and Comprehension—ability to read with understanding, to reason logically, and to use judgment.

9. Arithmetic—skill in working with numbers : adding, subtracting, multiplying, and dividing.

10. Patterns—ability to reproduce simple pattern outlines accurately.

11. Components—ability to identify important component parts in line drawings and blueprint sketches.

12. Tables—ability to read tables of numbers and tables of words and letters.

13. Mechanics—ability to understand mechanical principles and to analyze mechanical movements

14. Expression—knowledge of correct English.

In the *Counselor's Booklet* for the Flanagan Aptitude Classification Tests (FACT), job descriptions for thirty occupations are presented and specific tests are recommended for each occupation. Thus, for the job classifications of Accountant, the following Critical FACT Elements are recommended : Test 2—Codin, Test 3—Memory, Test 8—Judgment and Comprehension, Test 9—Arithmetic, and Test 12—Tables.

Some follow-up studies have been made of graduates of Pittsburgh high schools to whom some of the tests were administered. More careful study and research are required to establish the predictive validity of the FACT for various occupational classifications. This series of tests was published in January, 1954. Investigators will gradually add to the fund of information about the value of these tests.

General Aptitude Test Battery of the United States Employment Service is not generally available for use, but the fifteen tests which comprise the GATB measure the following aptitudes which contribute to occupational success : G—intelligence, V—verbal ability, N—numerical ability, S—spatial ability, P—form perception, Q—clerical perception, A—aiming, T—motor speed, F—finger dexterity, and M manual dexterity. There are eleven paper and pencil and four apparatus tests. Occupational Aptitude Patterns have been established for twenty fields of work, representing two thousand occupations, setting critical scores which will eliminate the lowest third of the standard scores of the employed sample. An Individual Aptitude Profile is prepared from the counselee's scores. This is compared with the twenty Occupational Aptitude Patterns to detesmine the fields of work that are most suitable for the person's abilities.

SUMMARY

Aptitudes may be defined as capacities and abilities for a given line of endeavor, such as a particular art, school subject, or vocation. Evidence from current research studies supports the theory that aptitudes are both innate and acquired : are pluralistic rather than unitary in character ; are more constant than variable for an individual; tend to fit the normal frequency distribution curve when a large, unselected population is measured on specific aptitudes and abilities.

It is the function of the school to identify aptitudes, to encourage the development of talents and abilities. and to provide educational and vocational guidance so that educational opportunities may be adapted to individual abilities and needs. In the evaluation of aptitudes, both specialists and classroome teachers should be involved in the appraisal made. The timn at which aptitudes should be evaluated is determined by whes.

such information will be most useful in the guidance processed Aptitudes should be evaluated by means of tests, supplemented by such other methods as interview, questionnaire, observational and anecdotal record.

The types of aptitude tests discussed in this chapter, include intelligence, prognosis for ability in school subjects clerical aptitude, manual dexterity, mechanical aptitude, musica aptitude, art aptitude, aptitude for specific vocations, and multiple aptitude test batteries. Intelligence tests, both individual and group, are used to measure general intelligence or academic ability for success in the usual school subjects. Prognostic tests usually comprise introductory skills related to such school subjects as algebra, chemistry, physics, Latin, and French.

Aptitude tests are used with increasing frequency as one among several types of evidence that aid in the selection or guidance of individuals for special occupations. So camplex are the mental, physical, and emotional characteristics which contribute to success is an educational career or in an occupation that only selected characteristics can be measured by aptitude tests. Other types of evidence may be supplemented by aptitude tests in reaching decisions, For example, individuals achieving high scores on scholastic aptitude tests are good risks for academic success in high school and college. Likewise, individuals achieving high scores on music and art aptitude tests are good risks for success in their respective fields. Clerical aptitude tests have value in predicting success in clerical work, typing, and stenography.

Manual dexterity tests provide important information about the ability of an individual to work rapidly and skillfully with the fingers, hands, and arms, as well as eye-hand coordination, for aspects of an occupation requiring these abilities. In a like manner, mechanical aptitude tests provide valuable supplementary data on those aspects of an occupation requiring ability to visualize space relations and ability to recognize and utilize tools and mechanical processes.

Professional schools for medicine, law, engineering, and nursing are increasingly using aptitude test batteries to select applicants who are most likely to succeed in achieving the courses of study. However, additional evidence based on the previous school record of the individual is employed to assess scholastic success, attitudes, and personality.

PROBLEMS FOR CLASS DISCUSSION

1. For a class, compare the intelligence (academic aptitude) tests scores with pupil achievement in academic subjects. How well does the academic aptitude test predict achievement ?

2. Indicate how aptitude tests might be used in the educational and vocational guidance of several teen-age youths whom you know.

3. To an increasing extent, tests are being used to select personnel in large industrial or business firms. Choose three different positions which might be found in any large firm and draw up a testing program for selecting the best applicant for each position.